# The Children's Cause

GILBERT Y. STEINER

*with the assistance of Pauline H. Milius*

# The Children's Cause

THE BROOKINGS INSTITUTION
*Washington, D.C.*

*Copyright © 1976 by*
THE BROOKINGS INSTITUTION
*1775 Massachusetts Avenue, N.W., Washington, D.C. 20036*

*Library of Congress Cataloging in Publication Data:*

Steiner, Gilbert Yale, 1924–
  The children's cause.

  Includes bibliographical references and index.
  1. Child welfare—United States.  2. Children—Law—United States.  I. Milius,
Pauline H., joint author.  II. Brookings Institution, Washington, D.C.  III. Title.
HV741.S75      362.7′0973      75-43465
ISBN 0-8157-8120-2
ISBN 0-8157-8119-9 pbk.


9 8 7 6 5 4 3 2 1

THE BROOKINGS INSTITUTION is an independent organization devoted to nonpartisan research, education, and publication in economics, government, foreign policy, and the social sciences generally. Its principal purposes are to aid in the development of sound public policies and to promote public understanding of issues of national importance.

The Institution was founded on December 8, 1927, to merge the activities of the Institute for Government Research, founded in 1916, the Institute of Economics, founded in 1922, and the Robert Brookings Graduate School of Economics and Government, founded in 1924.

The Board of Trustees is responsible for the general administration of the Institution, while the immediate direction of the policies, program, and staff is vested in the President, assisted by an advisory committee of the officers and staff. The by-laws of the Institution state: "It is the function of the Trustees to make possible the conduct of scientific research, and publication, under the most favorable conditions, and to safeguard the independence of the research staff in the pursuit of their studies and in the publication of the results of such studies. It is not a part of their function to determine, control, or influence the conduct of particular investigations or the conclusions reached."

The President bears final responsibility for the decision to publish a manuscript as a Brookings book. In reaching his judgment on the competence, accuracy, and objectivity of each study, the President is advised by the director of the appropriate research program and weighs the views of a panel of expert outside readers who report to him in confidence on the quality of the work. Publication of a work signifies that it is deemed a competent treatment worthy of public consideration but does not imply endorsement of conclusions or recommendations.

The Institution maintains its position of neutrality on issues of public policy in order to safeguard the intellectual freedom of the staff. Hence interpretations or conclusions in Brookings publications should be understood to be solely those of the authors and should not be attributed to the Institution, to its trustees, officers, or other staff members, or to the organizations that support its research.

# Foreword

The difficulty of drawing a rationally defensible line of demarcation between public and private responsibility for the general welfare of children is constantly apparent as politicians are confronted with proposals to expand or revise programs that care for, protect, and nourish children, and make cash payments to poor families with dependent children. That the government's role in child care, for example, should be limited to care for those children whose parents would otherwise be public relief cases is a principle increasingly attacked by some leaders of the women's movement, some child development specialists, and some public school teachers looking toward new job opportunities. Yet the principle is still defended by many others. Similarly, universal, free public education that is not accompanied by universal, free school lunches strikes some children's advocates as an incongruity, but at least an equal number regard it as a sensible way to husband public funds. Even where there is agreement in principle, moreover, as in public financing of day care for children of the poor, disagreement continues over whether arrangements for getting the job done should be made by federal or state authorities.

Child development policy is uncoordinated. Public involvement in the field is a federal-agency-by-federal-agency, congressional-committee-by-congressional-committee, state-by-state, or city-by-city assortment of unrelated decisions that are as likely to be contradictory as complementary. Accidents of geography or of congressional committee jurisdiction affect child welfare in ways that spokesmen for children too often fail to consider as they propose legislative or administrative changes. In hopes of promoting public understanding of the children's cause as traditional definitions of the appropriate limits of government activity in child welfare are being reexamined, this book examines the apparatus for making children's policy and evaluates substantive policy proposals against the background of tension between proponents of public rather than private responsibility and between advocates of federal rather than state responsibility.

This book had its origins in my earlier research on the politics of stability and change in public relief policy that led to the publication of *The State of Welfare* by Brookings in 1971. A central finding of that work was that the divisiveness of public relief politics is largely attributable to the growth in number and costs of dependent children. Whether a comparable divisiveness can be found in all aspects of children's policy, how the political system is organized to respond to the needs of children, how children's policy originates, why some advocates are more successful than others, and what are the limits of federal policy for children—all these presented themselves as unexplored areas of inquiry that are addressed here.

Many people helped with documents and materials from their files, with willingness to be interviewed and sometimes reinterviewed, and with comment on early drafts or fragments of drafts. I am particularly grateful to William L. Pierce, Carolyn Harmon, Saul Rosoff, Milton Senn, and Marian Wright Edelman. Several of them may disagree in whole or part with interpretations and judgments found in the book. Only Pauline Milius and I should be held responsible for judgments, interpretations, or errors of fact.

Helpful research memoranda were contributed by Joy Silver and Linda Gillespie. Both the preparation of the manuscript and preliminary editing fell to Donna Daniels Verdier. Alice M. Carroll edited the final version for publication; the index was prepared by Florence Robinson.

The Brookings Institution is grateful to Carnegie Corporation of New York for a grant to support this work. The Corporation took no part in its direction, and has no responsibility for the findings, but Barbara Finberg's wisdom, encouragement, and patience all helped. Finally, the views expressed here do not necessarily represent those of any of the persons whose assistance is acknowledged above, nor should they be ascribed to the trustees, officers, or other staff members of the Brookings Institution.

GILBERT Y. STEINER
*Acting President*

*July 1976*
*Washington, D.C.*

# Contents

# Abbreviations

| | |
|---|---|
| AAP | American Academy of Pediatrics |
| ACEI | Association for Childhood Education International |
| ADC | aid to dependent children |
| AFDC | aid to families with dependent children |
| AFT | American Federation of Teachers |
| AHA | American Humane Association |
| AMA | American Medical Association |
| ARC | Appalachian Regional Commission |
| ASFSA | American School Food Service Association |
| BCHS | Bureau of Community Health Services |
| CAP | community action program |
| CATCH | comprehensive approach to child health |
| CDA | child development associate |
| CDF | Children's Defense Fund |
| CNOCY | Council of National Organizations for Children and Youth |
| CWLA | Child Welfare League of America |
| C&Y | children and youth projects |
| DCCDCA | Day Care and Child Development Council of America |
| E/K/N/E | Elementary/Kindergarten/Nursery/Educators |
| EPSDT | early and periodic screening, diagnosis, and treatment |
| 4-C | Community Coordinated Child Care |
| FWA | Federal Works Administration |
| GAO | General Accounting Office |
| HEW | Department of Health, Education, and Welfare |
| HSI | Human Services Institute |
| HSMHA | Health Services and Mental Health Administration |

| | |
|---|---|
| JCMHC | Joint Commission on Mental Health of Children |
| LAT | local assessment team |
| MCHS | Maternal and Child Health Service |
| M&I | maternal and infant care |
| MSA | Medical Services Administration |
| NAEYC | National Association for the Education of Young Children |
| NAS-NRC | National Academy of Sciences–National Research Council |
| NCJW | National Council of Jewish Women |
| NCOCY | National Council of Organizations for Children and Youth |
| NEA | National Education Association |
| NICHD | National Institute of Child Health and Human Development |
| NIH | National Institutes of Health |
| NIMH | National Institute of Mental Health |
| NOW | National Organization for Women |
| NPA | National Planning Association |
| OCD | Office of Child Development |
| OEO | Office of Economic Opportunity |
| OMB | Office of Management and Budget |
| PCC | Parent and Child Centers |
| PHS | Public Health Service |
| SIDS | sudden infant death syndrome |
| SRS | Social and Rehabilitation Service |
| UAW | United Automobile Workers |
| WIN | work incentive program |
| WPA | Works Projects Administration |

# 1

# Private Families
# and Public Responsibilities

Child rearing is the least regulated important aspect of American life. "All children are dependent," Grace Abbott wrote in 1938, "but only a relatively small number are dependent on the state. Most of them are in some degree problem children, but only a few have such serious difficulties in adjusting to their environment that the state feels obliged to assume responsibility for their care."[1] Forty years later, that description of governmental reticence remains valid. When politicians consider legislation affecting children generally, they do so hesitantly and reluctantly, knowing that the American social system presumes that barring economic disaster or health crisis, a family should and will care for its children without public intervention.

But nonintervention serves as a basic guiding principle rather than an absolute. Federally supported public programs of compensatory services or cash assistance are readily accepted when the need for them results from circumstances over which either a child or the child's parents have no control. Most of the 15.5 million children in America under five and the 33 million between five and thirteen in 1976 are lucky enough to be provided a home by their biological parents; to be able to spend their pre-school years and after-school hours in or around their homes; to be fed adequate and reasonably nutritious meals at home; and to be examined and treated periodically by private physicians and dentists. Less lucky children are helped by federal or state governments because their parents are literally incapable of caring for them. Social intervention is commonplace when there is no natural household to which a child is attached

1. In an introduction to "Organizing for Administration of Child Welfare Services," in *The Child and the State* (University of Chicago Press, 1938), vol. 2; reprinted in Robert H. Bremner, ed., *Children and Youth in America: A Documentary History* (Harvard University Press, 1971), vol. 2, pts. 1–6, p. 755.

because of the death, physical or mental incapacity, or incarceration of parents. In other cases, mentally and physically able parents claim to be or are alleged to be unable to meet the needs of their children for care and development. Some parents may have or be thought to have too little understanding of health or of nutrition or of human behavior to raise their children without public intervention.

Just how many children do benefit from public programs is an imponderable. Nearly 8 million are recipients of aid to families with dependent children (AFDC) in any single month, but more than 9 million children live in low-income families and are intermittent beneficiaries. Twenty-five million participate in a federally subsidized school lunch program, and over 10 million of them—many from AFDC families—receive a free or nearly free school lunch. About 285,000 preschool children from low-income families are enrolled in Head Start programs. Economic dependency aside, about 3 million children are reported to receive social services from state and local public welfare agencies. Well over 2 million of these children are served in their parents' homes, some 250,000 in foster family homes, at least 65,000 in institutions, and perhaps 150,000 in the homes of relatives. Some, but not all, of the social services recipients are also cash relief clients. There are, in addition, around 140,000 potential recipients of public services who are served only by voluntary child welfare agencies.[2] With the recent "discoveries" of the need for services to handicapped children, of child abuse, and of deficiencies in medical screening of children, the trend in public intervention is upward.

The circumstances that presently lead to intervention—dead or absent parents, hunger, illness—produce no challenges on principle to government responsibility. Implementing the decision to intervene troubles everyone involved, however, because the modes of intervention are imperfect. Aside from economic need evidenced by family income, there is no way to monitor provision of minimum services to children in private families in the fashion that wages, hours, and occupational safety and health are monitored routinely in the private work place. And in those special cases where monitoring of child care does take place because of a history of child abuse or other extraordinary condition, judgmental issues remain. Children's minimum needs elude measurement. Can any substitute arrangement, whether institution or foster family, meet those

2. "Children Served by Public Welfare Agencies and Voluntary Child Welfare Agencies and Institutions, March 1971," DHEW publication no. (SRS) 73-03258, NCSS report E-9 (3-71) (April 27, 1973; processed), table 1.

needs? Is there an acceptable definition of a "suitable home"? Is there a trade-off between material and emotional needs that allows a deficit in the one to be compensated for by a surplus of the other? Do minimum needs extend beyond corporal protection and into comprehensive development?

The traditional pattern of restraint in the use of public intervention has recently been challenged by a developmental philosophy that argues it is not enough to protect children against abuse and against the most dramatic and evident diseases like polio and blindness, and it is not enough to throw a protective cover over orphans and abandoned children. Without forsaking these activities, it is said, government should reach out to insure the maximum development of every child according to his own potential. To do so will be to undermine some long-cherished values relating to family life. More important, perhaps, to do so will introduce more questions that cannot be answered definitively. Is development enhanced by early education outside the home? Does development require providing a nutritionally balanced meal or meals in a school setting? Is development affected by parents' access to relief from twenty-four-hour care, that is, access to a day-care facility? How does preventive dentistry or periodic medical screening affect development? Protective services produce plenty of problems by themselves, but the developmental issue is a good deal tougher for politicians because the asserted benefits are less obvious. Battered and abandoned children are visible. The failure to make optimum use of the early years of a child's life is not comparably apparent.

In the absence of compelling evidence to challenge the belief that traditional, unregulated family life is as satisfactory a child-rearing style as any alternative, wholesale social intervention on behalf of children per se is not likely. "The fact of the matter is," says Dr. Edward Zigler, first director of the federal Office of Child Development, "all the evidence I know still indicates that a family life for a child is satisfactory to the optimum development of that child." Noting that many children do get the kind of developmental services that are offered in public programs in their own homes, Zigler has emphasized the desirability of a conservative, diagnostic approach, "pinpointing things for particular children . . . children of high risk."[3]

If social intervention to serve children of high risk is an acceptable public activity while wholesale intervention for any purpose that lacks

3. *Child Care*, Hearings before the Senate Committee on Finance, 92:1 (Government Printing Office, 1971), pp. 213 ff.

specificity is not, the professional definition of high risk may fix the limits of intervention. Popular attention and political interest are both maximized as the number of high-risk cases increases from a tiny to a major fraction of the child population because such an increase involves the self-interest of a corresponding number of parents. Intervention is routine where the entire child population falls in the high-risk category: the mandatory use of silver nitrate in the eyes of all newborn infants is an illustration. Where the high-risk cases are few in number, the public policy response depends less on the pressures and efforts of a group acting in its own self-interest and more on the persistence and persuasiveness of groups moved by social altruism rather than by self-interest.

Proponents of the children's cause—in Congress and in the bureaucracy, on the one hand, and in voluntary associations, in the foundations, and among unaffiliated "concerned Americans," on the other hand—all continue to be concerned about its future. But those who are responsible for making public policy affecting children march to different drummers than do the advocates. The former are uneasy about the latter's faith that expressions of love and imprecise concepts like "developmental care," "maximum potential," and "services for all who need them" can become manageable public policy. This book tries to narrow the gap between the groups by providing some explanations of how and why it has developed.

## Ambivalence in Federal Policy

Within the last decade an old equilibrium that balanced public and private responsibility for children has become unsteady. The outer limits of the equilibrium are still readily enough agreed on. Governmental indifference to children without parents is intolerable. So is governmental effort to inculcate an ideology or to separate children from parents. Children who are dependent, abandoned, crippled, or neglected are a proper public concern. Routine day-to-day care, feeding, health, and development of the generality of children is not a public concern. But complex new issues have developed. Routine child care is impossible for mothers who work to satisfy economic or psychic needs. As the number of such mothers grows, is there a public responsibility for child care? Evidence has been offered alleging the unique importance to human development of the first five years of life. Can nonintervention in preschool development continue to be sustained?

Nonintervention in the generality of parent-child relationships was formally affirmed as a public value early in the century, and affirmed again in the recent past. In practice, however, ambivalence is the best description of federal-level responses to proposals that involve intervention. For example, the 1912 legislative package that created the federal Children's Bureau also restricted it. While the bureau was to interest itself in children generally, to "investigate and report . . . upon all matters pertaining to the welfare of children and child life among all classes of our people," it was not to deal with the welfare of particular children: "no official, or agent, or representative of said bureau shall, over the objection of the head of the family, enter any house used exclusively as a family residence."[4] Almost sixty years later, President Nixon spoke of the "sacred right of parents to rear their children according to their own values and understandings," while proposing legislation that would have pushed some parents to the use of child-care centers as a condition of welfare aid.[5] The Supreme Court recently reaffirmed its own twenty-eight-year-old conclusion that "It is cardinal with us that the custody, care and nurture of the child reside first in the parents, whose primary function and freedom include preparation for obligations the state can neither supply nor hinder."[6] Yet the Court's language was "first," not "exclusively."

Following the success in 1912 of the effort to formalize a federal interest in children through creation of a Children's Bureau, nearly a quarter of a century elapsed before the Social Security Act made permanent additions to a small list of federal policies benefiting children. In the interim, two statutes regulating child labor were struck down by the Supreme Court as exceeding congressional power. But a third legislative prohibition on child labor enacted in 1937 as part of the comprehensive Fair Labor Standards Act—after hope had been abandoned for the constitutional amendment awaiting ratification since 1924—was finally sustained. In child health, a maternity and infancy grant program—the Sheppard-Towner Act—was enacted in 1921, contested, sustained, then allowed to expire in 1929. It reappeared in the Social Security Act with an emphasis on services in rural and economically depressed areas.

4. *U.S. Statutes*, 62:2 (1911–12), pt. 1, chap. 73, pp. 79–80; reprinted in Bremner, *Children and Youth in America*, vol. 2, pts. 1–6, p. 774.

5. The President's Statement on Establishing the Office of Child Development, *Congressional Record*, vol. 115, pt. 7 (1969), p. 8985.

6. *Prince* v. *Massachusetts*, 321 U.S. 158, 166 (1944); and *Stanley* v. *Illinois*, 405 U.S. 645, 651 (1972).

As for income-support programs on behalf of children, the first White House children's conference—called in 1909—was specifically a Conference on the Care of Dependent Children. Conferees urged public pensions enabling widowed mothers to care for their children in their own homes. After Illinois led the states, in 1911, with a mothers' pension program, the cause swept through forty states in less than a decade. By 1934, however, only half the counties authorized to give child aid were doing so. Accordingly, the aid to dependent children title of the Social Security Act required that federally aided programs be statewide in operation. The New Deal accomplished that within the package primarily addressed to a federal interest in problems of unemployment and old age; in a kind of afterthought, sponsors included noncontroversial grants to the states for aid to dependent children—ultimately to become the largest federal public assistance program—and for child welfare services.

That afterthought of 1935 represents the most advanced stage of federal policy on behalf of children until at least the mid-sixties. It may also reflect the high point of Children's Bureau influence in policy development, either before or since.

Over a long period of years, supporters of greater federal activity on behalf of children could count on three varieties of objections: spinsters in the Children's Bureau should not intrude on parent-child relationships ("Tiger's cub or wolf's whelp, I would rather feel the rough caresses of the hairy paws of my savage mother, I would rather have her care and protection than that of an official animal trainer"[7]); children in need of extraparental care are a concern of organized religious groups whose voluntary activities should not be discouraged by public activity;[8] if any governmental unit should assume responsibility for children, it is local or state government, not national government. In the Children's Bureau, the extraordinary capacity to avoid controversy evidenced by a succession of chiefs—Julia Lathrop, Grace Abbott, Martha Eliot, Katharine Lenroot—ultimately overcame crude objections to federal grants administered by the bureau. Church opposition to what was seen as a threat to church-maintained facilities for dependent, neglected, and abandoned children diminished as federal financial superiority became evident and federal

7. Remarks of Senator James Reed (Democrat of Missouri), *Congressional Record*, vol. 61, pt. 9 (1921), pp. 8759–67; reprinted in Bremner, *Children and Youth in America*, vol. 2, pts. 7–8, p. 1015.

8. Edwin E. Witte, *The Development of the Social Security Act* (University of Wisconsin Press, 1962), p. 168.

legislation authorized the use of federal money for purchase of services from church units. Finally, the state plan concept introduced in the child-welfare titles of the Social Security Act mollified the concerns of defenders of states' rights by effectively insuring state control of program details despite the provision of federal money.

Aside from its role in the administration of a short-lived (nine months) child labor law and in the administration of the maternal and infant health legislation of the 1920s, the first two decades of the Children's Bureau were spent, in the language of the bureau's official history, "reconnoitering" and in expanding and deepening the bureau's investigating and reporting work.[9] Compared to specific responsibility for administration of inconsequential programs, a general license to reconnoiter, investigate, and report on behalf of a discrete segment of the population is a valuable instrument. If put in skillful hands, such a license allows its holder to select points of emphasis and minimizes the danger of a broader cause being drowned in day-to-day administrative trivia. Since both were skillful advocates, it is not surprising that the administrations of Julia Lathrop (1912–21) and of Grace Abbott (1921–34) are thought of as among the glory days of the Children's Bureau.

The framers of the Social Security Act of 1935 based their program in part on the product of bureau reconnoitering, investigating, and reporting. The Committee on Economic Security's plan for expansion of state-supported mothers' pensions into a federal-state program of cash aid to dependent children grew out of a bureau proposal. So did the Social Security Act's title V dealing with federal aid, especially in rural areas, for maternal and child health programs, crippled children's services, and child welfare services. Administration of the cash relief program went at first to the Social Security Board, then was shuffled around the subsequently established Department of Health, Education, and Welfare. The rest of the package came to the Children's Bureau, but the rural emphasis was a tag that said "Think small." It was written because several big cities —New York, Chicago, Philadelphia, among others—then provided public money to religious groups for the institutional care of children committed to their custody, and those groups led by the National Conference of Catholic Charities insisted on the rural provision. Had a federal-state pro-

9. Dorothy E. Bradbury, *Five Decades of Action for Children: A History of the Children's Bureau*, U.S. Department of Health, Education, and Welfare, Social Security Administration, Children's Bureau publication no. 358 (rev. ed., 1962), especially p. 20.

gram been authorized for urban areas, the Catholic Charities leaders fore-saw objections to the extension of public funds to religious groups. With an agreement to divide the child welfare territory in a manner that limited federal participation to rural areas, religious groups' reservations to the title were withdrawn.

The rural restriction stuck for nearly twenty-five years. When it was finally dropped in 1958, three-fifths of the nation's children were living in urban areas where federally supported child-welfare services were not available. Even then, removal of the rural limitation was acknowledged to be "somewhat of a controversial issue."[10] To accomplish it, supporters of change agreed to the creation of an Advisory Council on Child Welfare Services to assist the Department of Health, Education, and Welfare in promulgating rules and regulations governing the change. The council's primary function was to insure that public agencies not violate the turf of private social service agencies. There was cause for the latter to be con-cerned. By the late 1950s, public assistance had virtually run private char-ity out of business. In the children's area, the developments were especially dramatic: aid to dependent children not only dwarfed private charitable activity for needy children but its beneficiary total already exceeded that of old age assistance. As sponsor of the Advisory Council provision, Sena-tor William Purtell (Republican of Connecticut) made his objective plain. "Certainly, we do not wish this new program to operate in any way which would remotely indicate that the public welfare agency is preempt-ing this [child] welfare field."[11] Spending limits in child welfare precluded that possibility. Unlike the aid to dependent children authorization which was always open-ended and meant consequent federal spending was un-controllable, the child welfare authorization has always been finite. Fixed at $10 million between 1950 and 1957, it rose only to $12 million for 1958, to $17 million for 1959 and 1960, and to $25 million through 1962 when the Public Welfare Amendments of that year changed the ground rules. More important, elimination of the rural restriction was accompanied by an increase in actual federal appropriations from $10 million in 1958 to only $13.7 million in 1961 and—finally—to $18.7 million in 1962.

Over the first fifty years of its life, then, little leverage was available to the Children's Bureau in its role as lead federal agency concerned with

10. *Departments of Labor and Health, Education, and Welfare Appropriations for 1960,* Hearings before the Subcommittee of the House Committee on Appropria-tions, 86:1 (GPO, 1959), p. 582.

11. *Congressional Record,* vol. 104, pt. 14 (1958), p. 17986.

services for the protection and care of homeless, dependent, and neglected children, and of children in danger of becoming delinquent. At first lacking an operational role in this area, then severely restricted by the rural limitation, and finally with broad authority but little money, the bureau was not able to cut a wide enough swath to command political attention. Given an administrative responsibility by the Social Security Act, it used its meager resources to encourage high-quality service by the states. It could not begin to make substantial contributions to the actual costs of services to children. Consequently, "professional and facilitating services" —a bureaucratic euphemism for the employment and training of staff— tended to absorb most of the federal grants to the states for child welfare services through the early 1960s. As long as federal money represented an insignificant share of the combined federal-state-local expenditure for so costly a child welfare service as foster care, federal impact on the service was similarly insignificant. And the responsible federal agency could influence neither the states, nor congressmen who found the Children's Bureau not worth much attention, nor federal budget officials who found the bureau tractable. Looking back after fifty years, Children's Bureau leaders could have concluded that the early years of reconnoitering, investigating, and reporting were the best years. Subsequently, its leaders were accorded a respectful hearing by politicians, but the Children's Bureau neither asked for nor accomplished much in the way of federal initiatives on behalf of children.

### Staunch Purposes, Slender Programs

When John Kennedy's administration began an active search for new frontiers, the passive, "quality-oriented" Children's Bureau had little to offer. Cash assistance to dependent children had long since overshadowed child welfare services as a matter of public and political concern. The big thing in the Children's Bureau at the time was a 1960 report of the Advisory Council on Child Welfare Services that had recommended increased spending, increased professionalism in child welfare, and a new definition of child welfare services. The Kennedy-inspired Public Welfare Amendments of 1962 responded to those recommendations with an increased spending authorization, a new definition that legitimized substitute and preventive services rather than services only to children already in trouble, and a recognition of the desirability of professionalism in child welfare work. But it was too late to rescue child welfare from public assistance. The submissive and respectful bureau continued to be submissive and respectful as appropriations failed to reflect the increased authorization, thus making it impossible to implement the broadened definition. Bureau officials dutifully characterized the legislation as "the most significant legislation in child welfare since the passage of the Social Security Act."[12] As late as 1966, the bureau continued to believe that there was a future for child welfare services separate from services for children in AFDC families. "Let us do all that is humanly possible," said the bureau's director of social services, "to achieve the glowing future for child welfare services so surely and clearly perceived."[13]

That sure and clear perception of a glowing future was not widely shared. The failure of the 1962 welfare amendments to reduce the costs of AFDC led to political disenchantment with the social service profession. The separate and equal status of child welfare was washed out by a new requirement in 1967 specifying that child welfare and AFDC services be provided by the same organizational unit at the state and local levels. Actually and symbolically, the effect was to submerge child welfare within AFDC as child welfare lost its separate title V status in the Social Security Act and was grafted on to the AFDC title IV. The Children's Bureau was subordinated administratively to a new Community Services Administration. With the enactment of the 1967 welfare amendments, child welfare became a component of the federal-state public assistance program. Given the dimensions of the AFDC problem, it is not surprising that child welfare services—never very well explained to or understood by the Congress—should be thrown into the battle. It is surprising that the Children's Bureau meekly accepted its degradation, assuring itself until the end that things would work out.

Paradoxically, that same year—1967—Lyndon Johnson sent the first presidential message to Congress ever devoted exclusively to children. Asserting that "No new ventures hold more promise than these," the emphasis was on children in need of catch-up services. Johnson's twelve proposals ranged from the construction and staffing of facilities for the mentally retarded, to summer employment programs, to better means of

12. Mildred Arnold, "Expanding and Improving Child Welfare Services" (notes for meeting with Kentucky Child Welfare staff, May 2, 1963), p. 1.

13. Mildred Arnold, "The Future of Child Welfare" (paper prepared for delivery at Conference on Children's Social Services, Salvation Army, Chicago, Ill., Oct. 20, 1966; processed), p. 17.

providing child dental service, to a Follow Through program that would carry on the presumed benefits of preschool compensatory education for children in poverty areas.[14]

With Johnson's popularity already on the wane, response to his message was lackadaisical. President Nixon attracted bipartisan interest and enthusiasm, however, when he quickly embraced the children's cause. The new President's preinaugural Task Force on Education told him nothing happening in American education was more important than early childhood programs, and characterized the nonavailability of these programs to two-thirds of American children as "tragic." Coincidentally, the Task Force on Welfare urged federal financing for construction of daycare facilities. Within a month of his inauguration in 1969, Nixon followed Daniel P. Moynihan's advice and called for a "national commitment to providing all American children an opportunity for healthful and stimulating development during the first five years of life."[15] Two months later, Nixon explicitly pledged himself again to that commitment. Both the commitment to that age group and the follow-up pledge were unique. Perhaps realizing that he was on delicate ground, the President then took care to refer to "the sacred right of parents to rear their children according to their own values and own understandings."[16]

Those who looked for the flowering of public efforts on behalf of children felt encouraged. A conservative President unexpectedly had gone out of his way to signal sympathetic interest by talking of a national commitment to the first five years of life. Coincident with his pronouncements, there were other actions and reports that appeared to mark the beginning of a period of strengthened public activity on behalf of children.

• Robert Finch, President Nixon's friend who had chosen to become secretary of the Department of Health, Education, and Welfare, established an Office of Child Development (OCD) and lodged it in the Office of the Secretary. The action was meant to foreshadow a more activist in-house lobby effort than that carried on by the Children's Bureau, now an elderly bureau.

• State welfare directors were particularly encouraged by the OCD to

14. February 8, 1967 Message on Children and Youth, *Congressional Quarterly Almanac*, 1967, p. 56-A.

15. February 19, 1969 Message on Reorganization of the War on Poverty, *Congressional Quarterly Almanac*, 1969, p. 34-A.

16. From the President's Statement on Establishing the Office of Child Development; reprinted in *Congressional Record*, vol. 115, pt. 7 (1969), p. 8985.

request federal financing of day-care services for a wider population of children than those whose families received public assistance payments.

• A distinguished group of physicians, scholars, and laymen—the Joint Commission on Mental Health of Children—created with the awareness of Congress and sustained with federal money over four years of study and meetings, issued its report calling for a child advocacy program.

• A new concept, community coordinated child care (4-C), designed to accomplish advocacy for and planning of children's services at state and local levels, was formally implemented with selection of a group of pilot communities and states.

• The women's liberation movement was recognized as a reasonable and serious cause. The President named a Task Force on Women's Rights and Responsibilities, a subject that was widely assumed to include child care.

• In the Senate, Walter Mondale (Democrat of Minnesota) found twenty-two cosponsors for a comprehensive child development bill that would have legitimized public involvement in child care and development and authorized billions of federal dollars for the purpose.

• In the House, extensive hearings began on a bill introduced by John Brademas (Democrat of Indiana) to provide comprehensive preschool educational and day-care programs.

• The role of chairman of the decennial White House Conference on Children, a conference that had been a tradition since the administration of Theodore Roosevelt, was assigned to a White House staff member, a loyal Republican and Nixon biographer, who might be expected to gain a sympathetic hearing for conference recommendations at the highest administration levels.

• After the Westinghouse Learning Corporation issued an important report concluding that Head Start gains fade, congressional enthusiasm was unaffected, and the secretary of health, education, and welfare reacted by questioning the adequacy of the study's data base and the breadth of its coverage.

As it developed, some of the buds died, and many simply did not flower. The Office of Child Development proved to have no more political influence than the old Children's Bureau. Use of federal social-services money for day care on an almost unrestricted and unlimited basis was choked off when it became costly. The "child advocacy" program of the Joint Commission on Mental Health of Children, defined as Alfred J. Kahn has put it "in expansive terms," turned out to be a system that "has been proposed but is hard to find."[17] The 4-C program never gained the specificity it lacked when it was created. Child care, while included on the women's rights agenda, is neither prominent nor well defined. Senator Mondale's child development legislation was maneuvered through Congress only to be vetoed with a devastating presidential message. Subsequently, it was difficult even to find a sponsor in the House of Representatives for a fresh effort. The unruly White House Conference on Children became an embarrassment to be forgotten; its chairman left the administration soon afterwards. And while the findings of the Westinghouse Head Start study were taken in stride in the Department of Health, Education, and Welfare and in the Congress, those findings caused the President to back away from a planned initiative in child development. After a few flourishing years, the children's issue withered.

Most of this book inquires into how and why all this came to pass as indicative of the future of children's policy. Accordingly, the book deals with social altruism and self-interest as factors in the development of federal public policy affecting children, with stability and change in intervention policy, with the goals and the techniques of groups in and out of government that are concerned with making and implementing that policy. The book is not a catalog of federal programs related to children. Its particular emphasis, in substantive policy, is on preschool services, especially out-of-home child-care services, on school feeding, and on child health. Feeding and health both permit comparison between congressional and executive responses to new issues and old issues. Care, feeding, and health collectively subsume children's programs with universal applicability and programs targeted to selective categories of children.

17. Alfred J. Kahn, Sheila B. Kamerman, and Brenda G. McGowan, *Child Advocacy: Report of a National Baseline Study* (Columbia University School of Social Work, 1972), p. 13.

# 2

# Intellectualizing Day Care

Publicly financed day care for preschool children and for older children after school became an important political issue upon the publication of scholarly research findings dealing with the plasticity of the early childhood period, and the coincidental emergence of the female-headed family as the principal cause of the rising cost of public assistance. The idea of assuming public responsibility for early child development through a universal day-care system—with priority for poor children—occupied the attention of policy planners in a large segment of the human resources field, and achieved rapid success in Congress. For a time, opposition seemed to come only from the extreme right. But as it became clear that child development and out-of-home child care are not synonymous, the apparent consensus fell apart. If out-of-home care will not insure enhanced development, why should welfare mothers alone be expected to agree to it for their children? If public support of day care can be defended only as a technique for reducing welfare costs, is it reasonable to intrude on that "sacred right of parents" to rear their own children simply because a family is very poor or lacks a father?

A theory of early child development—as distinguished from ordinary child care—that would both justify and define expanded boundaries of public intervention had barely emerged from the intellectual world when the federal antipoverty program was put together in 1964. The politics of that program provided the opportunity to test the early development theory through Head Start, a preschool program for poor children. If it worked for the poor, expansion of preschool education up the economic scale could become a major social policy issue.

For its first four years, at least, Head Start was seen as providing (1) a program of preschool education that implemented the newest ideas in educational psychology; (2) an instrument for social change that imple-

14

mented the progress-through-community-action philosophy of political liberals; and (3) a way "that the child could serve as a handle by which the family might be grasped."[1] Moreover, it had a commonsense appeal to many persons who were indifferent to parent education, community action, and cognitive development: if some children in the United States were so deprived that they did not know such basic things as colors, a program that seemed quickly to wipe out those deficits was obviously a sensible effort. The commonsense appeal persists, but Head Start's other strengths have eroded. Proponents of so-called comprehensive child development legislation find that each of the components of the cognitive development–community action–parent education coalition has become a shaky base to build on: preschool programs may be no more satisfactory a path to optimizing child development than other techniques that both cost less and do less violence to traditional arrangements; community action seems not to be an ideal way to narrow in on child development; and irregular participation means parent development can be accomplished in only a relative handful of cases. Social and emotional development of children has now come to be the principal rationale for early intervention. Without a mechanism to measure those characteristics, however, it takes an act of faith to believe that noncognitive gains can more certainly be accomplished than can cognitive gains.

## An Era of Sporadic Federal Interest

Before Head Start, federal support for child care had been accomplished only when tied explicitly to national emergency—to winning a war or overcoming economic depression. In the depression of the 1930s, day-care centers were created to provide jobs. When Congress during the late 1930s earmarked $6 million for day-care programs sponsored by the Works Projects Administration, the preoccupation was with providing work for unemployed teachers, custodians, cooks, and nurses. "As one would expect," Sheila Rothman has written, "turnover in both clients and staff was very high, facilities were inadequate (the basements of schools or public buildings), and the entire effort was really a minor ven-

---

1. *Headstart Child Development Act*, Hearings before the Subcommittee on Employment, Manpower, and Poverty of the Senate Labor and Public Welfare Committee, 91:1 (Government Printing Office, 1970), pt. 1, p. 149.

ture in relief giving."[2] While the 1937 *Social Work Yearbook* saw WPA day care as recognition of a public responsibility for education and guidance of preschool children, in fact more stress was placed on nutrition and health services.[3] World War II made the WPA unnecessary, and the latter's day-care centers expired. National defense womanpower needs led to another round of federal support for day care, but that support lasted barely as long as the war. Experience with a changed distribution of private and public responsibility for child care brought about by these efforts might have led to a permanent shift in the direction of greater public responsibility. Experience resulting from expediency alone did not, however, alter custom: family care of children showed itself to be strongly resistant to change.

The public program that provided federal aid to the states for preschool and after-school care of children during World War II is often cited as a model for federal child-care support. This wartime experience under the Lanham Act and the continuing California program it spawned does yield important social and political lessons, but it does not suggest any major deviation from the general nonintervention tradition. Child care under the Lanham Act reached a relatively small number of children, and termination of the program hardly provoked a fight. The most instructive aspect of the California experience is its emphasis on a special class— working mothers in single-parent families.

The Lanham Act of 1940 authorized federal expenditures for operation and maintenance of hospitals, schools, and child-care centers built to meet the needs of workers in defense facilities. Legislative intent was clear all along: it never extended to federal sponsorship of child care outside the defense emergency framework. Even arguments suggesting that center-care support be perpetuated for children of war widows were brushed aside in the face of expressed congressional belief that mothers should be at home caring for their children, that jobs in shipyards and aircraft factories "belong to men," and that federal rather than state action could only be defended under wartime conditions.[4] Although more than three thousand day-care centers were sustained with $51 million of Lanham Act money, it was a win-the-war program, not a save-the-children program.[5]

2. "Other People's Children: The Day Care Experience in America," *Public Interest*, Winter 1973, p. 20.
3. Lela Costin, *Child Welfare: Policies and Practice* (McGraw-Hill, 1972), p. 192.
4. Rolla McMillen (Republican of Illinois), in *Congressional Record*, vol. 91, pt. 5 (1945), p. 6318.
5. Material on "Federally Assisted Day Care Programs," prepared by U.S. Depart-

Responsibility for administration of the act was lodged in the Federal Works Administration (FWA), an agency not really sympathetic to the use of Lanham Act money for child care, and one that never ceased to look ahead to termination of the program. The cooperating agencies, the Office of Education and the Children's Bureau, were torn between anxiety to provide facilities and anxiety to guarantee that the facilities and the care provided be of high quality.[6] With the three agencies reflecting three goals all involved in the grants-approval process, progress came hard. At the peak of the program, Lanham Act centers were caring for only 105,000 children, although an inflated 1.6 million enrollment figure continues to be quoted.[7]

The termination warning that the FWA delivered to the states early in 1945 brought strong reaction. But the FWA's move was attacked as premature, not as indefensible on its merits. The sponsor of legislation designed to extend federal assistance for another year expressed concern only about timing: "Why do we stop . . . before these wartime conditions under which it was wise and expedient to set up these child care centers with Federal funds have been materially eradicated to peacetime conditions?"[8] When President Truman agreed to continue federal support for six months beyond the original FWA plan, the bill was set aside, a reprieve attributable less to support for public child care than to the need for orderly reconversion.

The children's lobby—such as it was—had little to say on behalf of a continuing federal role in child care after FWA's early warning that the end was in sight. An ambiguously worded statement came from the Child Welfare League of America: "Joint planning and administration of day-care programs [require] a single Federal agency having resources in medicine, education, and social work. . . . The war has shown that such factors cannot be effectively dealt with entirely within the borders of particular States or counties."[9] Another came from the National Commission on Children in Wartime in the form of a proposal that federal child welfare

ment of Health, Education, and Welfare, appears in *Headstart Child Development Act*, Hearings, pt. 1, pp. 123–27.

6. William H. Chafe, *The American Woman: Her Changing Social, Economic, and Political Roles, 1920–1970* (Oxford University Press, 1970), p. 168.

7. Dorothy E. Bradbury, *Five Decades of Action for Children*, U.S. Department of Health, Education, and Welfare, Social Security Administration, Children's Bureau publication no. 358 (rev. ed., 1962), p. 61.

8. *Congressional Record*, vol. 91, pt. 2 (1945), p. A 4156.

9. *New York Times*, May 22, 1945.

funds be used "to provide day-care services for children whose mothers are employed or whose home conditions require such services."[10] One bill to implement a commission recommendation dealing with maternal and child health, crippled children, and child welfare services did reach the hearings stage in the Senate. Day-care centers and foster-family homes were among the eight welfare services to be assisted, but in two days of hearings, just one witness—a representative of the Congress of American Women—argued on behalf of a national program of day care modeled on the Lanham Act child-care centers for children of working mothers.[11]

So Lanham Act funds ended with the proverbial whimper. Only California, New York, and the District of Columbia centers did not promptly collapse. Congress, consistent at least with its posture that child care was a state function, appropriated funds for child-care centers in the District. Under the jurisdiction of the Department of Public Welfare, the centers were for the exclusive use of children of low-income, employed parents. Even under these restricted conditions, the centers lasted only from 1946 to 1953. The end came much sooner in New York where a compromise had continued state appropriations for care in New York City. In 1947 the New York State Youth Commission reported that neither World War II nor depression day-care needs any longer existed. Finding that local communities had not taken responsibility for day-care centers, that limited numbers of children were benefited at great expense with no assurance that the neediest were being served, and that the day-care program conflicted with the philosophy of the aid to dependent children program, the commission concluded that state-aided general day care should be ended.[12] It did end on January 1, 1948.

Only the California children's centers were permanent survivors of the program begun under the Lanham Act. The California program's emphases on language and educational development and social experiences, together with its staff training requirements and low teacher-pupil ratios (one to five), cause it often to be cited as the prototype for a national program. What is less frequently mentioned—and probably less well known—is that the program reaches only a tiny fraction of California children; that it still exists primarily to preclude welfare dependency; and

10. U.S. Children's Bureau, National Commission on Children in Wartime, Building the Future for Children and Youth: Next Steps Proposed by the N.C.C.W. (April 1945).

11. Maternal and Child Welfare Act of 1945, Hearings before the Senate Committee on Education and Labor, 79:2 (GPO, 1946), pp. 124–25.

12. Youth Services News, April 1947, pp. 2–4.

that in recent years, at least, it has been paid for in large part by the federal government.

From 1946 to 1957 the centers were voted support "only very reluctantly" by the California legislature. Their mission was "to continue serving children whose parents needed work as a result of the slowness of economic reconversion and the continued drafting of men into the armed services."[13] Although authorization was extended indefinitely by a 1957 act, it was not until 1965—after the invention of Head Start—that persistent efforts to change the stated purpose of the California program to "supervision and instruction" from "care and supervision" finally succeeded.[14] While instruction superseded care in the justification, constraints on admission remained tight. The orientation has consistently been toward single-parent working mothers, who would be even heavier burdens on the total tax load if they did not work to support themselves.[15] By 1972, single-parent families accounted for 80 percent of the 24,000 children served by the centers.

The California children's centers were ideal candidates for federal financing under provisions of the 1967 amendments to the Social Security Act that authorized unlimited three-to-one matching of funds for services to past, present, and potential welfare recipients. Alerted by efficient staff work, California's legislature enacted the necessary bills. The centers shifted their emphasis from children of low- and middle-income working mothers who paid income-related fees to children of potential welfare recipients and of actual recipients in work training—and, in so doing, also shifted most of the cost to Washington. That manner of federal financing of day care became a "frustrating, sometimes impossible task" in the judgment of one center director, but it saved state money.[16] By mid-1973, for example, of the 1,328 children in San Diego's sixteen centers, 425 were from welfare families and most of the remaining 903 qualified as former or potential clients. When restraints on the amount and use of federal social services money were proposed that year, California's superintendent of public instruction wrote HEW Secretary Caspar Weinberger, in a "Dear Cap" letter, that such restraints would cause "irremedi-

13. Marjorie Stern, "California Children's Centers," *American Teacher*, December 1971; reprinted in *Congressional Record* (daily ed.), March 7, 1972, p. S 3569.

14. Theresa S. Mahler, *A Brief on the California Children's Center Program* (rev. ed., Calfornia Children's Centers Directors and Supervisors Association, 1966).

15. Ibid.

16. Letter from Docia Zavitkovsky, June 15, 1973.

able harm,"[17] a euphemism for "our whole program would be in jeopardy because we would have to go back to paying for it ourselves."

In short, close examination of the California program indicates that it never was sustained solely as a child development activity. Rather, it has been sustained through most of its life as a way of freeing low-income mothers from actual or potential dependence on welfare assistance. To the extent that child development was consistent with that objective, the child development cause would also be served.

Although the Korean War came only a few years after the termination of Lanham Act support, renewed defense-mobilization activity associated with the war led to no renewal of interest in child care as a national issue. (The 1950 White House Conference on Children and Youth, where publicly supported child care might have been a big issue, passed it over in the conference platform.) Federal aid to impacted areas for community facilities, including day care, discussed in 1951 as one way to offset the dislocation caused by Korean War mobilization, generated no enthusiasm in the Truman administration. Acknowledging a need for day care as mothers entered defense work, Federal Security Agency administrator Oscar Ewing held that "such care is basically a local responsibility," and that federal help would "be required only as a supplement to existing local resources."[18] Catholic Church opposition was expressed by Monsignor John O'Grady, the formidable lobbyist for the National Conference of Catholic Charities, who took the position that mothers should not be encouraged to leave their children.[19] Supporting groups never organized to make a major push in 1951. And while the 1952 Democratic platform favored day-care facilities for the children of mothers doing defense work, 1952 was not a good year for the Democrats. When President Eisenhower promptly fulfilled his campaign commitment to end the war, defense-related day care became moot.

Five years would elapse before public child care was again to be mentioned in Congress. Then, in 1958, the first of a series of "cold war" day-care bills was offered by Senator Jacob Javits, Republican of New York, to provide day care for the children of working mothers ("It is surely as important now, during the cold war, for the Federal Government to give financial support to a day-care center program as it was during World

17. Letter from Wilson Riles to Caspar Weinberger, Feb. 14, 1973.
18. *Defense Housing and Community Facilities,* Hearings before the House Committee on Banking and Currency, 82:1 (GPO, 1951), p. 101.
19. Ibid., p. 292.

War II."[20]). Not until the next regular White House Conference on Children and Youth was held in 1960 was publicly supported child care provided further visibility—and then it was not much. That conference issued six hundred and seventy recommendations, the product of eighteen separate forums on eighteen separate topics. Somewhere in the pile was something on growth and development, but even the Children's Bureau found it discouraging to try to sort things out.[21] Later in 1960, a National Conference on Day Care for Children was sponsored by the Women's Bureau and the Children's Bureau. Its planners, a group representing voluntary women's associations, labor, management, national social agencies, education, and health agencies, hoped to stimulate community interest and leadership in day care. One of the conference's twenty-five recommendations called for an effort to obtain day-care funds from local, state, and federal sources. Another proposed day care for all children needing it from infants to adolescents as a part of every community child welfare program but did not offer criteria for determining which children "need" such care.[22]

First signs of high-level interest in publicly sustained day care (in other than a national emergency) were forthcoming in a letter read at the national conference from then President-elect Kennedy. In the letter addressed to Elinor Guggenheimer, one of the organizers of the conference, Kennedy declared himself in favor of day-care centers for "children of working mothers and of parents who for one reason and another cannot provide adequate care during the day."[23] A year later, President Kennedy sent a welfare message to Congress proposing legislation to implement his earlier statement. The point of the message was that people receiving public assistance deserve more than a check, they deserve services, which might help them get off assistance. As part of this plan, day-care programs were to be provided so that mothers could work. Kennedy wanted a small authorization—$5 million the first year and $10 million thereafter—to aid local programs.[24]

20. *Congressional Record,* vol. 104, pt. 10 (1958), p. 12430.

21. HEW, Social and Rehabilitation Service, Children's Bureau, *The Story of the White House Conferences on Children and Youth* (1967), p. 26.

22. Gertrude L. Hoffman, *Day Care Services, Form and Substance: A Report of a Conference, November 17–18, 1960,* HEW, Social Security Administration, Children's Bureau publication no. 393-1961, and U.S. Department of Labor, Women's Bureau bulletin no. 281-1961, p. 48.

23. Ibid., pp. 13–14.

24. *Congressional Quarterly Almanac,* 1962, p. 884.

The welfare amendments passed, but it took another year (1963) before even an $800,000 supplemental appropriation was achieved through the urging of Senators Javits and Ribicoff, the latter fresh from service as Kennedy's first secretary of HEW. This was the first federal financial assistance for child-care purposes since 1946. Ribicoff, a Democrat of Connecticut, emphasized day care as a way of getting mothers off welfare and out to work and provided reassurance that there was "no intention of providing services for the purpose of relieving parents of the care of their children while they run errands or seek recreation."[25] Neither Ribicoff nor Javits suggested possible positive benefits for the children to be served. As concern over the cost of public assistance mounted, more political leaders advocated sending welfare mothers to work and providing day care for their children. But a reluctance to encourage any but the most poverty-stricken mothers to work appeared even in the statements of strong day-care advocates like Javits and Ribicoff. The case for publicly supported child care continued to be tied to the low-income working mother, to the mentally retarded and otherwise handicapped, and to children of migrant agricultural workers.

During the decade and a half between liquidation of the child-care program established under World War II's Lanham Act and the Kennedy request in 1962 for a small day-care appropriation, no serious attention was paid at the federal level to the possibility that organized child care could be a way of getting important positive benefits to children. Keeping low-income mothers off welfare succeeded national defense manpower needs as the stated purpose of day care. In each case, enabling part of the population to work, not improving child development, was the public policy objective. Child care happened to be the impediment to work to be dealt with, but the impediment might have been lack of transportation or a comparable impersonal problem. Even the most socially conscious politicians put the argument in those terms because they then had no basis to argue the grander case of day care as a possible developmental force in children's lives.

### Experience and Intelligence

"When radical change takes place," Daniel P. Moynihan once explained to leaders of the day-care movement, "it comes through knowledge, not slogans, not simply enthusiasm, but through the impact of

25. *Congressional Record*, vol. 109, pt. 6 (1963), p. 7555.

knowledge."[26] Beliefs in fixed intelligence and predetermined development of children were unchallenged by contrary knowledge until comparatively recently. "These beliefs," J. McVicker Hunt has written, ". . .
dominated thought among a great majority of the leaders of psychology
and education and among a major share of the intellectual leaders of
America, from the days of the nineteenth century debates over Darwin's
theory of evolution through World War II."[27] Research pursued in the
1950s and the first part of the 1960s cast doubt on beliefs in fixed intelligence by suggesting that outside influences may affect the rate of early
development of human infants. Hunt's own findings on intelligence and
experience appeared in 1961. Their central conclusion was that experience
programs the development of the human brain.[28] The conclusion is of
profound significance for child development. It means "that the counsel
from experts on child-rearing . . . to let children be while they grow and to
avoid excessive stimulation was highly unfortunate."[29]

From that time on, there could not be a public policy debate over child
care that did not become a debate over child development. If Hunt was
right, the stakes involved in child-care policy were much higher than had
been realized. Child-care centers were more than a matter of maternal
convenience or a technique for reducing welfare costs. Potentially, at least,
they were investments in human development and could become instruments of social change. Nursery schools had been used by middle-class in-
tellectuals during the 1950s as a presumed socializing technique for children. The focus of these schools was on emotional rather than cognitive
growth. As Hunt and others unveiled their conclusions, new attention
focused on both the clientele and the curriculum of the nursery school and
of kindergarten. The distinction between care, cognition, and compensatory education for preschool children became important.

Over the next decade, some complicated questions would be asked and
studied. A nasty argument would develop over the relative significance
of genetic and environmental factors in accounting for human intelligence, an argument, in short, over the validity of the proposition that
experience programs the development of the human brain. Even among
those who accepted that proposition, there would be questions about the
clear benefit to be shown from organized child development efforts in

26. Speech to board of directors of Day Care and Child Development Council of
America, quoted in *Voice for Children*, vol. 2, no. 10 (November 1969), p. 3.
27. Vernon L. Allen, ed., *Psychological Factors in Poverty*, Institute for Research
on Poverty Monograph Series (Markham Publishing, 1970), p. 48.
28. J. McVicker Hunt, *Intelligence and Experience* (Ronald Press, 1961).
29. Ibid., p. 362.

formal preschool settings compared to parents' own efforts to intervene. Does the particular "mix" of children matter? What does organized development do for cognition? Are any measurable benefits permanent or do they fade? What of the social and emotional side? What are the ultimate economic benefits of emphasizing cognition?

Before these kinds of disenchanting issues were pressed, however, theory and practice in child development were pushed ahead significantly by the publication in 1964 of a much-quoted volume by Professor Benjamin Bloom of the University of Chicago, and by the invention of the Head Start program.

Bloom's book resulted from five years of effort to synthesize longitudinal studies undertaken during the previous fifty years in various parts of the world. Those studies, involving repeated observation and measurement of the same children from birth through ten or more years of age, constituted the principal data base. Supplementary evidence came from studies in which a sample of individuals was tested or observed two or more times, from studies in which the effects of particular educational or other conditions were being determined over a limited time span, and from school records. Bloom focused on some thirty human characteristics, including height, weight, certain body processes, intelligence, and verbal aptitude.

The findings on the several characteristics differed. But the general findings on a large number of characteristics, especially characteristics like verbal ability, so-called general intelligence, general school achievement, attitudes of dependency and of aggressiveness, showed a pattern of very rapid development in the early years followed by slower and slower development. The range within which fluctuations occur becomes narrower with increasing age. For general intelligence, for example, Bloom concluded that around the age of four, one has accounted for around 50 percent of the variation possible for any particular child. The limits of variation become shorter and shorter as the child approaches ages twelve to eighteen. Moreover, "the importance of the influences which affect the growth of . . . [each human] characteristic is likely to be far greater in the periods of most rapid development than it is, at least quantitatively, in the periods of least rapid development."[30] Without taking a position on the relative importance of heredity and environment, Bloom left no room for continued belief in predetermined development and fixed intelli-

30. Benjamin S. Bloom, *Stability and Change in Human Characteristics* (Wiley, 1964), p. 204.

gence. "We cannot imagine any research worker or any research in disagreement with the basic proposition that *the environment is a determiner
of the extent and kind of change taking place in a particular characteristic* . . . the evidence is clear that the increments for a particular characteristic are in part determined by the environment."[31]

Since the environment can be controlled or adjusted, its introduction
as a variable makes a major difference in the ability to predict individual
human characteristics at maturity. Thus the issues of social responsibility
and of public policy are raised. Bloom observes that many authorities
regard as desirable a number of positively stated characteristics which, at
their optimal level, enable an individual to be "a productive contributor
to the society as well as to lead a satisfying and useful life."[32] A large proportion of individuals should be able to attain these characteristics to some
minimal degree. Accordingly, more desirable child-rearing environmental
conditions should be identified and created. Those more desirable environmental conditions would have to be based on recognition that the half-
development of general intelligence and of intellectuality is achieved by
age four, of height by age two-and-a-half, of aggressiveness in males by
age three, and of dependence in females by age four. For all of these
characteristics, in short, the most rapid period of development is in "the
first five years of life."[33] It was a phrase that would have political consequences.

Bloom's willingness to address himself to the question of social responsibility might have been expected to open a low-keyed discussion among
educational psychologists, social reformers, and politicians extending over
several years, at least, and posing for broader consideration the costs and
consequences of one or another social policy addressed to the first five
years of life. Instant solutions seemed unlikely for the challenge with
which Bloom's book concluded:

Put briefly, the increased ability to predict long-term consequences of
environmental forces and developmental characteristics places new responsibilities on the home, the school, and the society. If these responsibilities are
not adequately met, society will suffer in the long run. If these responsibilities
are neglected, the individual will suffer a life of continual frustration and
alienation.[34]

What Benjamin Bloom, J. McVicker Hunt, and a handful of others

31. Ibid., p. 209.
32. Ibid., p. 228.
33. Ibid., pp. 204–05.
34. Ibid., p. 231.

had done was to suggest that existing policy did not adequately meet society's responsibility to children. Public intervention for development did not begin until age six, yet all children grow and develop at a much faster rate in the first five to seven years of life than at any subsequent period. If children pass through their most important period of development before they ever become part of the educational system, then preschool developmental services should be as compelling a public obligation as protection of preschool children against neglect and dependency.

Creative research provided a theory to justify such a move, but the research did not fix public policy priorities. If intervention were expanded to cover "development," services might be provided either in the home or out of the home in organized centers. And such services could be concentrated on children who start with manifest environmental disadvantages and might, therefore, gain the most, or they could be extended to children with normal environmental advantages to assure whatever marginal growth is possible. The questions of "how to do it" and "to whom to do it" have been important to both the research and the political communities since the appearance of Bloom's book. The "how" question was further complicated as it intertwined with debate over the overhaul of the public relief system originally established in the Social Security Act of 1935. The "to whom" question produced anxiety among many middle-class families who did not want to exclude their children from the benefits of "development," but who could not persuade themselves that the concept of mother caring for small children in the home without government intervention was obsolete.

## From Experiment to Institution

Neither Hunt's *Intelligence and Experience* nor Bloom's *Stability and Change in Human Characteristics* directly triggered public policy activity. Whatever their importance for later efforts to effect social policy change, the short-run importance of these works was in the coincidence of their timing with the political needs and purposes of the Kennedy and Johnson presidencies.

There was no reference to research conclusions about early childhood when the original antipoverty task force—created by direction of President Kennedy—proposed a massive community-action program.[35] Pre-

35. James L. Sundquist, ed., *On Fighting Poverty: Perspectives from Experience* (Basic Books, 1969), pp. 34 ff.

school children were not then pinpointed. Project Head Start, characterized in retrospect by Adam Yarmolinsky, who was Sargent Shriver's deputy
during the development of the war-on-poverty legislation, as "perhaps
the most favored offspring of the entire effort," was not invented until
six months after enactment of the Economic Opportunity Act.[36] Only as
Shriver and his associates refined community action, in hopes of developing both a more comprehensive program and one that would show quick
results, did they introduce the idea of targeting community-action efforts
to a variety of groups, including preschool children.

Head Start was proposed by a panel of "action-oriented people in the
fields of pediatrics, child development, education, social service, psychology, and psychiatry," chaired by Dr. Robert E. Cooke, professor of
pediatrics at the Johns Hopkins University School of Medicine.[37] Cooke
was not a haphazard choice. Members of the Kennedy family, whose intense personal interest in problems of mental retardation stemmed from
the tragic life of their mentally retarded sister, had had earlier contact
with him. Cooke had helped educate the family to the nature of child
health and human development, had pushed the case for a national institute of child health, and had later served with Eunice Kennedy Shriver
on the advisory council of the National Institute of Child Health and
Human Development. The mandate given to Cooke was to "assemble a
panel of experts to consider the kinds of programs which might be most
effective in increasing achievement and opportunities for the children of
the poor."[38] He did so, and the panel's conclusion favored preschool
programs that would provide the child maximum opportunity to develop
his potential. Such programs would be comprehensive, including health,
education, and social services.

In a letter to Shriver, Cooke wrote that there "already exists adequate
understanding of the problems and processes involved to permit an immediate and massive intervention in the poverty cycle."[39] The report
itself said because children of poverty lack "the kinds of experiences and
opportunities which are available to more economically advantaged families," many of them are unable to utilize the typical school situation.
Thus it was necessary to identify the child's special needs and deficiencies
and provide the necessary compensatory experiences.[40]

36. Ibid., p. 40.
37. Headstart Child Development Act, Hearings, pt. 1, p. 146.
38. Ibid., p. 147.
39. Ibid.
40. Ibid., p. 154.

Cooke's panel did not seem to anticipate that Head Start gains would be dissipated by the public school experience. The report does state that Head Start activities "need to be carefully integrated with the program for the school years,"[41] but it offers no suggestions about how to do this. The underlying assumption seems to be that if the right blend of experiences and services is provided the poverty child, he will be able to move easily into the public school system.

The panel would have preferred earlier public intervention in the child's life. Indeed, Dr. Cooke later said that it was "concern with the enormous influence of environment . . . in the early months and years of life" that led him to organize the Head Start effort "under Mr. Sargent Shriver's direction in December, 1964." Dr. Cooke said that from the beginning his committee was "convinced that earlier intervention would have to occur for maximum yield; but, considerations of cost, of personnel shortage, or organization difficulties with a younger age group, impelled us to begin first with the immediate group who were entering school."[42] Cooke himself agreed completely with the evidence that the later the intervention the more solidified the defects and deficiencies.

Moynihan's suggestion of knowledge as a prerequisite for change is confirmed by the development of Head Start. But it was largely by chance that the knowledge provided in the specialized writings of Bloom, Hunt, Cooke, and Jean Piaget found its way to policy. It was the earlier tie between Cooke and the Kennedys that made preschool development an item on the political agenda in 1964, for without Shriver, Cooke had no access. Without the war on poverty, Shriver had no vehicle for a preschool program. Without President Johnson's decision that the war on poverty was "my kind of program. . . . Move full speed ahead," there would have been no economic opportunity legislation.[43] To put it differently, the preexistence of the antipoverty program provided the environment for creating Head Start. The latter, in turn, implemented some of the conclusions of the educational psychologists. Had there not been a war on poverty, those conclusions might have remained academic for an indefinite time. Once in place, Project Head Start itself generated a further expansion of interest in and study of early childhood, but it was neither in-

41. Ibid.
42. Ibid., p. 149.
43. Remarks made to Walter Heller on Nov. 11, 1964, and repeated by him in a speech at Indiana State College, Indiana, Pa., March 26, 1965; quoted in Sundquist, *On Fighting Poverty*, p. 21.

vented as nor did it ever become an appropriate model for a universal preschool program.

Unexpectedly finding themselves next to the centers of power, the scientists of child development too readily acquiesced as Head Start was moved from experiment to established institution without wide-ranging debate about likely costs and benefits, or about likely alternatives. Some of its own planners ultimately came to speak of "the naive environmentalism which caused Head Start to be oversold in the early days. . . . We were captured by the notion that these kinds of minimal interventions, which are nothing but token programs, would make a difference in children's lives."[44] Those observations were made after evaluation studies had demonstrated that for all of its popularity, "the largest and most important social action experiment mounted in behalf of needy children in the history of our nation"[45] was of dubious value as an investment. The cognitive gains achieved by its children during the Head Start experience faded by the early years of school. But no cautionary word had been uttered in the early days by the White House or the Office of Economic Opportunity.

President Johnson shared the hope of Shriver's panel of experts that preschool experiences would give poverty children a boost in school. The President's position was that "education must begin with the very young," that the child of poverty is handicapped even before he begins school, is usually a year behind before he reaches the third grade, and three years behind if he reaches the eighth. But, Johnson said in a 1965 education message, preschool programs had shown "marked success" in overcoming this handicap, citing programs in New York and Baltimore as evidence. The President said his budget would include "up to $150 million" for OEO community-action preschool programs to begin in the summer of 1965 and serve children who would enter school in the fall.[46]

About $17 million, for about 100,000 children, was what OEO planners had expected to spend during the summer of 1965. But the demand was far greater than anticipated—due in large part probably to the way the program was sold by Shriver and his staff. Public announcement of Head Start came at a White House tea party in February reported, to the delight

44. Edward F. Zigler, "Child Care in the 1970's" (remarks at the Idaho Early Childhood Conference, Spring 1972); reprinted in *Congressional Record* (daily ed.), Aug. 16, 1972, p. E 7527.

45. Ibid., Aug. 15, 1972, p. E 7519.

46. *Congressional Quarterly Almanac*, 1965, p. 1374.

of Head Start's first national leaders, on the society pages. Thereafter, Shriver sent personal letters to thirty-five thousand school administrators, mayors, welfare administrators, and community officials. The requests poured in and the OEO decided to support a much larger program than originally planned, ignoring the Cooke panel's warning that "during the early stages of any programs assisted by the Office of Economic Opportunity, it would be preferable to encourage comprehensive programs for fewer children than to attempt to reach vast numbers of children with limited programs."[47] Instead of 100,000 children, 561,359 children were enrolled in 11,068 centers in the summer of 1965.

Sar Levitan has pointed out that the OEO staff saw value in a rapid expansion of Head Start for more reasons than early education of poor children. Head Start was extremely popular in contrast to some of the OEO's other programs. Its rapid expenditure of money would help the OEO secure a larger appropriation in 1966, and it could serve as a catalyst in the formation of community action agencies.[48] In fact, both of these purposes were served. And five years later, Head Start's popularity would again be a wedge, utilized this time by a coalition of child-care activists, community-development groups, and women's organizations on behalf of a proposal to expand the scope of out-of-home child care as the preferred instrument of child development. But whether Head Start has produced evidence to sustain the choice of that preferred instrument is open to question.

If Head Start is a disappointment, it is not because it has harmed children. Although Edward Zigler argues that Head Start was understaffed and underfinanced from the beginning, and insists that "small token programs may have as many negative consequences as positive ones,"[49] no claim is made that Head Start has had negative consequences. Nor is the disappointment that it failed to capture public approval. To the contrary, it was an instant popular success, and also a congressional favorite from the beginning. The disappointment in Head Start results from the quick willingness of some federal bureaucrats and their advisers to suggest that they had found the key to manipulating environmental conditions that might optimize if not maximize growth and development of the preschool child.

Head Start achieved its instant and continuing popularity by focusing

47. Headstart Child Development Act, Hearings, pt. 1, p. 154.
48. Sar Levitan, The Great Society's Poor Law: A New Approach to Poverty (Johns Hopkins Press, 1969), p. 137.
49. Headstart Child Development Act, Hearings, pt. 1, p. 157.

essentially on one model of service, organized centers serving preschool children. That exclusive focus was adopted as a matter of adminstrative policy, not of statute. The Economic Opportunity Act of 1964, and the subsequent amendments to it which wrote a Head Start program into law, anticipated maximum community group freedom in choosing services. In an internal memorandum to the secretary of health, education, and welfare late in 1971, the director of the Office of Child Development acknowledged that HEW could not "demand that prime sponsors of existing Head Start programs change the Head Start Center format without encountering serious political repercussions."[50] The subject was not being discussed in a vacuum. Pending legislation would have specifically authorized several alternative forms of services to children including in-home services, child-development training for parents, prenatal care, and others. At the same time, the bill would have protected Head Start projects by giving them priority in financing. "Thus, it would be unrealistic," the memorandum admitted, "to suggest that new legislation will enable us to easily alter existing Head Start programs in the immediate future."

That this conclusion could be reached more than two years after the first disillusioning report about the Head Start model only emphasizes the dilemma that first became apparent in the early months of 1969. Head Start centers were so great a popular and congressional success that it was virtually impossible to alter the program either by administrative action or by statutory authorization for alternative models. "Whatever the many evaluations of Head Start may indicate," the secretary of HEW was told, "the Head Start experiment is now viewed as a success by many among the scientific community, the Congress, and the public."[51] Yet, there was doubt about Head Start's effectiveness in cognitive development. Alternative ways of manipulating children's environments might be more effective or equally effective at less cost.

From Lyndon Johnson's January 1965 education message to Richard Nixon's February 1969 message on reorganization of the antipoverty program, Head Start's value as an instrument of early education had not been in dispute. To be sure, J. McVicker Hunt, who chaired a Task Force on Early Child Development, wrote President Johnson's policy assistants as early as December 1966 that the beneficial effects of Head Start for deprived children could be lost unless special attention was continued on

---

50. "Response to September 30 OCD Management Conference Action Item #3: The long-term role of Project Head Start—Information Memorandum," from Edward Zigler to Elliot Richardson (Nov. 23, 1971), p. 4.
51. Ibid., p. 2.

into grades one, two, and three. That prescient concern, however, was preceded by assurances that "the early reports of the effectiveness of Head Start are favorable."[52]

Such was the Washington view of Head Start through all of the Johnson administration. Daniel P. Moynihan has described the circumstances attending receipt during the first weeks of the Nixon presidency of the findings of the first large-scale evaluation study of the program:

The president's February 19 message was about to be sent to the Congress, complete with a strong endorsement of Head Start, when word arrived for OEO that a massive evaluation study, carried out by the Westinghouse Learning Corporation and Ohio University, had come forth with the finding that had in effect been predicted by Coleman: Head Start wasn't working. The children were getting their teeth fixed, but little else that could be quantified. The president's message was modified, in an attempt, as much as anything, to telegraph the blow. Head Start was described as still "experimental," it had demonstrated not only how difficult but how important it was to get at the mysteries of early learning, it fixed teeth. The message ended with the nice passage: "We do not pretend to have all the answers. We are determined to find as many as we can . . . not every experiment succeeds. . . ." But this to small effect.[53]

The Westinghouse study involved a post-hoc sample of children from over a hundred centers across the country who had gone on to local area schools and a matched sample of control children from the same grades and schools who had not attended Head Start. Both groups were administered a series of tests covering various aspects of cognitive and affective development to learn the extent to which Head Start children differed in their intellectual and social-personal development from comparable children who had not attended. The answer, in essence, was "not much." Aside from a slight but significant superiority of full-year Head Start children on some measures of cognitive development, "the Head Start children cannot be said to be *appreciably* different from their peers in the elementary grades who did not attend Head Start in most aspects of cognitive and affective development measured in this study."[54] Among the

52. Memorandum to Joseph Califano, Jr., Douglass Cater, and James C. Gaither in response to Gaither's request for report of progress and description of recommendations likely to come from the task force (Dec. 4, 1966; processed), p. 5.

53. *The Politics of a Guaranteed Income: The Nixon Administration and the Family Assistance Plan* (Random House, 1973), p. 150.

54. Westinghouse Learning Corp., Ohio University, "The Impact of Head Start: An Evaluation of the Effects of Head Start on Children's Cognitive and Affective Development," executive summary (June 1969; processed), p. 5.

nine major findings of the Westinghouse effort, the most positive dealt not with children's measurable cognitive gains or social-emotional development but with parents' strong approval of the program and its effect on their children.

Response to Westinghouse was mixed. Harvard's Sheldon White explained to Representative John Brademas one day that "with all of the faults of the Westinghouse study, one must accept its assessments of the present effectiveness of Head Start. . . . I know of 30 other evaluations of Head Start, done on a much smaller scale, and I would say the Westinghouse results are more positive than many of the others."[55] Critics of the work, including leaders of the Day Care and Child Development Council of America, complained generally that its scope was too narrow, and its technique and methodology faulty.[56] "Some of us knew that with that set of questions, that set of answers was inevitable," Urie Bronfenbrenner, who had served on the earlier Head Start task force, told an interviewer.

But "that set of questions" and "that set of answers," as we have seen, was enough to transform a planned strong endorsement of Head Start by President Nixon into an ambiguous endorsement. In Congress, the Westinghouse study produced very little reaction, and no thoughtful reaction at all. "To me," said Representative James Scheuer, Democrat of New York, "the shopping list of negatives arrived at by the Westinghouse study provides graphic and dramatic evidence of the need for further strengthening, expansion and improving of the program."[57] At appropriations hearings, Democratic Representative Dan Flood of Pennsylvania, Labor-HEW Appropriations Subcommittee chairman, and Jule Sugarman, Head Start's director, reassured each other:

MR. FLOOD: Headstart is the sort of program which lends itself to cooperation.
MR. SUGARMAN: I think that is true.
MR. FLOOD: Everybody connected with it is rather enthused about it?
MR. SUGARMAN: I think so.
MR. FLOOD: Yes. And that helps.[58]

55. *Comprehensive Preschool Education and Child Day-Care Act of 1969*, Hearings before the Select Subcommittee on Education of the House Committee on Education and Labor, 91:1 and 2 (GPO, 1970), p. 51. For a summary of White's views generally, see Sheldon White and others, *Federal Programs for Children: Review and Recommendations, Summary*, HEW (1973), vol. 4.

56. *Voice for Children*, newsletter of the council, vol. 2 (April 1969), p. 1.

57. *Congressional Record*, vol. 115, pt. 9 (1969), p. 11930.

58. *Departments of Labor and Health, Education, and Welfare Appropriations for 1970*, Hearings before a Subcommittee of the House Committee on Appropriations, 91:1 (GPO, 1969), pt. 8, p. 212.

A few months thereafter, the OEO's review of all Head Start research and evaluation carried on between 1965 and 1969 was published. It found the studies "rather uniformly" to indicate that while Head Start children did not lose what they gained through the experience, they did tend to level off to a plateau which allowed other children to catch up to them.[59] The review of over a hundred research projects also confirmed the Westinghouse finding that parents generally approved of Head Start. Moreover, parents make a difference: the children of parents who had a high level of participation performed better on tests of achievement and development.[60]

The situation headed for a stand-off. Head Start remained popular among its participants, and acceptable to the Congress. If it seemed not to be accomplishing a fundamental objective, its defenders argued that it accomplished other objectives. Early in 1970, with child development hearings going on in both houses, an evaluation of Head Start impact in local communities reassured bureaucrats that the program was an important social force in American society. Kirschner Associates studied fifty-eight communities with full-year Head Start programs, recorded 1,496 institutional changes, and grouped them neatly in four categories:[61]

|  | Number | Percent |
|---|---|---|
| Increased involvement of the poor at decision-making levels | 305 | 20.3 |
| Greater employment of the poor as paraprofessionals | 51 | 3.4 |
| Greater educational emphasis on the educational needs of the poor and minorities | 747 | 50.0 |
| Modification of health services and practices to serve the poor better and more sensitively | 393 | 26.3 |

Kirschner concluded that by "pragmatic, quiet actions rather than by violent confrontation," Head Start had achieved its goal of making local

59. Edith Grotberg, *Review of Research 1965 to 1969 of Project Head Start*, HEW, Office of Child Development, Bureau of Head Start and Early Childhood (1969), p. 40.

60. Ibid., p. 34.

61. Kirschner Associates, Inc., *A National Survey of the Impacts of Head Start Centers on Community Institutions*, prepared for HEW, OCD, Project Head Start, contract no. B89-4638 (1970), p. 6.

institutions more responsive to the poor[62]—institutions, the report pointed out, that were traditionally run by and for the middle class.

In defending the program against the Westinghouse-induced loss of fervor, Head Start theoreticians complain about the scant attention given Kirschner. Edward Zigler characterizes it as "a moving document . . . momentous."[63] Calling it "one of the most important social evaluations of the last ten years," the director of the Office of Child Development told a conference on early childhood that "in communities where there is a Head Start Center, the entire community is becoming mobilized around the needs of children."[64] Kirschner never captured the attention that Westinghouse did, however, because dependence on Kirschner appeared to be a fall-back position and because its appeal was relatively narrow. The universe in favor of enhancing cognitive development of children is enormously larger than that concerned with changing local institutions. Support for a broadened educational effort is easier to come by than is support for peaceful revolution.

If Westinghouse did discourage a planned presidential initiative on behalf of Head Start expansion, the pre-Westinghouse absorption in early cognitive development had been an important element of the initial interest in support for Head Start. The latter, in turn, showed that public programs for children as young as three could be established. That demonstration and its enthusiastic reception nearly everywhere led to a willingness to accept public intervention in development of preschool children. In short, if the original stated hopes for cognitive gains turned out to be less valid than at first believed, Head Start's unique contribution has been to give intellectual respectability to out-of-home child care under public auspices.

62. Ibid., p. 15.

63. Press conference, June 26, 1970 (transcript prepared by Ace-Federal Reports; processed).

64. *Congressional Record* (daily ed.), Aug. 15, 1972, p. E 7519.

# 3

# The Transfiguration
# of the Children's Bureau

Commingling community action with preschool education and child care bothered enough congressional supporters and opponents of each as early as 1968 to result in a directive to the President to study the feasibility of transferring or delegating Head Start from the Office of Economic Opportunity to another agency of government. Subsequently, the Nixon pre-inaugural Task Force on Welfare recommended delegation of Head Start specifically to a program within the Department of Health, Education, and Welfare labeled community coordinated child care—then only a dimly perceived vision in some bureaucrat's mind. A month after his inauguration, President Nixon announced his intention to delegate the operation of Head Start to HEW,[1] but did not say where in HEW. An obvious and logical possibility was the Children's Bureau. Instead, the decision was for a new agency. Taken together with earlier and later decisions by the administration and by Congress, the result is a transfiguration of the Children's Bureau that recognizes its continued existence yet superimposes over it an Office of Child Development to lead the children's cause. But the idea of glorifying the cause implicit in this arrangement can only be successful if the Office of Child Development can inherit, invent, or otherwise acquire viable programs to distinguish it from the old bureau.

## The Bureau and Its Critics

The traditionalism and the maternalistic style of the Children's Bureau discouraged the child-development activists of the sixties from using the bureau as the focal point for an expanded program of federal intervention

1. February 19, 1969, Message on Reorganization of the War on Poverty, *Congressional Quarterly Almanac*, 1969, p. 33-A.

36

in early childhood. Neither aggressive in style nor innovative in program, the bureau seemed out of touch with the issues of children in poverty, the special problems of black children, child-care programs for working mothers, early education for cognitive development. If the Children's Bureau's style refuted the assertions of its original opponents that it would lead to "the establishment of a control, through the agencies of government, over the rearing of children,"[2] its style also left unsatisfied those who believed that the agencies of government should equalize opportunities for children.

## Old Bureau, New Issues

By the end of the Johnson administration, there was cause for the bureau's leaders to have become discouraged. While its very earliest emphasis on combating infant mortality had led to responsibility for administration of the Sheppard-Towner Act through the 1920s, the most important governmental programs affecting children in the depression, war, and postwar periods were assigned elsewhere despite expressed bureau interest. Even the Great Society did nothing to halt the downhill slide of the bureau that began in the depression. Politicians were unwilling to entrust the Children's Bureau with much responsibility outside the area of foster care and adoption services, important but second-level activity totally overshadowed in the 1960s by aid to dependent children, school lunches, and Head Start.

A case in point is the public assistance program for dependent children. Martha M. Eliot, the fourth chief of the bureau, has pointed out that in the early 1930s more and more bureau effort was concentrated on investigating and describing to the public the effect of the depression on children and youth, on maternity care, and on the stability of family life.[3] The reports dealt with the effects of the unemployment of fathers, and of the absence from the home of mothers who went to work; the problem of "latchkey" children and their lack of supervision; the shortage and poor quality of day-care facilities for infants and young children; the shrinking of state programs of mothers' aid. Legislation to establish a federal relief

2. Senator Weldon B. Heyburn (Republican of Idaho) during Senate consideration of the Children's Bureau bill, in *Congressional Record*, vol. 48, pt. 1 (1911), p. 189; reprinted in Robert H. Bremner, ed., *Children and Youth in America: A Documentary History* (Harvard University Press, 1971), vol. 2, pts. 1–6, p. 765.

3. "Six Decades of Action for Children," *Children Today*, vol. 1 (March–April 1972), p. 4.

system to be run by the bureau languished in Senate committees during the Hoover administration, but with the coming of the New Deal, prospects seemed good for a coordination of federal relief and child welfare services under the leadership of the bureau. Instead, President Roosevelt opted first for a temporary Federal Emergency Relief Administration. After Roosevelt's Committee on Economic Security undertook to develop a permanent program to provide economic protection against old age and unemployment, the Children's Bureau successfully urged inclusion of federal aid to dependent children (ADC). In the committee's early deliberations, it was assumed that the ADC program would fall to the bureau. But it lost again. The resulting Social Security Act put ADC under the Social Security Board while assigning to the bureau responsibility only for more traditional services: maternal and child health (a revival, in effect, of the Sheppard-Towner Act); crippled children's services; child welfare services other than money, and especially those provided in rural areas beyond the reach of voluntary, sectarian agencies.

Some of the bureau's critics trace their concern about its political inepititude back to the development of the Social Security Act. In the course of doing the background work for the dependent children program, the bureau tied the level of support for ADC to that provided for orphans of war veterans. The different group working on the old age assistance program tied support in that category to the level envisioned by the then-popular Townsend plan. Not only did the bureau start by fixing its expectation level for children below the level others were fixing for the aged, it also failed to note that the Veterans' Pension Act allowed a separate grant for an adult caretaker. When ultimately noted, it was deemed politic not to try to effect a change in the pending ADC title. The upshot was that while the Children's Bureau managed to plan an ADC program, its product did not provide for federal sharing at a level comparable to that of old age assistance, nor did it extend benefits to the caretaker group in the manner of its purported model. Fifteen years would elapse before a separate caretaker benefit provision was finally adopted, and the disparity between individual ADC payments and those in the adult categories was never overcome. All of this was perhaps political accident, not necessarily bungling, but it dimmed the image of the bureau held by social reformers.

Public relief activity in the Bureau of Public Assistance then proceeded to eclipse Children's Bureau services over the next twenty-five years. There was no way for the bureau to make a splash; it may have presided over the birth of ADC, but bureau programs were the "add-on" to ADC by the time the latter reached its teens. In 1963 the bureau was made administratively responsible to HEW's Welfare Administration. When the Welfare Administration was metamorphosized into a Social and Rehabilitation Service in 1967, public assistance was its principal responsibility, the Children's Bureau a minor one.

At the time the Nixon administration decided—too quickly, it later became evident—on a children's program as one of its big initiatives, the Children's Bureau was perceived as dinky, depressed, uninspired, and uninspiring. It was not a likely receptacle for new programs. Neither Mary Switzer, administrator of the Social and Rehabilitation Service (SRS), nor Jule Sugarman, Head Start's associate director, had a good word to say about the bureau. The latter, a few weeks after being made associate chief of the bureau, while waiting for transfer of Head Start to HEW, wrote an "eyes only" confidential memorandum proposing an intact transfer of Head Start personnel and program responsibility to the bureau. Nine months later, in December 1968, his "administratively confidential" response to Switzer's request that he consider the future of the Children's Bureau took a different line. His "Program and Administrative Assumptions" lauded the SRS. Assuming that the service would both stimulate and develop services for children, and would be an advocate for children, Sugarman went on to argue that SRS was no one's captive and had coordinating experience. "With these advantages, SRS could do things in the children and youth areas that no one else can do," he wrote. The Children's Bureau, Sugarman said, was another story. "The problems in the administration of the Children's Bureau are so severe that they can only be overcome by (a) drastically reducing its role through incorporating it into a new organization, or (b) substantially modifying its organization and leadership at several levels."[4]

Given Sugarman's important role as director-presumptive of Head Start, and given the nine months he had had to study the Children's Bureau from the inside, the second memorandum effectively destroyed any chance that Head Start would be assigned to the bureau. His build-up of the SRS caused professional social workers and friends of the Children's Bureau to view Sugarman with some suspicion before the Head Start transfer was ever made. These critics in and out of the bureaucracy noted that Mary Switzer's impending retirement would soon leave her job open. On the other hand, Children's Bureau Chief P. F. DelliQuadri, a social

4. Memorandum from Jule Sugarman to Mary Switzer (Dec. 26, 1968), p. 3.

work school dean, was just fifty-four, had only been appointed the previous summer, and would presumably be around for a while since that job was considered professional and, therefore, not subject to turnover because of the 1968 election results. DelliQuadri's predecessor, Katherine Oettinger, was only the fifth chief in the life of the bureau. She had been appointed by Eisenhower and served through the Kennedy and Johnson administrations. Her predecessor, Martha Eliot, was a Truman appointee who had carried over until her retirement in Eisenhower's second term. The three great chiefs who preceded Eliot—Julia Lathrop, Grace Abbott, and Katharine Lenroot—were all nonpolitical. When Oettinger was named deputy assistant secretary for population and family planning a few months before the 1968 election, and DelliQuadri was recruited for the bureau job, the assumption within the child welfare community was that HEW Secretary Wilbur Cohen was protecting the Children's Bureau against the possibility of a Nixon-appointed chief. Oettinger was sixty-five in 1968; her replacement would thus have been likely relatively early in the life of a new administration.

Just ten days into the Nixon presidency, the SRS's Switzer made some suggestions to HEW Secretary Robert Finch about reorganization of the Children's Bureau, "as you consider the person who should be appointed Chief."[5] DelliQuadri was obviously not to benefit from the tradition of carrying over the bureau's chief from administration to administration. In presenting Finch with a devastating assessment, the Switzer memorandum went beyond the views of the bureau Sugarman had given her a month earlier. Nor was it the first time Switzer had complained to the new secretary about the bureau. As she reminded Finch: "At every opportunity I have had to talk with you, or any of your staff, I have indicated that one of my major problems is the Children's Bureau."[6] The bureau, it seemed, would not be receptive to Switzer's effort to introduce a priority into its concern for children—to devote as many resources as could be utilized effectively to help the poor, and particularly those on public assistance. The bureau would not fully cooperate in efforts to bring joint energies and resources within the SRS to bear on the specific problems of the disadvantaged. Because of bureau intransigence, the SRS was less successful in the effort than would otherwise have been the case. Indeed,

5. "Reorganization of the Children's Bureau," memorandum from Mary E. Switzer to HEW Secretary Robert Finch (Jan. 30, 1969).
6. Ibid.

the bureau personnel and their traditional supporters in the welfare field had not even agreed to the emphasis, let alone been energetic in supporting it.

In essence, the problem is philosophy, structure and people, particularly those in the top spots now in the CB. The proposed restructuring of the CB would assume that we can move into the top administrative posts of the CB individuals who are concerned not only with children, but who are concerned with the priorities and objectives of the Department and SRS.

Much of the program should revolve around the services features of the Aid to Families with Dependent Children (AFDC) program. If we are to provide any solutions or even alleviate the problems of disadvantaged families, I am convinced it must come through rehabilitation of the disadvantaged parents and children who are served by this program.

But the AFDC program is not enough to meet the needs of all disadvantaged families, many of whom do not need or want to be involved in "welfare" programs. For them we should be able to use Head Start and day care programs to complement what is available under AFDC.[7]

Switzer proposed two moves to emphasize that new policies and directions were contemplated by the new administration. The first was to create a new organization within the SRS which would incorporate the Children's Bureau into "something like a Family and Youth Administration," while the second was to introduce several new top officials—"including some youthful leaders."[8] Both steps would be regarded as degrading the bureau and the bureau's leaders. Finch might have been disposed to avoid hasty decisions about degrading a statutory agency with an outside constituency of middle-class matrons save for the congressional directive that the transfer or delegation of Head Start out of the Office of Economic Opportunity be studied and the results made known early in 1969.[9] That directive, and the strong language in the Switzer and Sugarman memorandums, made the forthright approach seem one that would create a new home for Head Start and would weaken the Children's Bureau all at once.

No study ever took place. After President Nixon announced his decision to delegate Head Start out of the OEO, the new Republican secretary of HEW convened an ad hoc advisory committee, chaired by

7. Ibid.
8. Ibid.
9. The directive was contained in the Vocational Education Amendments of 1968 (H.R. 18366; P.L. 90-576); for a discussion of the amendments, see *Congressional Quarterly Almanac*, 1968, pp. 500–04.

the old Democratic administration's budget director, Charles Schultze. It held a couple of days of meetings early in 1969. The committee members—including specialists from Health, Education, and Welfare and local community action leaders, a handful of whom were Head Start parents— were by no means despondent. The perception of the committee was that HEW, under the sympathetic leadership of the President's friend, Robert Finch, was on the upswing, and the OEO was facing an uncertain future. Faced with a choice within HEW, however, the majority of Schultze's group could develop little enthusiasm for either the Office of Education's professional educators or the Children's Bureau's professional social workers, and had misgivings about the SRS where the preoccupation was with making public assistance payments to the states and inventing work training programs for relief recipients. Work training for adults and Head Start for children need not be incompatible, but child development considerations are no match for efforts to reduce the relief rolls. Head Start in the SRS, it was feared, would quickly be transformed from "developmental" to "custodial" care.

The Schultze committee opted for a wait-and-see compromise: Head Start should be delegated to a new agency of HEW, an Office of Child Development (OCD), which should be lodged at least for the time being in the Office of the Secretary.[10] The committee also suggested that consideration be given to transferring the day-care programs supported by the Children's Bureau to the new OCD. Finch agreed to it all, and went beyond. It would not do to have an agency of little consequence reporting directly to the secretary. Accordingly, he endowed the OCD with "high prestige and visibility" by announcing that it was expected to become the focal point for a new initiative in child development. As for the Children's Bureau, Finch spelled out its depressing future. "I plan to upgrade and transfer the day care, and over time, other early childhood programs operated by the Children's Bureau to this new Office."[11] The bureau would become solely a staff research agency. Things did not quite work out that way. Still, the great days of the Children's Bureau had clearly come to an end.

10. "Report of the Chairman of the Head Start Advisory Committee" (March 10, 1969; processed), p. 8.
11. The Statement of HEW Secretary Robert Finch on the Transfer of Head Start and the Creation of the Office of Child Development, *Congressional Record* (daily ed.), April 14, 1969, p. E 2889.

*Reorganization: A Commitment without a Plan*

Jule Sugarman, who had recommended that the bureau's role be drastically reduced through incorporation into a new organization, displaced DelliQuadri who would not preside over the bureau's humiliation. Sugarman became acting chief of the bureau, and a few months later when the OCD was formally established with the delegation of Head Start, Sugarman also became acting director of the OCD. As Representative Dan Flood put it to Sugarman that spring: "They made you very important in the past few months?"[12]

Sugarman had become important enough that friends of the Children's Bureau, particularly those influential in the foster care and adoption areas of the child welfare spectrum, let it be known that there would be opposition to a Sugarman appointment as director of the OCD. At that point, no decision had been taken about the administrative location of or program responsibilities to be assigned to the Children's Bureau. As a statutory agency, it could not be liquidated by simple administrative order. Partly, at least, because of Sugarman's devastating assessment of the bureau, Finch had committed himself to transferring day care and early childhood programs out of the bureau and into the OCD. He got half way. After both Sugarman and Sugarman's internal and external critics were finished, the bureau was decimated.

Sugarman had had twelve years of routine assignments in various parts of the federal structure before joining the OEO in its first days. At forty-one, he could have qualified—at least from her vantage point—as one of the "youthful leaders" Mary Switzer suggested to the secretary. But the world of child welfare professionalism objected to Sugarman's appointment as director of the OCD on at least two counts. First, any umbrella agency for children's programs overshadowing the Children's Bureau should be headed by a professional social worker with formal training. Second, an OCD leader should have relevant experience in the children's field other than Head Start experience. It was one thing to decide against assigning Head Start to the Children's Bureau. A Sugarman appointment as director of the OCD would seem to assign the Children's Bureau to

12. *Departments of Labor and Health, Education, and Welfare Appropriations for 1970*, Hearings before a Subcommittee of the House Committee on Appropriations, 91:1 (Government Printing Office, 1969), pt. 6, p. 504.

Head Start, and that was more than could be accepted gracefully by groups determined to protect preexisting programs.

Secretary Finch had said, when appointing Sugarman acting director of the OCD, that no final decision on Sugarman as director had been made.[13] A decision was made within a couple of months. James Farmer, assistant secretary for administration and the department's spokesman on the subject, explained that the nominee would have to be a scholar, which Sugarman was not, and expert in community relations as well as in child development. "The man we are looking for must be a specialist in early childhood. A scholar who is strong on research, he must also have the ability to relate to constituent communities."[14] Ultimately, Edward Zigler was brought from Yale University to serve as the OCD's first director. Defining the OCD job to exclude Sugarman who had close ties to Head Start meant that the latter was losing its role as model for federal children's programs.

In the six months between Secretary Finch's announcement of his intention to create a focal point for a new initiative in child development and the specific administrative reorganization to accomplish it, welfare reform became the centerpiece of the Nixon domestic social program. The shape of the reorganization of children's programs reflected lack of faith in the Children's Bureau, uncertainty about Head Start, and the importance of the welfare policy question. The Office of Child Development was to be organized into three bureaus: the Bureau of Head Start and Early Childhood, which would operate the Head Start and Parent and Child Centers programs; the Children's Bureau, which kept its research function and was assigned responsibility for Community Coordinated Child Care, but lost most of its operating responsibilities, including those in maternal and child health assigned now to the Health Services and Mental Health Administration; the Bureau of Program Development and Resources, which was to be concerned with programs for older children. But most important, HEW's Social and Rehabilitation Service retained major responsibility for money and policy in the children's field, including all day care under the Social Security Act's public assistance and child welfare services titles.

Neither the Office of Child Development nor the Children's Bureau nor the Office of Education became the focal point for the Nixon administration's asserted interest in programs and policies affecting children.

13. *Washington Post*, Feb. 22, 1969.
14. *Voice for Children*, vol. 2 (November 1969), p. 1.

The disappointment of the bureaucrats in each of the agencies was less significant, however, than was their concern over the White House's willingness to perpetuate scattered responsibility for federally sponsored child care. Without unified responsibility, there was little likelihood of moving all such child care into conformity with Head Start's low adult-child ratios; comprehensiveness, including education, nutrition, and health; and parent involvement. Independent child-care programs getting federal money were run under the child welfare services title (IV-B) of the Social Security Act; title I of the Elementary and Secondary Education Act; the provision for social services to families receiving aid to families with dependent children (title IV-A of the Social Security Act); the provision of the work incentive (WIN) program entitling poor families involved in training or employment to child-care services; and assorted other pieces of legislation including Model Cities, Concentrated Employment, and the Education Professions Development Act. Federal interagency day-care requirements presumed to be applicable to all programs had been promulgated but were not enforced.

With no uniform standards and with administrative responsibility scattered, the biggest stakes over which a battle could be expected were child-care standards under the administration's proposed family assistance plan for welfare reform. Creating an OCD and delegating Head Start to it included no commitment for anything more than continuing Head Start. By itself it did not mean support for an expanded federal role in child care, nor that all existing child care was to be remodeled in the image of Head Start.

The signals were plain, and, especially in view of the Westinghouse findings, they were not unreasonable. Head Start was acceptable on its own terms, a program for the poor to be reported on the society page rather than as political news. It was not to be dependent on the Office of Economic Opportunity. But it was not to be put in the hands of the educational professionals in the Office of Education, nor in those of the child welfare workers in the Children's Bureau. Local and parent control of Head Start continued to be acceptable.[15] The administration was not ready to discard any child-care models because it was keeping its options open about how to handle child care in the blockbuster it was preparing: family assistance and "workfare" to replace the thirty-five-year-old family welfare program. What the administration did not count on was a con-

15. See "Report of the Chairman of the Head Start Advisory Committee."

gressional initiative that would emphasize comprehensive development services for children rather than day-care services for welfare mothers. But neither family assistance nor comprehensive child development became law, leaving the Office of Child Development an agency without a program.

### The OCD Inheritance

The Office of Child Development was invented to dramatize a new administration's planned policy initiatives in the children's field, and to stifle any claim by the Children's Bureau for control of those initiatives. Anticipating some new—albeit still undefined—federal activity, the OCD's architects began by assembling the Children's Bureau from HEW, Head Start from the OEO, and several on-going experiments. The Children's Bureau transfer to the OCD was clearly a demotion, the only way perhaps to state no confidence in a statutory agency. Head Start came just as its bloom was wearing off, its lasting value under challenge, its growth at an end. By the time the OCD inherited Head Start the number of individual projects, enrollment totals in full-year programs, and federal appropriations all were showing stability rather than growth. Head Start was in no jeopardy, but a highly decentralized program with little prospect for further growth could not be expected to help much in demonstrating the value of the new Office of Child Development. However, two of the experimental activities inherited by the OCD—Community Coordinated Child Care, and Parent and Child Centers—still seemed promising.

#### Coordinating Child Care

One inheritance that made it easier to flesh out the initial case for an OCD was Community Coordinated Child Care (4-C), the product of a Federal Panel on Early Childhood, itself formed early in 1968. Coordinating the varieties of child-care programs existing under diverse auspices seemed a sensible enough idea. If 4-C could be made useful, the credit would go to the Republican administration that had professed a commitment to the first five years of life. If 4-C proved useless, it could be junked as Great Society nonsense.

The Federal Panel on Early Childhood was a consequence of the proliferation of child-care activity in the middle sixties as the Children's Bureau reconsidered its limited day-care horizons and both the Welfare

Administration and the Office of Economic Opportunity began new programs. Whether OEO should operate as well as plan programs for poor children confused and troubled some of its strongest congressional sympathizers. One of them, Senator Joseph Clark (Democrat of Pennsylvania), chairman of OEO's oversight subcommittee, heard an associate commissioner of education explain in June 1967 that his relationships with the OEO tended to be closer than those with "any of the agencies which are within our own [HEW] department," and wondered whether that was a desirable situation. Why, Clark asked the OEO's Sargent Shriver, should not the poverty program shed all of its operating responsibilities and become a planning and coordinating body exclusively as "many of the professional administrators" suggest?

A tart response about the limits of public administration theory and the practicalities of presidential preferences ("Presidents don't always necessarily follow exactly what Woodrow Wilson's school thinks best") got Shriver through the interrogation.[16] That, however, was not the end of it. To many in the Congress, presidential preference was not an adequate justification for significantly different kinds of child-care programs to be operated in the OEO and in HEW, among other places, with no effort at coordination. Under OEO auspices, community change and Head Start were the motivations; under HEW auspices, parental failure or work experience for adult welfare dependents were the primary justifications. While the consequences of these different approaches were not examined in detail, the 1967 amendments to the poverty legislation did instruct the OEO and HEW to get together to coordinate day-care programs provided under their respective jurisdictions. The legislative hope was that the agencies would attain a common set of program standards and regulations and mechanisms "for coordination at the State and local levels."[17]

Early in 1968 the White House dutifully arranged to have established a Federal Interagency Panel on Early Childhood with responsibility for coordination of all federally supported early childhood programs whether in or out of HEW.[18] At the same time, Jule Sugarman moved from the

16. *Examination of the War on Poverty*, Hearings before the Subcommittee on Employment, Manpower, and Poverty of the Senate Labor and Public Welfare Committee, 90:1 (GPO, 1967), pt. 9, p. 2838.

17. *Economic Opportunity Amendments of 1967*, H. Rept. 866, 90:1 (GPO, 1967), p. 50.

18. For a detailed discussion of the composition of the panel and its initial plans, see *Voice for Children*, vol. 1 (September 1968), p. 7.

OEO to HEW in anticipation of the eventual shift of Head Start. As an experienced bureaucrat, Sugarman, who was named chairman of the panel, knew enough to emphasize his skills as an administrator sensitive to waste and duplication. Under his leadership, the panel created the Community Coordinated Child Care Program, an instrument that could forestall further complaints about the absence of coordination. The 4-C philosophers dreamed of all early childhood programs in a community, whether run by public welfare, Head Start, a profit-making group, or private charity, joining in the purchase of equipment and supplies, jointly recruiting personnel, making joint use of health caregivers, sharing the services of a nutritionist, and creating common staff training programs.[19] If they also dreamed of common adherence to high standards of care, no one said so explicitly. Writing a year after initiation of 4-C, Sugarman claimed a less grand purpose: "to encourage agencies providing day-care and preschool services to work together to stretch their resources, cut out waste and duplication, and improve and expand the quality and scope of their services."[20]

As it turned out, most attention was paid to coordinating matters of little importance, probably because matters of great importance like day-care program standards are inherently too divisive to permit coordination. Jointness has an abstract appeal that loses strength when it becomes evident that there must be one leader, one front group. So, in practice, 4-C meant local communities were invited to decide whether they wished to be led by a local welfare agency, a local community action agency, a Model Cities agency, or perhaps a committee operating out of the mayor's office. The designated leader would then be in a position to strengthen its own hand in the continuing competition for support for child-care services, while the followers got nothing more than a slight improvement on prices of supplies.

Seven years after its invention, 4-C was in extremis. The Office of Human Development, an umbrella agency that encompassed the OCD and sundry other seemingly good ideas (Aging, Juvenile Delinquency and Youth Development), had ceased any mention of the 4-C program in budget presentations. In the interim, both a National Academy of Sciences assessment panel and the Appalachian Regional Commission—a technical assistance contractor—had filed some unenthusiastic observa-

19. Jule M. Sugarman, "The 4-C Program," *Children*, vol. 16 (March–April 1969), p. 76.
20. Ibid.

tions about the administration and the conceptualization of 4-C.[21] And the grass roots supporters of 4-C found themselves unable to overcome 4-C's central problem—its inability to define a role. The most serious challenge to the existence of 4-C, however, was not lack of purpose or accomplishment, but a Civil Service Commission finding that the contractual arrangement for obtaining field staff was illegal.

Community Coordinated Child Care was sometimes referred to as a "CAP (community action program) for kids," but it lacked the critical ingredient of community action: relatively free money to support community-designed programs. The national 4-C effort, far from being an open-handed parallel to the OEO's community action program, was really penniless. Once a group of enthusiastic locals in a place like Denver, Colorado, organized themselves appropriately for recognition as a so-called 4-C pilot project, the reward was a $9,000 grant and "technical assistance" from the Day Care and Child Development Council of America (DCCDCA). The latter's role was to contract with an on-site coordination specialist in each pilot location. The specialist, who would be expected to provide information on federal law, regulations, administrative arrangements, and instances of successful coordination, could be a private nonprofit organization interested in day care, an educational institution, or a specialist from one of the disciplines associated with day care. The $9,000 grants to the pilot projects that were supposed to serve as demonstrations of the value of the 4-C concept and the $400,000 technical assistance contract with the DCCDCA as well as a later contract with the Appalachian Regional Commission were carved out of Head Start appropriations. Without a legislative mandate and with no line item in its budget, the OCD spent about $850,000 a year to support 4-C field projects and staff coordination activity.

At the outset, the word from Washington was that formal coordination was the probable key to the vault: "Communities that make such coordinating efforts may be eligible to receive joint funding from a number of different Federal sources." Again, from the same source: "Recent trends suggest that future legislation in the day-care and preschool areas may

21. National Research Council–National Academy of Sciences, Division of Behavioral Sciences, *Report of the Panel on the Assessment of the Community Coordinated Child Care Program*, prepared for U.S. Department of Health, Education, and Welfare, Office of Child Development (1972) (Gilbert Steiner was one of six members of the assessment panel); Appalachian Regional Commission, *ARC/OCD Contract Report*, prepared for HEW, OCD (1973).

include preferences for coordinated communities."[22] By the time the DCCDCA filed its report with HEW a couple of years later, there seemed to be a different understanding of how the money was to come: "It was recognized that this [$9,000] was a token amount insufficient for normal operations, but pilots were expected to generate additional sources of funds."[23] The disappointing actuality was that creation of a 4-C mechanism did not bring a financial reward worth the effort. In the District of Columbia, for example, 4-C's planning participants "made the false assumption," explained the local coordinator, "that because of their efforts in the development of a 4-C program a windfall of Federal monies would be forthcoming to support day care and pre-school programs in the District."[24] Instead, organized 4-C groups had a license to go hunting Model Cities funds or money available under the social services title of the federal public assistance legislation. But that hunting license was readily available; it did not require the creation of a 4-C committee.

The DCCDCA final report's list of "impressive accomplishments" by the 4-C program was a head count: numbers of communities known or thought to be organizing a 4-C effort, numbers of 4-C pilot programs in existence and the number that had satisfied all program criteria, numbers of communities that had convened their first organizational meeting on the way presumably to developing a 4-C program, and numbers of communities that had requested information on the program.[25] The substantive results, the specific benefits of organization as 4-C communities, could not be found as "impressive accomplishments" or elsewhere. Accomplishments were measured not by services provided to the target population, nor by new ideas generated, nor by resources made available on behalf of a stated objective, but by a count of formal organizations created to fulfill an unspecified task.

Enough people shared uncertainty about 4-C to provoke the OCD director to include a request for an assessment of the program in a study package he proposed to the National Academy of Sciences–National Research Council around the middle of 1971. By then, the DCCDCA had left the 4-C scene, its technical assistance activity widely regarded as a

22. Sugarman, "The 4-C Program," pp. 76–77.

23. Day Care and Child Development Council of America, Inc., "Community Coordinated Child Care: A Federal Partnership in Behalf of Children," prepared for HEW, OCD (Dec. 31, 1970; processed), p. 5.

24. Kenneth Johnson, in Voice for Children, vol. 2 (November 1969), p. 6.

25. DCCDCA, "Community Coordinated Child Care," p. 2.

failure. A comparable function had been bought from the Appalachian Regional Commission. The national 4-C program was still a one-professional-plus-one-secretary operation in HEW, still lacked congressional authorization, and still had no financing other than that diverted from Head Start appropriations. The possibility that the entire activity was of dubious legality had not yet been formally raised. But there were grounds for such a belief. In providing technical assistance personnel, the Appalachian Regional Commission, like the DCCDCA before it (and like the National Capital Area Child Day Care Association which was to succeed the ARC as the contractor), was really providing the functional equivalent of OCD regional personnel, yet the ARC staff were outside the authorized civil service system. Whether the use of Head Start money to sustain the 4-C effort could be justified legally was also being avoided by the OCD. Whatever the legality, some Head Start supporters had negative views about the morality of the arrangement. After the fact, the chairman of the NAS-NRC assessment panel—a specialist in the economics of child care— privately characterized the financing aspect as "disgraceful."

The assessment panel, reporting in June 1972, found little to be cheerful about. Lack of central direction in 4-C, according to the panel, resulted in failure to build a strong national 4-C movement. Specifically, the panel's findings were: inadequate federal staffing, lack of coordination of interagency effort, no use of the Federal Panel on Early Childhood, absence of central definition of 4-C's role, poor functioning of the federal regional 4-C, no local agency participation, lack of support for 4-C in the OCD, little help for local 4-Cs from regional offices, insufficient inventiveness in finding funds, and impediments to coordination caused by rivalry and group conflict. Yet the panel could not bring itself to proposing termination of the 4-C program.[26] Instead, it made recommendations for redirecting the coordination effort. The report upset 4-C's regional staff, caused some disagreement within the OCD which limited its distribution, and produced no immediate effect. While the 4-C chief explained that most of the recommendations referred to policies over which the OCD had no control, conditions that led to those findings of the report over which, presumably, the OCD had some control also remained unchanged.

The latter point became apparent a year and a half later when the Appalachian Regional Commission filed a report on its experience in

26. NRC-NAS, *Report of the Panel on the Assessment of the Community Coordinated Child Care Program*, pp. 33 ff.

providing regional staff for 4-C. That report, like the earlier one, suggested that the central 4-C office was not providing strong leadership.[27] Conclusions in the ARC report are backed up by assessments of the ARC project, and indirectly of 4-C itself, by the regional 4-C staff—known as child development program coordinators—and the assistant regional directors for the OCD. They pictured 4-C to be weak as a centrally directed federal program coordinating the work of many agencies for children, albeit unobjectionable as a collection of locally initiated efforts to do "something" for children. Each effort could proceed without reference to the central office. One coordinator stated this view most clearly: "Except for the 4-C pilots, I have always had questions on the rationale for [federal] monitoring [of] what are essentially volunteer efforts which in most instances we are not funding."[28] Whatever happened in 4-C happened because a group of local people worked for it; the efforts of the Washington office were indiscernible and irrelevant to people active in 4-C.

Local 4-C workers had their own troubles when they tried to organize themselves. They agreed that the central office's function is to provide support, and "commitment." They did not agree that it carried out that function. After pulling together an unofficial Shoestring Conference in Washington in the fall of 1971, enthusiastic local workers thought they could sustain a grass roots drive.[29] A year later, the local workers attempted to form their own mutual support organization—National 4-C—claiming that support and commitment were not forthcoming from Washington. But National 4-C's stated goals of sharing information, assisting each other, and speaking out together for the interests of children emphasized fraternity, not specific policy goals. The group met a few times, elected officers, adopted by-laws, and assessed dues. Members produced a few position papers for each other, but they "have not done much for about a year," a founder of National 4-C told an interviewer in 1974.[30] National 4-C's lack of progress stemmed from its inability to decide whether it should be independent of the OCD, act as an adviser to the OCD, or

27. Appalachian Regional Commission, ARC/OCD Contract Report, p. 32.

28. Memorandum from Stanley Subarsky to Marian Seifert, March 16, 1973, in ARC/OCD Contract Report, p. 107.

29. Memorandum report from Jean Ruffin to the NAS-NRC 4-C Assessment Panel, Sept. 28, 1971; it describes the background, discussion, and conclusions of the conference.

30. Telephone interview, Gwendolyn Morgan, April 5, 1974. As executive secretary of the Massachusetts 4-C committee, Morgan was principal organizer of the 1971 Shoestring Conference in Washington.

affiliate with some other national organization. Conflict over the definition of its role was a constant drag on National 4-C's ability to get beyond organization and into substance. The organizers received little encouragement from the OCD; they even had difficulty getting an appointment with the acting director.[31]

The fuzziness of the 4-C concept is its most striking characteristic. From the beginning, no compelling case was made for a local umbrella agency over child-care programs. Well-established health and welfare councils already existed at the local level, and community action agencies spawned by the poverty program also existed. Neither group was ready or willing to be displaced, but a new umbrella would have to displace them. Why it should and what it would do was unclear to high officials in HEW and even to some of the field officers who were under contract to help guide communities in the creation of 4-C programs. One DCCDCA field officer, for example, in a region that included four 4-C pilot projects, told an interviewer that he had found the concept vague from the very beginning, and hence difficult to explain to others.[32] Further acquaintance with the program did not dispel his confusion. At the highest level of HEW to which 4-C percolated, the problem was the same. "When you don't know what a thing is, and when people who should be able to do so simply cannot explain it to you—what position can you take?" a bewildered member of the under secretary's staff asked an interviewer. Briefings on 4-C were characterized as "un-understandable."[33] The result was a neutral posture in the Office of the Secretary, perhaps a good break for the 4-C proponents.

The 4-C program did no real harm. It provided a way for enthusiastic people of goodwill to be involved in social improvement. It has no permanent significance for federal child-development activity. If 4-C ever had any potential value, it was political rather than substantive. But by indecision, indifference, and inability to take hold of and exploit 4-C as a grass roots mechanism, the OCD's leaders lost the opportunity to use 4-C to badger congressmen or an HEW assistant secretary on behalf of the children's cause.

31. Interview, Theodore Taylor (DCCDCA), April 1, 1974.
32. Memorandum report on interview with Robert Carr, from Jean Ruffin to the NAS-NRC 4-C Assessment Panel, Sept. 30, 1971. Mr. Carr later was administrative assistant to Congressman John Conyers (Democrat of Michigan).
33. Memorandum report on interview with James Edwards, assistant to the under secretary of HEW, from Ivor Wayne to the NAS-NRC 4-C Assessment Panel, Sept. 7, 1971.

## Parent and Child Centers

Following early reports of physical and cultural deficits in children entering Head Start, President Johnson in 1966 set up a White House Task Force on Early Childhood Education under the direction of J. McVicker Hunt, professor of psychology at the University of Illinois, whose work on *Intelligence and Experience* had furnished some of the theoretical basis for Head Start. One of the Hunt task force proposals was a pilot program of Parent and Child Centers (PCC), a proposal Johnson instructed the Office of Economic Opportunity to implement. According to the theory, help provided by the PCC would include day care for children under three, health and welfare services, meals, and extensive counseling for parents. In addition, the centers were to serve as a training ground for child development specialists, and where possible were to be associated with universities "to provide greater research and experimentation in the fields of child development and education."[34]

The aim was to try to break the poverty cycle through intensive work with poor families, especially the mothers of children under three. At the centers and in their homes, these mothers would be taught about the developmental, health, nutritional, and educational needs of their children, and the mothers' own needs would be attended to. Through such intervention, program specialists hoped it would be possible to produce children who ate better, had improved physical and mental health, and were "more imaginative and creative."[35]

The planners of Parent and Child Centers envisioned a two-year experiment to see what could be learned. Depending on the results, the program would be dropped or expanded. Although a highly critical evaluation was made during the first year,[36] no action was ever taken. The centers survived in part because they were overlooked at the time of the change of national administration, in part because they were available a few months thereafter to help in forming a new Office of Child Development in HEW. Within the OCD, the PCCs limped along with no hard questions asked about their objectives, accomplishments, or relationship to other OCD programs for children and families.

Whatever the PCC program has done, it has done for very few people

34. From the President's February 8, 1967 Message on Children and Youth, *Congressional Quarterly Almanac*, 1967, p. 56-A.

35. Interview, Sylvia Pechman, OCD, Parent and Child Centers, Dec. 26, 1973.

36. Kirschner Associates, Inc., *A National Survey of the Parent-Child Center Program*, prepared for HEW, OCD (March 1970).

at high cost. While the anticipation was that the pilot programs could be "duplicated throughout the country without the expenditure of astronomical sums of money," they have not been.[37] The same thirty-six centers established at the outset existed in 1974, no more, no less. Nor have these centers served as many families as expected. Many of the families have been in the program longer than expected as repeaters. Instead of participating with only one child in the birth-to-three target range, many parents have enrolled again with subsequent children. And parents who worked in the programs tended to hang on because of the lack of other jobs.

The thirty-three regular Parent and Child Centers enroll about seventy-five to a hundred families each.[38] If each had the maximum hundred families, about thirty-three hundred families would be served throughout the country. But that figure would not be an accurate measure since it is widely agreed that only about a third of the families are deeply involved and perhaps another third partially involved. An in-house estimate made at the end of 1973 was that the program had served between five thousand and ten thousand families since it began in 1967.

With total budgets averaging in the neighborhood of $200,000 a year, Parent and Child Centers thus became a very expensive way to deliver services. Even if the inflated figure of one hundred families per center is used in the calculation, the average annual expenditure is $2,000 per family. If only the fifty or so really involved families are counted, the cost rises to $4,000 per family—with total costs perhaps three to six times this amount, depending on the number of years the family is in the program. Parent and Child Center proponents will argue that $2,000 or even $4,000 is not too much to pay for the improved physical and mental health of a family, both parents and children, but there is no evidence that such benefits result from the expenditures.

A major national survey of the impact of the PCCs on both parents and children is not encouraging on the benefits side. Having made positive assumptions about how "long-term" (in the program) parents would act compared with "new" parents, the investigators report a series of preliminary findings at odds with their initial assumptions or hypotheses:

More long-term parents express concern about the adequacy of their mothering, and admit to feeling overwhelmed at times, than do new parents.

37. Alice Keliher, "Parent and Child Centers: What They Are and Where They Are Going," *Children*, vol. 16 (March–April 1969), p. 63.
38. Sylvia Pechman, "Seven Parent and Child Centers," *Children Today*, vol. 1 (March–April 1972), p. 30.

Long-term parents are more pessimistic, express more powerlessness, and feelings of helplessness than new parents. . . .

Long-term and high-involved parents are more dependent on others than are new or low-involved parents. . . .

There are no major differences in terms of use of any of these resources (housing authority, state employment office, or job training) either in terms of longevity or of involvement.

There are no significant differences between new and long-term parents in terms of the number of visits which are made to the doctor during the child's first year of life.

No differences were found between what new parents eat and serve their children and what ongoing parents eat and serve their children.[39]

As for children in the program, the evaluation concluded that the data are "supportive of the hypothesis that PCC has an impact on children," although the evidence "is not strong."[40] To reach that conclusion, evaluators measured impact by the use of two standard tests. On each of them, the performance of PCC children was compared with that of children entering Home Start (another OCD program) and with norms based on a standard population sample. While analysis of the Preschool Inventory Test results indicated that the PCC does have an impact on the school readiness of children, the data also suggested that with maturation this initial advantage of PCC over other low-income children is not sustained.[41] Even that was a more encouraging conclusion than the one reached on the basis of the Denver Developmental Screening Test:

Mean score comparisons between PCC and Home Start boys and girls at every age group show only two significant differences. . . . One of these differences favors the Home Start children. Since two significant differences out of a possible 39 comparisons could be expected on the basis of chance alone, it can be concluded that there are simply no differences between PCC and Home Start children, among either boys or girls, at any age, in terms of the data collected.[42]

Both PCC literature and spokesmen for the program say it was not intended primarily as a research effort. "This was to be a service program,

39. Monica and Douglas Holmes and Dorie Greenspan, "The Impact of the Parent-Child Centers on Parents: A Preliminary Report," prepared by Center for Community Research, New York, for HEW, OCD (February 1973; processed), vol. 2, pp. 5–15.

40. Monica and Douglas Holmes, Dorie Greenspan, and Donna Tapper, "The Impact of the Head Start Parent-Child Centers on Children: Final Report," prepared by Center for Community Research for HEW, OCD (December 1973; processed), p. III-16.

41. Ibid., p. II-17.

42. Ibid., p. III-9.

in which research was handmaiden to service rather than vice versa. . . . The 'experimental' aspects of the program were to be innovations in content and delivery of service, not experimental research."[43] Accordingly, in-house evaluations of the PCCs are after-the-fact observations of the "this is what we see" variety. If parents and children seem to be doing things differently (or say they are) after involvement in the program, the presumption is that the differences are the result of the PCC experience. Questioned about the program's impact, a program specialist answered that after PCC involvement "people look different, kids do too," and that nonprofessional staff more often speak to children in sentences than in words or phrases. These are modest accomplishments for a program that set out to "demonstrate what could be done to prevent developmental deficits by helping parents both before and after their babies are born."[44]

Director Edward Zigler and his associates in the Office of Child Development developed early doubts about the value of their PCC inheritance. In their view, despite its very high cost, the experiment failed to document anything in the research and demonstration sense. The program could have made a real contribution in the discussions of infant day care—whether, for example, such care is feasible outside of a university atmosphere. While the original PCC guidelines expressed reservations about infant day care, program critics argue that flexibility would have been appropriate as day care became a larger policy issue. Zigler clearly hoped to get useful data on infant day care from the PCCs. In the spring of 1971, with comprehensive child development legislation an apparent live issue, he told an inquiring congressman that the PCC experiment could make a contribution to the "tremendous controversy among experts as to what happens to children this young (birth to three) who are separated from their parents. . . . I think these 32 centers will give us the base line data to tell us whether this Nation should move ahead in very massive day care and child care for very young children in group settings."[45]

But OCD programs each exist in a vacuum, quite separate from other OCD programs, although most of them—whether home or center based—have similar objectives and often use similar techniques to achieve them.

43. Joan Costello, *Review and Summary of a National Survey of the Parent-Child Center Program*, HEW, OCD (1970).

44. Keliher, "Parent and Child Centers," p. 63.

45. *Departments of Labor and Health, Education, and Welfare Appropriations for 1972*, Hearings before a Subcommittee of the House Committee on Appropriations, 92:1 (GPO, 1971), pt. 4, p. 558.

The PCCs were supposed to be providing much the same services for families of very young children (birth to three) that Home Start, a program introduced by Zigler, was designed to provide for families of three- to six-year-olds. Yet, there has been no connection between the two undertakings. (An after-the-fact explanation by Zigler's staff is that he did not wish to "dump a good idea on a bad thing.") Similarly, there is little interaction between most PCCs and Head Start programs in the same vicinity. Nor is there generally a connection between Home Start and Head Start programs, both of which serve three- to six-year-old children and their families. When the OCD set up the Child and Family Resource Program to serve children from the prenatal period through age eight, it financed eleven new projects rather than build on existing PCC or Home Start undertakings. In the case of infant day care, despite Zigler's expectations, the national PCC staff remained wary and continued to discourage centers from establishing full-day, full-week programs. The PCC staff went its way while others in the OCD went their ways.

The White House Task Force on Early Childhood Education had proposed the Parent and Child Center plan as a demonstration program focused on infants and on ways to enhance their physical, emotional, and intellectual development. In some centers, however, the needs of parents received the most attention. Rather than serving as educational programs, the PCCs provided therapy for the mothers. Center staff found parents so preoccupied with their own crippling problems that they were unable to concentrate on their children's needs. The presumption seems to have been that once the parents' own needs were taken care of they would be able to start thinking about their children. In other centers, both education and parent support were clearly less important than routine care and affection for the children. The Kirschner evaluation of the program's first year suggested the need for a decision about the program's purposes, because, given its resources,

a PCC cannot do both jobs well. The major policy question implied has not really been faced: Is this a program to assist in the development and education of infants and toddlers, or is it a program to lift parents out of poverty? Can one be done without the other? The relative effectiveness of these approaches can best be tested over a considerable period of time and with the proper design, record keeping and other normal concomitants of systematic longitudinal research.[46]

46. Kirschner Associates, *A National Survey of the Parent-Child Center Program*, p. 407.

Four years after the Kirschner evaluation, the OCD was presented with another report on the Parent and Child Centers, this one by David Goslin, a sociologist then in transition between the Russell Sage Foundation and the National Academy of Sciences–National Research Council. Goslin inquired into the implications of the centers for the design of future programs. Goslin concluded that the program should be continued for several more years. But his fifty-seven-page report explained that evaluation was difficult because parents often did not participate in PCC activity. Moreover, parents resented being used as research subjects, an attitude that hampered data collection. Goslin fell back for support on what he described as "intuitive, necessarily subjective judgments," along with staff and parent testimonials that "good things do happen with considerable frequency in many programs."[47]

The recurrent PCC answer to all of this has been that the program's focus is service, not research. Three Parent-Child Development Centers are accorded separate status as experiments in research and development strategy. It has been a slow experiment. Planning for these centers began in 1969, a model-building and -testing stage extended to the fall of 1975, followed by a replication experiment "calculated to produce the critical policy relevant information on which decisions about the wider operational use of models must depend."[48] So whether there is much to be learned from the half-dozen significant model variations tested in the three development sites (Birmingham, Houston, New Orleans) must await the results of replication in other places.

Without the three centers representing the research and demonstration component, and viewed simply as a service activity, the PCCs offer a high-cost service to a relative handful of poor mothers. Neither the OCD nor the HEW leadership is sufficiently insistent on weighing the benefits against the costs, and addressing the future of the PCC program as a service program. It may simply be thought, of course, that $6 million is a small price for a program in an agency badly in need of programs.

47. David A. Goslin, "Children Under Three and Their Families: Implications of the Parent and Child Centers and the Parent Child Development Centers for the Design of Future Programs," a report to the OCD (April 30, 1974; processed), p. 9.

48. Mary E. Robinson, project manager, "The Parent-Child Development Centers: An Experiment in R&D Strategy" (paper prepared for delivery at Society for Research in Child Development Symposium, Denver, Colo., April 13, 1975; processed), p. 6.

# 4

# The Bureaucratization
# of Child Development

Any newly created agency is likely to inherit some failing programs that its leaders would rather renounce and is equally likely not to inherit some programs that its leaders covet. Those decisions are often beyond agency control. So, at the outset, Office of Child Development leaders could only accept what was passed on to them, and regret some losses. New programs, however, particularly experimental efforts, are agency-controlled investments, and the OCD has made several. Unlucky in its inheritance, the OCD compounded its troubles by prolonged loyalty to some unimpressive investments.

Expecting to marry Head Start's concern for children to its own broader interest in workfare-in-lieu-of-welfare, the Nixon administration had quickly created the child development office to spotlight the children's side of that plan. Welfare reform, so called, never came to pass, leaving the administration stuck with an OCD of its own making. Running a status quo Head Start and some inherited enterprises in which it had little confidence was not a sufficient justification for an Office of Child Development. Consequently, when he was named first director of an agency in need of a program, Edward Zigler, a Yale psychologist, seemed in a position to innovate and to diversify. Aside from an obvious constraint involving Head Start—too popular to drop, but not valuable enough to expand—he was free to abandon whatever he judged to be misguided programs of the Great Society years, or to adopt and expand experimental efforts begun in that period. Zigler came to the job persuaded of the commitment of the national administration to children. "It has been transmitted to me both in words and deeds," he said a few days after his appointment.[1] When he left after two years, Zigler was less sure of the

1. Press conference, June 26, 1970 (transcript prepared by Ace-Federal Reporters; processed), p. 3.

administration's commitment. Equally important, however, Zigler's experience led many political leaders to doubt that anyone knows how to honor such a commitment satisfactorily. During his tenure, Zigler tried to innovate by encouraging the idea of a credential for semiskilled child development associates, and to diversify by varying the Head Start model. But the philosophers of child development have been unable to produce a compelling package to graft onto Head Start, and the OCD has been degraded in the Department of Health, Education, and Welfare's administrative hierarchy, its new responsibilities limited to making grants to combat child abuse.

Taken all in all—Parent and Child Centers and Community Coordinated Child Care, both inherited programs, together with the newer demonstration and service efforts mounted since the OCD's creation—there is still no federal child-development program. Taken separately, the new programs sponsored by the OCD to provide a credential for child-care workers and to diversify Head Start are fuzzy in conception and sloppy in execution, while child abuse is properly characterized by the Child Welfare League as merely "the above surface tip of a huge iceberg" because it focuses on battered children alone in the whole stream of neglected children.[2]

## Credentials for Children's Caretakers

It has never been within the power of the Office of Child Development unilaterally to extend child development services to additional millions of preschool and elementary school-aged children. Nevertheless, the evidence at hand when the OCD was created—the increasing attention being paid to day care, the rapid growth in kindergarten and other early childhood programs during the sixties, President Nixon's own family assistance proposal, and the competing but widely supported child development bill— suggested a likely mushrooming of preschool programs. How to find qualified staff for all of these preschool centers at some bearable cost was, in the judgment of the OCD's leaders, a priority goal for the office. In this environment, the concept of a semiskilled profession of child development associate (CDA) evolved and flourished. Though the immediate pros-

2. *To Establish a National Center on Child Abuse and Neglect*, Hearings before the Select Subcommittee on Education of the House Committee on Education and Labor, 93:1 (Government Printing Office, 1973), p. 149.

pects for expansion of preschool programs have since faded, the CDA enthusiasts do not acknowledge this. Moreover, problems associated with fixing a training curriculum for the child development associate and judging the achievements of trainees resist solution.

Edward Zigler's ideas for a new semiskilled child-care profession assumed that daily activities in child-care programs need not be in the hands of fully certified teachers with college degrees, but require a caretaker with both natural and acquired skills. What was needed, Zigler held, was a program or process to train child-care workers (those already on the job and those entering the field) in less than four years and outside of the traditional college classroom. Instead of requiring a certain number of college credits, CDA training would be individually based, taking into consideration individual knowledge, experience, and natural skills in working with children.[3] Each candidate's abilities would be assessed against what it was thought a child development associate should be able to do (the "competencies"), and training would then be tailored to fill in the gaps. Some particularly able and experienced people would require little or no training; candidates would more commonly need two years (or more) to achieve the competencies. Although academic work would be involved, the emphasis would be on in-service or on-the-job training. The child-care workers so trained would not replace, nor serve as aides to, college trained teachers. Instead, the CDA would have responsibility for the daily activities of a group of children under the direction of a master teacher—who in small centers would not need to be in residence.

The appeal of the CDA concept is understandable. If child-care programs are going to expand, and if adults to staff them are going to be more than casual laborers, a need for trained staff should be anticipated. Zigler put the issue: "Are we going to provide children of this nation with developmental child care or are we going to merely provide them with babysitting?"[4] It would be prohibitively expensive to pay such staff as much as fully certified public school teachers, however—particularly if the low child-adult ratios of the 1968 federal day-care requirements were in effect. In September 1971, Zigler discussed this problem with the Senate Finance Committee: "I think that the idea that we are going to have a children's center sitting in L.A. or in New York City or anywhere that is manned by Bank Street MAs, as ideal as that might be, is idealistic. The costs are too

3. Edward Zigler, "A New Child Care Profession: The Child Development Associate," *Young Children*, December 1971, pp. 71–74.
4. Ibid., p. 71.

high and you would not need these qualifications in a woman or man taking care of 15 children."[5] Yet programs of reasonable quality would require some form of staff training and assessment. The CDA credential seemed a sensible compromise between cost and quality. The idea had two additional virtues: it left access to the field open to local community people since the only prerequisite to CDA training was that the applicant be seventeen (later lowered to sixteen), or a high school graduate; it would not threaten already-employed child-care workers who could if they chose —the procedure would be a voluntary one for them—be trained and assessed on the job for the CDA credential.

The leaders of the OCD clearly intended that the federal government would ultimately make the CDA a minimum requirement in staffing federally financed child-care and preschool programs whether Head Start, day care, or whatever. In its 1973 *Guides for Day Care Licensing* the OCD suggested that centers enrolling thirty or more children require at a minimum one half-time staff member who has: "(1) a B.A. or A.A. with 12 hours in child development or a related field, or (2) a high school diploma and 3 years of early childhood or day care experience, or (3) a CDA certificate."[6] The competence requirement was separate from the basic staff-child ratios that the *Guides* recommended. In 1972 the OCD had inserted more binding language regarding the employment of CDAs in its proposed revision of the 1968 day-care requirements, but its changes had successfully been fought off by the Office of Management and Budget.

Zigler's ideas were well received by the early-education specialists to whom they were first proposed. The need for a child-care profession seems to have been taken for granted, and discussion instead focused on how such a profession might be brought into being. The mechanism tentatively agreed to was a consortium of professional organizations directly concerned with the education of young children. Accordingly, the OCD selected the National Association for the Education of Young Children (NAEYC) to consider the feasibility of forming such a consortium. In addition, the OCD set up two task forces: one to decide what skills or competencies should be required of the CDA, the other to decide what training would be necessary to produce such skills.

5. *Child Care*, Hearings before the Senate Committee on Finance, 92:1 (GPO, 1971), p. 214.
6. U.S. Department of Health, Education, and Welfare, Office of Child Development, Bureau of Child Development Services, *Guides for Day Care Licensing*, DHEW publication no. (OCD) 73-1053, p. 23.

By September 1971, the NAEYC had concluded that a consortium would indeed be the best way to implement the CDA program. Noting that such an approach "represents a substantial departure from current practice," the NAEYC's feasibility study suggested that a consortium would give the new professional credential far greater respect and visibility than could be had were training and recognition offered by a single agency.[7] Nonetheless, the NAEYC raised some basic questions about the venture: how the CDA gets into the career ladder; how recognition can be achieved from the various states; whether it is "fair" to build up hopes for jobs when they are not available for "fully qualified teachers." It raised other questions about the competencies themselves: whether by selecting specific competencies the OCD would be defining the model approach for programs for young children; whether there are such things as universal competencies; whether they were relevant to minority groups. Not much attention has been paid to most of these questions since the NAEYC raised them save for considerable effort to gain minority participation and approval. And for all its searching questions, the NAEYC failed to address the most elementary one: How certain is the need for CDAs?

After more than a year of CDA planning—especially, though not exclusively, with the early-education groups: the NAEYC, the Association for Childhood Education International (ACEI), and the American Association of Elementary/Kindergarten/Nursery/Educators (E/K/N/E) —the OCD set about the job of broadening the base of support for the CDA idea. Preliminary to an $800,000 grant made in June 1972 for creation of a formal consortium of organizations, other groups concerned with children but not exclusively with early childhood education were approached. Some of them were not happy about having been included only at a late date. Nor were they content with the secondary positions they were expected to assume vis à vis the three early-education groups, which were to get the only permanent seats on the board of the proposed consortium, an arrangement that the Day Care and Child Development Council of America (DCCDCA), for example, could not afford to abide. Thus the difficult task of making peace fell to the staff of the Child Development Associate Consortium. It did so in part by getting the board of the consortium expanded from twelve to seventeen seats. (But both the American Home Economics Association and the Child Welfare League

7. National Association for the Education of Young Children, "Feasibility Study for Child Development Associate Project" (Sept. 1, 1971; processed), p. III-2.

continued to hold out. In 1975 they were not among the consortium's claimed membership of more than thirty national organizations and individuals concerned with early childhood education and development, ethnic-minority populations, and training and certification.) In addition to its organizing tasks, the consortium staff was directed by the OCD to develop a prototype assessment system, that is, a way of deciding whether competencies have been achieved.

## The Need for CDAs

From the outset, neither the OCD nor the consortium has questioned the need for a child development associate; they have simply assumed and proclaimed it. Nor have they reconsidered their assumption despite various changes in circumstances. Among those changes are the dramatic and unexpected drop in the birthrate in the 1970s and the decision of the federal government not to become involved in a major way in the child-care field. In 1970 the prospects were more promising; but CDA planners have not acknowledged and perhaps do not even realize how much the picture has changed. The data on which both the OCD and the consortium continue to rely are outdated. Earlier, when the projections were more reliable, they were applied indiscriminately and inaccurately. The use that the OCD and the consortium have made of two supply and demand studies is illustrative. One is a *Monthly Labor Review* article of July 1970, the other a 1973 report on CDA strategies and alternatives conducted by the National Planning Association (NPA) for OCD.

In November 1971 when Edward Zigler made public his plans for a new child-care profession at the NAEYC annual conference in Minneapolis, he linked the great need for it to the likelihood of increased federal activity in the child-care-child-development field. While citing an existing need for trained child-care staff—current trends would increase kindergarten and nursery enrollment from 3.9 million in 1968 to 6.3 million in 1980—Zigler asserted that pending legislation could make the need much greater. Quoting Department of Labor estimates that 23,000 new teachers a year "will be needed" to cope with accelerated preprimary enrollment, Zigler declared: "This increase, plus the proposed increase for child care contained in various pieces of pending legislation, makes it clear that our nation must develop new institutional forms if we are to produce trained individuals in large enough numbers to meet the demand."[8]

8. Zigler, "A New Child Care Profession," p. 72.

There were two defective aspects of Zigler's characterization of the Labor study. First, the study did not state that 23,000 teachers "will be needed" each year, only that that number might be needed. One prerequisite was increased federal support for early childhood programs. Thus, the number was not 23,000 "plus" other new positions created by federal child care programs; the number included any such new positions.

The 23,000 and 6.3 million figures that Zigler used were taken from a *Monthly Labor Review* article of July 1970 which examined the growth in nursery and kindergarten programs from 1964 through 1968. The author, Janice Neipert Hedges, concluded that if the 1964–68 trend in enrollment rates continued, instead of the 3.9 million three- to five-year-olds in preprimary programs in 1968, there would be 6.3 million of them in 1980 (90 percent of five-year-olds, 40 percent of four-year-olds, and 20 percent of three-year-olds). Hedges suggested, however, that because of the growing awareness of the "importance of early education," the expected surplus of elementary school teachers, and the possibility of increased federal activity in the field, growth might well be accelerated in preprimary programs between 1968 and 1980.[9] So that instead of 6.3 million children in such programs in 1980, 7.6 million might be enrolled then (100 percent of five-year-olds, 50 percent of four-year-olds, and 30 percent of three-year-olds). If this were the case, and if there were one professional for each twenty children in the classroom, Hedges calculated that 23,000 trained persons would be needed each year to cope with the expanding preprimary population. But these 23,000 would not be needed if the 1964–68 enrollment rates—that is, growth leading to 6.3 million children by 1980—continued. Ironically—and significantly—the point of Hedges's article was not to proclaim the need for a new child development profession but to suggest that the 23,000 potential preprimary openings represented an expanding job market for the anticipated surplus of roughly a million elementary school teachers.

The OCD literature has at times used the 23,000 and 6.3 million figures together although the 23,000 figure is meaningful only in conjunction with the 7.6 million projection. In 1973, for example, Jenny Klein, OCD's project director for the CDA effort, wrote that "kindergarten and nursery school enrollment is expected to reach 6.3 million by 1980," while quoting Department of Labor estimates that "between now and 1980, we will need

9. Janice Neipert Hedges, "Prospects for Growth in Preprimary Education," *Monthly Labor Review*, vol. 93 (July 1970), p. 40 and passim.

23,000 new teachers in early childhood education each year."[10] Later, Dr. Klein maintained that the 23,000 figure was probably low since it was based on previous growth rates. If any new federal programs were enacted, she assured an interviewer it would be much larger.[11]

A figure surprisingly close to the 6.3 million Hedges projection appears in the National Planning Association study done for the OCD. Relying on a population projection series which had been revised downward by the time it submitted its report to the OCD, NPA estimated that there would be 11.9 million three- to five-year-olds in 1980 (12 percent more than the 10.7 million of 1970) and that about 6.3 million or 52 percent of them would be in formal group programs.[12] Assuming these projections are accurate and assuming that turnover staff and unqualified staff in existing programs would be replaced with qualified people (CDAs), NPA estimated that early childhood programs could absorb approximately 13,000 CDAs a year from 1974 to 1980.[13]

Neither Hedges nor NPA could foresee that beginning in mid-1971 the birthrate would begin a dramatic drop, reaching record lows in 1972 and 1973. The population projections used by each of them have since been revised downward. Thus, instead of the 11.9 million three- to five-year-olds that NPA expected in 1980, the Census Bureau by February 1975 had estimated the number would be only about 9.6 million.[14]

It appears then that even the more conservative of Hedges's projections —6.3 million three- to five-year-olds in preprimary programs in 1980— is not likely to be borne out. Assuming, as Hedges did in this instance, that 90 percent of all five-year-olds, 40 percent of four-year-olds, and 20 percent of three-year-olds would be in preprimary programs in 1980, only

10. Jenny Klein, "A New Professional for the Child Care Field—The Child Development Associate," *Child Care Quarterly*, vol. 2 (Spring 1973), pp. 56–57.

11. Interview, Jenny Klein, Aug. 31, 1973.

12. Hedges used a Series C projection, probably from U.S. Bureau of the Census, *Population Estimates and Projections*, series P-25, no. 381 (December 1967). The NPA used a Series E projection from U.S. Bureau of the Census, *Population Estimates and Projections*, series P-25, no. 470 (November 1971).

13. Arnold Kotz and others, "The Child Development Associate Policy Planning and Programming: Strategies and Alternatives," prepared by National Planning Association, Washington, D.C., for HEW, OCD (September 1973; processed), vol. 1, p. I-12.

14. *Population Estimates and Projections*, series P-25, no. 541 (February 1975), p. 9. The 9.6 million figure is the middle (Series II) of the bureau's three projections. The high is 10.7 million three- to five-year-olds in 1980; the low, 8.7 million. Census considers its middle figure the most accurate guide for the short run.

about 4.7 million children would be in such programs in 1980 on the basis of the 1975 Census projections of the number of children of those ages in 1980. Even assuming the larger enrollment rates of 100 percent, 50 percent, and 30 percent in the three age groups that Hedges used to reach her 7.6 million and 23,000 figures, only about 5.6 million children would be in preprimary programs in 1980, according to the 1975 population projections. In October 1974 there were about 4.6 million three- to five-year-olds in preprimary programs, or about 700,000 more than the 3.9 million in 1968.[15] An average of 280,000 additional children would have to be enrolled each year to reach 6.3 million by 1980. That outcome seems unlikely. While the percentage of three-, four-, and five-year-olds in preprimary programs is apt to be greater in 1980 than in 1974, the total population of children of those ages is expected to be smaller in 1980 than in 1974—about 10.5 million in 1974; about 9.6 million in 1980.

The important consideration is not that the Hedges and NPA projections are too high, but that the OCD and the CDA Consortium have acted as if they were unaware of that fact. The OCD did not complete its executive summary of the two-volume NPA study until the spring of 1974, well over a year after the Census Bureau first revised downward the projections on which the study was based. Ironically, one of the NPA's major recommendations was for "an automatic data system" to overcome the "serious deficiencies in the data, such as gaps, duplications, and ambiguities as to what is included in the statistics which are available."[16] As late as November 1974 the consortium prepared an overview, "Who Is Taking Care of the Children," which relied solely on the then-outdated NPA data for its statistics on how many three- to five-year-olds there will be in 1980, referring all the while to the "ever-increasing numbers of children under six."[17]

The CDA training guide, issued by the OCD in April 1973, states in its discussion of supply and demand that "the number of children ages one through six in preschool programs is expected to increase another three

15. The 4.6 million figure was arrived at from data contained in *Population Estimates and Projections*, series P-25, no. 541 (February 1975), and in *Population Characteristics*, series P-20, no. 278 (February 1975).

16. Kotz and others, "The Child Development Associate Policy Planning and Programming," Executive Summary, p. 14.

17. Child Development Associate Consortium, Inc., Credentialing and Community Relations Department, "Who Is Taking Care of the Children in the Day Care Center, Nursery School, and Other Child Development Programs Across the Nation" (November 1974; processed), p. 2.

million by 1980, to about 28 [sic] million."[18] By the time of a 1975 re-printing, the OCD came to realize something was wrong with that formulation of anticipated demand, but did not realize how much was wrong. The later printing eliminated "in preschool programs" without, however, reconsidering the demographic projection. In fact, according to the Census Bureau's 1975 projection, there should be about 20 million one-through six-year-olds in 1980.

Admittedly, the OCD involved itself in CDA training only on a limited scale. It sustained thirteen pilot training programs and Head Start supplemental training. "We're not going out and training the world," the CDA director told an interviewer who suggested the desirability of precise data about need.[19] But either by design or sloppiness, the OCD is encouraging a wasteful overproduction.

### Competencies, Constructs, and Capacities

To qualify for the child development associate credential, candidates are expected to possess forty-two "competencies"—a blend of abilities, skills, and knowledge. These competencies, first set out in 1971 by a task force of early childhood educators and described by the OCD as "an operational definition of what should occur in a developmental child care program," are said to distinguish the qualified from the unqualified child-care worker.

Unhappily, progress toward making child development an exact science is too limited to give desirable specificity to the CDA credential requirements. While six "organizing constructs" are unchallengeable objectives—for example, advance physical and intellectual competence, build positive self-concept and individual strength; set up and maintain a safe and healthy learning environment—the particular skills needed to accomplish them defy objective measurement. How can it be known with confidence whether a trainee has acquired the competence to "recognize and provide for the young child's basic impulses to explore the physical environment"? And can a certificate of competence really assure that a trainee will "be able to assess special needs of individual children and call in specialist help where necessary"?[20]

18. HEW, OCD, *The CDA Program: The Child Development Associate, A Guide for Training,* DHEW publication no. (OCD) 73-1065 (April 1973), p. 6.
19. Interview, Jenny Klein, Aug. 31, 1973.
20. A statement of the competencies appears in *The CDA Program: A Guide for Training,* pp. 11–16.

Nor are skeptics about the validity of the forty-two educational competencies reassured by a further listing of nine "capacities" that are considered essential to the effectiveness of the CDA. The list includes the capacity to be sensitive to children's feelings and the qualities of young thinking; to be able to establish orderliness without sacrificing spontaneity and child-like exuberance; to feel committed to maximizing the child's and his family's strengths and potentials. Like the competencies, only the complete absence of the capacities may be recognizable.

Providing trainees with missing competencies—those they do not have either as natural abilities or as acquired skills—is the function of CDA training programs. Without any reexamination of long-range needs, a dozen CDA pilot training programs were put in place under the OCD's direction a year after the presidential veto of child development legislation. Established principally at community colleges or small four-year institutions, the pilots were expected to be innovative and to uncover problem areas likely to need technical assistance over the long haul. Pilot projects, however, do not overcome inadequacies in conceptualization. The inadequacies are simply documented by the projects. Consider the pilot program at a small southern institution, where the training is described as "built upon a role-centered curriculum, integrating a variety of role possibilities." Upon completion of this training, the child development associate must be able "to project comprehensive knowledge of responsive, early learning environments," presumably meaning that the CDA must have the competencies. Within each of six training "dimensions" ranging from child care to activity planning to professional development, three objectives are sought: specific skills, subjective education objectives, and "celebrative objectives which are exclusively personal and subjective experiences characterized by joy."[21]

Not all of the pilot project descriptions triumph so successfully over understandable English. Nearly all of the pilots, however, recognize that there is no way of knowing whether they are successful. So, one municipal CDA council pinpointed as a problem area "the possible need for technical assistance in developing evaluative tools in assessing clients' progress." A state college frankly acknowledged that it did not know how to define competency or recognize the achievement of competency: "Program will need all the assistance available in developing criterion [sic]

21. "CDA Pilot Training Program Abstracts" (compiled by Child Development Associate Consortium, Inc., for CDA training workshop, May 15–17, 1973, Silver Spring, Md.; processed), p. 1.

(yardsticks for measuring competency). This is a critical factor as we must define each individual competency that we wish to teach so that the student as well as the trainers can determine when the competency is achieved."[22]

A pilot program operated by a state consortium requested technical assistance "in the development of an instrument to evaluate competencies and performance in the field," a need comparable to that expressed by a state university operating a pilot project. Another participating institution made the same point, using a language of its own, however, as it listed for future technical assistance: "Formative evaluation in preparation for summative consortium evaluation."[23]

## The Consortium's Assessment System

The eighteen subcontractors hired by the consortium staff in 1973 to work on assessment instruments produced so many indicators of competence that the CDA staff had to confine itself to "the identification of a pool of items as a base for further refinement."[24] (Specifically, that meant arranging the identified indicators on file cards, coding them, sorting them into four functional categories, then further subdividing them.) Late in 1973 the staff presented CDA board members with the pool of items: more than a thousand indicators of competency ranging from entries like "soap is available" to "abides by child's choice of activities." The search for a defensible assessment system continued as both the consortium and OCD leaders agreed that a simple checklist was not the goal. If the product were "only a checklist of 999 items, I'd throw it in the wastebasket," explained the OCD project director.[25]

In more recent efforts, the consortium staff has divided the six basic competency areas into thirteen functional areas, while offering examples of things the candidate might do in each functional area. But the staff has emphasized the examples are not meant to be a complete list of possible behaviors—"The observer should add any evidence which he feels may be useful in making a decision."

The assessment system recently agreed upon by the consortium board

22. Ibid., p. 6.

23. Ibid., p. 1.

24. Child Development Associate Consortium, Inc., "A Review of a Procedural and Conceptual Framework for Developing the CDA Assessment System" (Sept. 6, 1973; processed).

25. Interview, Jenny Klein, Aug. 31, 1973.

avoids the use of either a checklist or a test in favor, in its own words, of a "judgment-referenced system."[26] The CDA candidate's competence will be determined by a four-member local assessment team (LAT) composed of the candidate, the candidate's trainer, a community representative chosen by the candidate from a pool of persons assembled by the candidate's training program or center director, and a professional evaluator trained by the consortium—the only nonlocal person. To be deemed competent, the candidate requires the votes of any three of the four members. Over the objections of its staff, the consortium board permitted this less-than-unanimous vote to establish competency—a decision presumably representing a victory for local over national standards. It may also be a victory for community control, for the candidate, trainer, and community representative can approve candidates notwithstanding the dissent of the consortium representative. The chief of the consortium's design and assessment division, aware of the problems under the present arrangement, acknowledges that the candidate "is a captive of the general quality of the center in which he (or she) is trained."[27] While the consortium staff worries over the issue and while the board presumably could reverse itself at some future time and require a unanimous vote to establish competency, in 1975 the consortium began awarding CDA credentials under the any-three-of-four arrangement. Given the difficulty in making the system operational at all, major subsequent change in the process is likely to be hard to accomplish.

There are other problems facing the assessment system. A basic one, readily acknowledged by the consortium staff, is that it is not yet possible to tell whether this or any system can distinguish between competent and incompetent candidates. What has been put in place is regarded as workable, credible, and adequate to begin operation. Suppose, however, a control group of persons without the CDA credentials were put in jobs comparable to those filled by child development associates. Could behavioral differences be detected?

The cost of the assessment system is also a source of concern, if only subsurface concern. Consortium leaders assert their first obligation is to the quality of the product, the second to its cost-effectiveness. While they have said they would abandon the project rather than compromise quality to lower costs, the hope is for a system that initially might cost the federal

26. Child Development Associate Consortium, Inc., *Toward an Assessment System: Efforts to January, 1975* (Washington: CDA Consortium, 1975.)

27. Interview, William Foskett, April 2, 1975.

government several hundred dollars a trainee but that ultimately would be self-supporting, or nearly so. Whether trainees would ever be expected to pay their own way and what a reasonable cost might be, no matter who pays, are questions that have neither been settled nor been faced explicitly. Thus far, the CDA candidate is charged a $5 application fee and $15 for the assessment process, but $20 is not expected to cover the cost of the evaluation alone, to say nothing of training. While the OCD has paid for the thirteen pilot training programs and for training CDAs via Head Start Supplemental Training, it will not create new institutions to provide CDA training on a nationwide scale—"Large scale implementation of the CDA concept will depend," according to OCD literature, "upon training institutions redirecting their own resources around competency-based preparation strategies for child care staff."[28] Even with unassailable "competency-based preparation strategies," few training institutions can redirect their resources without reasonable assurance that their service will be paid for.

External problems facing the CDA venture also remain unresolved. The most obvious, again, is the issue of need or demand. Another is how to get the CDA credential accepted in the face of reservations held by education associations. While the states set licensing standards by law for public school teachers, those standards are worked out by the various education associations who oppose a federal move into the licensing field, even in this area only distantly related to traditional teaching. Three education groups—the American Association of Colleges for Teacher Education, the Association of Teacher Educators, and the National Association of State Directors of Teacher Education and Certification—are represented on the CDA Consortium board, and other education groups including the Council of Chief State School Officers, the National Education Association, and the American Federation of Teachers are members of the consortium. When the board voted in March 1975 to begin awarding credentials to CDA candidates, the representatives of the three education groups voted no, arguing that such licensing is legitimately a state function—and no doubt looking at the present and projected surplus of already certified elementary school teachers. From the outset the various education groups have opposed the use of the word *credential* to signify what a competent CDA will receive, preferring instead *letter of recognition* or *certificate of proficiency* or some such term that would not be

28. *The CDA Program: A Guide for Training*, p. 7.

confused with legal certification. The argument cannot have escaped the majority of the consortium board that nevertheless opted for *credential*. But it is one thing to issue a credential and quite another to give it practical significance.

On the other hand, to the extent that federal money pays for child-care programs, the old rule that he who pays the piper shall call the tune may apply to setting standards for child-care workers or CDAs. In this instance, however, paymaster and standard-setter are not one. The OCD does not control all federal child-care money and cannot insist on its own standards as a condition for support. It is entirely conceivable that the OCD will have its credential, but that the anxiety elsewhere in the federal structure to reduce welfare dependency will preclude an insistence on duly-recognized child development associates in child-care programs other than Head Start.

In sum, the fading interest in day care and child development as national policy objectives does not help the case for the CDA activity. Lack of demand, excess teacher supply, and a continuing inability to define the CDA job specifications are making the CDA venture more academic than Zigler ever intended it. A new profession for children's caretakers gives scant promise of becoming a cornerstone of a program for the Office of Child Development.

### Diversifying Head Start

Comprehensive preschool programs are expensive. In the case of Head Start, by the beginning of the 1970s a combination of high costs and fading cognitive gains legitimized questions about the validity of its emphasis on child development. Some doubters, in and out of Congress, preferred an emphasis on providing more custodial care for children of working mothers and others needing such service. Others thought it possible and desirable to reduce costs without sacrificing the comprehensive array of services—health, educational, nutritional, psychological, and social—that are central to the Head Start philosophy. Head Start appropriations were virtually stabilized at 1968 levels. Faced with a static Head Start budget and a Head Start program that was in his view losing its innovative character and becoming an orthodoxy, Edward Zigler set about while director of the Office of Child Development to revamp the Head Start format.

Zigler spelled out his position in a memorandum to HEW Secretary Elliot Richardson on the long-term role of Head Start. The question to be asked, Zigler maintained, was what is the optimal means of helping deprived children, not whether full-day, full-year Head Start was better than no preschool care. Alternate arrangements had to be considered because there was neither the money nor the staff to provide full-week programs for all children needing them and because "different program models could be more beneficial to some children and their families than the Head Start center mode of delivering services." What Zigler wanted to promote was "a diagnostic, rather than a 'single panacea,' approach to child development services. . . . We would propose to limit the five-day per week comprehensive center Head Start service to those children who are identified as being at greatest development risk. Other children might be served through Home Start programs or less intensive (e.g., two days per week) center participation."[29] Among the children identified as being at greatest developmental risk were foster children, physically or emotionally handicapped children, and children from seriously disorganized homes regardless of income level.

Both the Economic Opportunity Act of 1964 and practical political considerations prevented the OCD from requiring Head Start sponsors to alter existing center-based programs. Instead sponsors would be persuaded to do so. Experimental programs demonstrating alternative ways of delivering comprehensive services to children were the chosen method of persuasion. Experiments conceived for this purpose—Health Start, Home Start, and the Child and Family Resource Program—were each designed to deliver Head Start-type services but in varying mixes and to children of varying ages. Health Start projects were intended to provide effective health services to disadvantaged preschool children not served by Head Start. Home Start, on the other hand, is meant to provide a range of services to the three- to six-year-old in his home comparable to those the child would receive in a Head Start center. The Child and Family Resource Program, the newest and most ambitious of the three undertakings, "works closely with other community agencies to provide services in response to individual family needs. . . . [It] is designed to provide family-oriented comprehensive child development services to children from the

29. "Response to September 30 OCD Management Conference Action Item #3: The long-term role of Project Head Start—Information Memorandum," from Edward Zigler to Elliot Richardson (Nov. 23, 1971), p. 5.

prenatal period through age eight in accordance with assessed needs."[30] As the administrators explain it, the purpose is to change Head Start from a program with many centers to a center with many programs. The results are in on two of those three programs, and they are depressing.

### Health Start

By 1970, no case was being made that developmental benefits (or gains) accrued from summer-only Head Start enrollment. Nevertheless, more than two hundred thousand children were enrolled that summer. The Office of Management and Budget reminded OCD Director Zigler that the effects of summer Head Start were difficult to discern. The message was clear: spend more wisely, or stop spending. The OCD's decision was to continue to phase down summer Head Start and to develop a summer demonstration program that could show measurable results. As one vehicle for meeting his commitment to the OMB to improve use of summer programs, Zigler decided on Health Start, a demonstration program intended to provide poor children not enrolled in Head Start with health services similar to those provided to Head Start's enrollees. Screening, follow-up treatment, and health education were the critical components. Health Start did provide health services to some ten thousand children in each of its two years of life. The program failed, however, to demonstrate optimum ways of organizing those services.

Health Start's managers and its monitors agree that it suffered from a lack of clearly defined objectives. One outspoken critic, an evaluator under contract to the OCD, had followed the program from the beginning: "No one had an idea of what the program was supposed to be. It should screen some kids. There was no concept of a demonstration program, of putting together a delivery system for health."[31]

The OCD guidelines failed to provide consistent direction and definition to Health Start. Guidelines for the first year were imprecise, to put it mildly, in that they gave equal weight to providing service in areas of scarce health resources and to developing techniques of coordination of health resources. Each may be an appropriate objective for a demonstration program, but the guidelines were no help where a choice had to be made between coordinating resources and expanding service, between

30. HEW, OCD, "Child and Family Resource Program Fact Sheet" (n.d.; processed).
31. Interview, Jim Kennelly, June 20, 1974.

creating a health center and increasing a complement of visiting nurses. For the second year, the OCD's bureaucracy revised the guidelines and made the development of techniques of coordination the program's main goal. Those who had taken the other road were out of step.

Nor did the administration of Health Start give it the needed direction. Through its first year, Health Start had no director. In its second year, it had a director, but little direction.[32] For much of the life of Health Start, program responsibility was delegated to OCD staff who were also in charge of Head Start health services. Understandably, Head Start services took precedence. But there was no continuity of direction in Head Start's health program either. Dr. Gertrude Hunter, director of Head Start health services, left the OCD just as Health Start was beginning in June 1971. An Air Force nurse on loan to the OCD became acting director responsible for implementing a new Head Start health strategy, a new Head Start health education curriculum, and the new Health Start program all at once. She has since described the administration of Health Start as "management by crisis,"[33] recalling that Dr. Hunter left on a Friday and training for the Health Start project coordinators began on the following Sunday.

Second-year guidelines did include a section on program administration. The national role was to assume "direct responsibility for the quality and successful operation of Health Start programs through a national Health Start director," but the director's duties were not described. The national staff was to provide training, communication, and coordination for everyone involved in Health Start. A national committee of collaborating HEW agencies was to assist in everything from planning to evaluation.[34]

In practice, the national office performed even less of a role than the sketchy guidelines would suggest. The interagency committee has been described as a "bomb-out" by Health Start's second-year director who arrived at the OCD in April 1972.[35] By then, the new guidelines for the second year had been written and training sessions had already been planned. The director, asked to spend some of his time on Head Start

32. Leona M. Vogt and others, "Health Start: Final Report of the Evaluation of the Second Year Program," prepared by Urban Institute for Office of Child Development (December 1973; processed), p. II-3.

33. Interview, Lee Burner, June 27, 1974.

34. Ibid.

35. Interview, Jim Kennelly, June 20, 1974.

health services, gave less than full attention to Health Start. Eventually, he lost interest in a dying program.

Nor did the regional offices provide leadership for Health Start. The 1971 guidelines indicated that the regions were to prepare regional plans for Health Start, although nothing was said about the contents of the plans. Not surprisingly, most of the regions did not prepare plans for a program that allocated them $75,000 for a minimum of two projects. The plans that were filed were lost somewhere in the OCD, according to a subsequent evaluation report.[36]

Poorly conceived and weakly administered, Health Start—planned as a demonstration program but operated as a small-scale service program— terminated quietly after two years. No advocates rose to speak in its favor. The program was too small—thirty projects compared to fifteen hundred Head Start projects—to build an effective constituency. Edward Zigler, the apparent originator of the idea, left the OCD in June 1972. The OMB budget examiner for the OCD moved to another job. Head Start's acting health services director had too much thrust upon her too suddenly. The Health Start director, belatedly appointed, perceived little top-level interest in Health Start and became discouraged. Among interest groups, the American Academy of Pediatrics (AAP) had the closest ties to the program, but the AAP was ambivalent. Originally, it had not endorsed Health Start, claiming that a summer program was too short to affect a child's health. Adding year-round follow-up to the program made the academy more supportive, but Health Start never ranked high on the AAP list of interests.[37]

An independent evaluation of Health Start's first year by the Urban Institute was devastating; from every indication, the second year's record would be no more encouraging. When OCD leaders were preparing their 1974 budget, the office needed programs, but not badly enough to try to sustain Health Start. Consistent with previous OCD administration of Health Start, however, even the decision to terminate was badly handled. Without bothering first to inform Health Start's director, OCD officials simply reallocated Health Start funds to support services for handicapped children enrolled in Head Start.

36. Leona M. Vogt and Joseph S. Wholey, "Health Start: Final Report of the Evaluation of the First Year Program," prepared by Urban Institute for OCD (Sept. 29, 1972; processed), p. IV-6.

37. Joe N. Nay, Leona M. Vogt, and Joseph S. Wholey, "Health Start: Interim Analysis and Report, Working Paper: 961-2," prepared by Urban Institute for OCD (Jan. 3, 1972; processed), p. II-2.

## Home Start

When the OCD Home Start program was being explained to a congressional subcommittee, proponents argued that the effects of home life are far more long-lasting and continuous than those that could ever be expected from a few hours a week in a developmental center alone. Programs that help parents do a better job as parents would, therefore, give "a greater payoff for the child" than would center-based programs. But parents would not be told by "some expert" how to raise their children. Rather, education-in-parenthood would be carried out by community people "well trained in a circumscribed course." Three or four different approaches were to be tested in fifteen Home Start projects "to see what the bugs are in it, what is more effective."[38] Home Start would show through its "carefully defined experiments" what can be accomplished in home-based programs in benefits to the child and to the family. Later, when the projects were under way, they were said to make more sense than center care "from a developmental viewpoint" and "in trying to get the most cost-effective program." Home Start, it was said, is both cheaper for the sponsor and more logical for some children.[39]

Home-based parent-education programs were not invented by the OCD nor do OCD officials make any such claim. What is different about the Home Start venture from perhaps two hundred predecessors is its size, comprehensiveness, and the fact that Home Start has been systematically evaluated.[40] What also may be different about Home Start is that it lacks the sophistication and specificity of curriculum and objectives that distinguished some earlier research efforts.

Of the four stated objectives of Home Start, two have to do with strengthening parents' role in the education and development of their children. A third objective is to demonstrate and evaluate methods of delivering comprehensive child-development services to children for whom a center program is not feasible. The fourth objective is to determine the relative costs and benefits of home- and center-based programs

38. *Departments of Labor and Health, Education, and Welfare and Related Agencies Appropriations for Fiscal Year 1972*, Hearings before a Subcommittee of the Senate Commitee on Appropriations, 92:1 (GPO, 1971), pt. 2, p. 1351.

39. *Departments of Labor and Health, Education, and Welfare and Related Agencies Appropriations for Fiscal Year 1973*, Hearings before a Subcommittee of the Senate Committee on Appropriations, 92:2 (GPO, 1972), pt. 4, pp. 3666 and 3687–88.

40. HEW, OCD, "Home Start Fact Sheet" (June 1973; processed).

where both are feasible. Selected by regional and federal OCD staff, Home Start projects must be home-based, associated with a Head Start program or other agency able to receive a Head Start supplemental grant, have a local parent policy committee, and make use of community resources.[41] Each of sixteen projects serves about eighty families for a total of about 1,250 families. The number of children reached is sometimes set at 1,250 by the OCD (one per family), and sometimes set at 2,500 (presumably two per family). To be eligible for Home Start, families must have at least one child in the three-to-six age range and must meet Head Start income guidelines.

Most Home Start families are intact two-parent households, according to a three-year profile compiled in 1974. One or more parents is employed in more than half of the families, although in less than half of the families is there regular work. In about two-thirds of the families the annual income does not exceed $4,000. About 30 percent of the families are single-parent ones. In most families the home visitor works principally with one "focal" parent, who is usually the mother. In about a sixth of the families, both parents are considered "focal parents." Slightly more than half of the focal parents have been to high school Another third have from one to eight years of schooling. More than two-thirds of the focal parents are unemployed. In most families there is only one "focal" child in the three-to-five age range. Sixty percent of the focal children are white; the next largest group—about 17 percent—are black.[42]

Home Start guidelines describe the nutritional, health, psychological, social, and educational services to be provided to Home Start children and families. The guidelines are strong on good intentions, weak on how to accomplish them. Basically they direct Home Start programs to use community resources when available. When public services are not available, projects may purchase them for Home Start children, but not for parents. Guidelines for particular services are only admonitions to home visitors to do the best they can. The nutrition component, for example, "is aimed primarily at helping parents make the best use of existing food resources, through food planning, buying, and cooking."[43] Similarly, the objective in the health area is to provide Home Start children with the

41. Ann O'Keefe, Home Start program director, "The Home Start Program: Guidelines," prepared for HEW, OCD (December 1971; processed), pp. 2–3.

42. These data are assembled from "(B-F) Worksheets" of "National Profile: Family Characteristics" for Year II, Quarter IV (ending March 31, 1974), compiled by Abt Associates, Cambridge, Mass., for OCD (processed).

43. O'Keefe, "The Home Start Program: Guidelines," p. 3.

same health services that Head Start children receive, and, if they are not available, to pay for them. The educational program "must fit the needs of the locale" and "must develop and expand the role of parents as their own children's most influential educators." Despite earlier assurances that home visitors would be trained in a "circumscribed course" and that three or four approaches would be tried, none is prescribed.

THE HOME VISITOR. Because Home Start is an individualized worker-to-family program formally guided only by hortatory language, the role of the home visitor assumes critical importance. The home visitor is "a teacher, a sympathetic listener, a helper, advisor, and a *friend* [OCD's emphasis] to the entire family being served. She encourages and helps in literally dozens of ways." In recruiting and selecting these hired friends, the emphases are said to be on "friendly attitudes, suitability of cultural and language background, and successful experience as a parent, rather than on academic credentials."[44]

Contrary to OCD descriptions, the typical home visitor is not a community resident selected more for her indigenousness and her experience as a mother than for her academic credentials. The vast majority of Home Start staff, about two-thirds of whom are the home visitors themselves, are white females between the ages of twenty and forty with some previous related experience in preschool education. About two-thirds of the staff have children. More of them have school-aged children than have preschoolers. Among the home visitors alone, fewer than 10 percent have not completed high school, and well over half have some college experience although most of them do not have a college degree.[45]

The home visitor generally serves only from eight to twenty families. Nonetheless, the *Report of the Second Annual Home Start Conference* notes that home visitors' heavy workloads often make it difficult for them to seek and obtain community services.[46] How home visitors who have friendly attitudes but also have difficulty securing community resources are going to make the poor mothers in their caseload early childhood specialists is not clear. What the home visitor herself should know about early childhood education is left to the local projects to decide and impart.

44. HEW, OCD, *The Home Start Demonstration Program: An Overview* (February 1973), p. 3.

45. Data assembled from "(B-S) Worksheets" of "National Profile: Staff Characteristics" for Year II, Quarter IV (ending March 31, 1974), compiled by Abt Associates, Cambridge, Mass., for OCD (processed).

46. HEW, OCD, *Report of the Second Annual Home Start Conference* (1973), p. 7.

Home visitors' training, say the OCD materials, should involve at least one week of preservice training "(two or three would be better) in all the many areas that they will have to deal with as home visitors and support staff."[47] The preservice training should be followed by continued in-service training of perhaps one day a week. Other frequently given advice from the OCD suggests turning everyday learning experiences into excit-ing learning experiences and turning "worthless junk and trash" into "worthwhile (and beautiful) toys and playthings."[48] The guidelines say that parents should be taught various approaches to child rearing and ways to encourage language development and social and emotional de-velopment. They offer no specifics on how to accomplish that objective.

CHEAPER, DIFFERENT, OR NEITHER? If home-based services are substan-tially cheaper to provide than center care, a case can be made for them even if they do not accomplish all the things that center programs do. If home-based services are more expensive, then the case for them must rest on effectiveness. One impediment to arriving at such judgments is the lack of agreement on what constitutes effectiveness for either home care or center care. Should effectiveness be judged solely on the basis of a child's cognitive gains at the end of the program or should an attempt be made to measure improvements in social, emotional, or physical health, home environment, and the like? The advantage of evaluations based on cog-nitive or achievement test gains is that they can be made—such results are measurable, while an instrument to measure "improved sociability" is not at hand. But there is a problem in making judgments solely on the basis of cognitive gains or achievement test scores, as Head Start has dis-covered. Such gains fade after the child has been out of the program for several years, if no other special help such as Follow Through is provided. Partly in response to the evidence of this fading, Head Start supporters have come to urge that evaluations consider other factors like improve-ments in physical or emotional health, and in family functioning.

A comparable lack of clarity about program purpose complicates as-sessment of Home Start. When discussing their hopes for the experiment, Home Start bureaucrats say they are looking for a Home Start model with as good results as a Head Start center. Yet, they find it difficult to specify the kinds of results other than that they would involve much more comprehensive data than children's test scores.

At the outset, Home Start proponents assumed that home-based pro-grams would be cheaper than center-based programs. By early 1973, OCD

47. Ibid., p. 51.
48. Ibid., p. 53.

literature was asserting that home-based programs appear to be "economically feasible" and have the advantage over center-based programs that they reach other children in the family besides the Home Start child.[49] A summary of evaluation findings released by the OCD in early 1975 concluded that the average expenditure for each Home Start family was $1,344, "roughly comparable to the cost of center-based programs." But it is not completely clear that the benefits of Home Start are equal to those of Head Start, although the OCD states that "in general Home Start children made gains comparable to those of Head Start children, and both Home Start and Head Start children made many statistically significant gains over the randomly selected control group." Areas in which Home Start children did not do as well as Head Start children were nutrition, immunizations, and day care. Where they were better off than their Head Start counterparts was in "things mothers teach their children," which in reference to Home Start seems to belabor the obvious.[50]

When Edward Zigler proposed a home start program several years ago, he maintained that its benefits would be "far more long-lasting and continuous" than those likely to result from a few hours a week in a developmental center alone.[51] Now the yardstick that Home Start staff seem to be using is the Head Start one—to produce results at least comparable to those achieved by Head Start programs.

The OCD program statement suggests that the benefits of Home Start will not fade with time as it has been established the cognitive benefits of center programs do. It is not yet possible to judge the validity of that claim. While the OCD's "tentative" plans call for a follow-up of a sample of Home Start children into their early school years, one of the most consistent findings of early intervention studies is that cognitive gains children make in home-based programs do fade also.[52] One informed

49. HEW, OCD, The Home Start Demonstration Program: An Overview, p. 2.

50. HEW, OCD, "The Home Start Evaluation: Highlights of Findings" (Jan. 12, 1975; processed), excerpted and abstracted from D. Deloria, C. Coelen, and R. Ruopp, National Home Start Evaluation: Interim Report V, Executive Summary (Ypsilanti, Mich.: High/Scope Educational Research Foundation; and Cambridge, Mass.: Abt Associates, Inc., 1974). To compare Head Start and Home Start children (and a control group in neither program) the evaluators used the Preschool Inventory, the Denver Developmental Screening Test, the Schaefer Behavior Inventory, a parent interview, a child food intake questionnaire, height and weight measures, a mother behavior observation scale, and several other measures.

51. Departments of Labor . . . Appropriations for Fiscal Year 1972, Hearings, pt. 2, p. 1348.

52. Interview, Joy Frechtling, Oct. 26, 1973.

opinion, that of Home Start's external evaluator, Dennis Deloria of the High/Scope Foundation, is that there will be no differences between a Home Start family and a non-Home Start family after the former has been out of the program for three or four years. Although he does expect Home Start to do better than Head Start in preparing parents to work with their children, Deloria doubts that the program is intensive enough for the benefits to be sustained. Moreover, the mother would need a different kind of help to deal with older children—what she was taught about infants and preschoolers would not apply to teenagers.[53] All of this suggests that home-based programs are faced with the same kind of problems that center-based programs face. While both approaches may be able to produce changes in the target child, it is not possible to sustain them without a more profound intervention.

"HELP HAVE-NOTS BE HAPPY." A "national Home Start song," sung by delegates from the sixteen programs at the annual Home Start conference, refers to "walls made of shingles, and walls of stone and brick; some of them are flimsy and some of them are thick; but all these walls are home to the folks who dwell inside; who join hands and hearts as partners; their horizons open wide, to great beginnings and greater planning and happy doings."[54] Unfortunately, the musical uplift obscures the particulars of the flimsy walls and of the real horizons of the Home Start target population. The inherent futility of any effort to achieve "happy doings" by intervening at the level of parent-child interaction alone becomes apparent when the Home Start song is replaced by actual descriptions of Home Start projects:

The Franklin, North Carolina Home Start Program

serves very isolated areas with homes that have no running water, no electricity, few facilities, no means of transportation, and no telephones, in a very mountainous area.

. . . one of the biggest problems home visitors encounter is getting families to accept and trust them, due to the desire of the families to be independent and self-sufficient.

. . . the average family income in the county is $1,500.

The Cleveland, Ohio Home Start program is in an area

characterized by decaying, gutted, overcrowded buildings, littered streets, poor lighting, no playgrounds, and no vegetation.

. . . less than five per cent of Home Start families are employed.

The Reno, Nevada Home Start Program:

The cost of living is very high and welfare payments are very low. There is a

53. Interview, Dennis Deloria, Nov. 2, 1973.
54. HEW, OCD, *Report of the Second Annual Home Start Conference*, p. 35.

long waiting list for low-income housing, and evictions pose a major problem. . . . Life, in general, is regulated around the casinos; thus, some home visits
are made at night because the mothers work in the casinos during the days.[55]

"Help have-nots be happy," a local Home Start director urged colleagues at a national conference. That exhortation is a fair summary of
both program philosophy and operating instructions to the home visitors
who carry out the Home Start mandate. Like so much of the Office of
Child Development attempt at a program, however, it is more exhortation
than substance, more goodwill than good sense.

### Child Abuse: OCD's Ultimate Reward

It is a dual irony of the children's cause that since an Office of Child Development was created with high-level expressions of interest and support,
major program responsibilities anticipated for the office either never came
to pass or were assigned elsewhere, while the office's self-initiated efforts at
innovation are hardly more encouraging than the few experimental programs it inherited with reluctance. The irony is compounded by the emergence of prevention and treatment of child abuse—the term describes
physical battering of children by parents, but is used sometimes to describe neglect, sexual abuse, and emotional abuse, as well as nonaccidental
injury inflicted by strangers—as the single new initiative of recent years in
the children's field. After comprehensive child development legislation
was laid to rest, and with both public assistance-related day care and traditional child welfare services lodged outside of the agency that had been
designed as the federal "focal point" for children's services and programs,
it did get a new responsibility in connection with child abuse. The OCD
neither sought the responsibility thrust upon it in this area, however, nor
is there much more for it to do than make grants once or twice a year.

No one knows the incidence of child abuse. There is neither a uniform
definition nor uniform reporting. Having surveyed the child abuse literature, Stephan J. Cohen and Alan Sussman conclude that "information indicating the incidence of child abuse in the United States simply does
not exist."[56] David Gil, who is among the most careful students of the
problem, has written that official reporting figures bear no relation what-

55. HEW, OCD, *The Home Start Demonstration Program: An Overview*, pp.
25–26, 29–32, and 38.
56. "The Incidence of Child Abuse in the United States," *Child Welfare*, vol. 54,
no. 6 (June 1975), pp. 432–41.

ever to actual incidence, and suggests the outer limits of each to be 6,600 versus 4 million cases a year.[57] Politicians, pediatricians, and social reformers use figures between Gil's outer limits. Mario Biaggi, a New York policeman turned congressman (Democrat), told the House of Representatives that an estimated 60,000 cases would be reported over a year, "an estimate that is less than 15 per cent of the total cases that will actually occur." His predicted total would work out to approximately 400,000 cases. Biaggi asserts that child abuse is "an epidemic—of such proportions that if it were the plague or some other communicable disease, a state of emergency would have been declared and special task forces set up to deal with the problem."[58] Writing in the *Harvard Educational Review*, Richard J. Light uses figures of 200,000 to 500,000 cases of physical abuse annually and adds to them 465,000 to 1,175,000 cases of severe neglect or sexual abuse.[59] Vincent de Francis, director of the American Humane Association's (AHA) children's division, says his "guesstimate" runs around 25,000 to 30,000 cases of child abuse each year, but "for every reported case there is an unknown number of unreported cases—perhaps 10, or maybe 100 cases which are never reported to the authorities."[60] That calculation, of course, could run the total to 3 million cases.

On the other hand, the AHA use of 25,000 to 30,000 as the number of cases is just half the 60,000 figure cited by Senator Walter Mondale in his statement opening hearings on the subject in 1973;[61] by Representative John Brademas who handled legislation on the House side and said that 60,000 cases reported annually "is the widely accepted estimate";[62] and by Chairman Carl Perkins (Democrat of Kentucky) of the House Education and Labor Committee ("There are over 60,000 reported, and a countless number of unreported cases of the abuse and neglect of innocent children"[63]). Those who use the 60,000 figure depend on a position paper by Dr. C. Henry Kempe, a pediatrician who is director of the National Center for Prevention of Child Abuse and Neglect.[64] Some senators ap-

57. "Violence Against Children," *Journal of Marriage and the Family*, November 1971, p. 639.

58. *Congressional Record* (daily ed.), Dec. 3, 1973, p. H 10494.

59. "Abused and Neglected Children in America, A Study of Alternative Policies," *Harvard Educational Review*, vol. 43 (November 1973), pp. 566–67.

60. "Protecting the Abused Child"; reprinted in *Child Abuse Prevention Act*, Hearings, p. 328.

61. *Congressional Record* (daily ed.), Dec. 20, 1973, p. S 23646.

62. Ibid., Dec. 3, 1973, p. H 10490.

63. Ibid., p. H 10491.

64. "Child Abuse (The Battered Child Syndrome)"; reprinted in *Child Abuse Prevention Act*, Hearings, p. 180.

parently have other sources. Senator Bob Packwood (Republican of Oregon), a strong supporter of protection legislation, says that "estimates have indicated that as many as 60,000 incidents of child abuse a year go unreported."[65] Senator Edward Kennedy (Democrat of Massachusetts) has his own figure: "Over 250,000 cases of child abuse and neglect were reported last year,"[66] and so does Senator Alan Cranston (Democrat of California) who says that "some 100,000 cases of child abuse" occur annually.[67]

Since the actual incidence of child abuse is unknown, its rate of growth is also unknown. Nonetheless, in providing formal endorsement of a plan for subcommittee hearings on child abuse, Senator Harrison Williams (Democrat of New Jersey), chairman of the Committee on Labor and Public Welfare, wrote Walter Mondale that "the media has begun to turn its attention to this phenomenon and it has become clear that brutality against children by their parents has been dramatically and tragically increasing. This fact is confirmed by recent studies showing child abuse to be on the rise in the United States."[68] As David Gil points out, however, there is no basis to the claim that the incidence of abuse has increased in recent years.[69] Since there are no accurate counts over different periods of years, no conclusion is justified about increased incidence. But whether child abuse has or has not increased, awareness, interest, and concern have grown. Since they are mutually reinforcing, Gil says, an impression of change in incidence results.

The problem of public policy to combat child abuse turned into a classic confrontation between the philosophers of the New Federalism and the philosophers of the Great Society. Both could agree that the magnitude of the problem was simply unknown, perhaps unknowable, and also agree that whatever the magnitude the goal was to reduce the incidence to zero. But it was not agreed that the Children's Bureau's earlier success in stimulating mandatory state reporting laws had made an appreciable difference.[70] When Walter Mondale hammered on HEW per-

65. *Congressional Record* (daily ed.), July 17, 1973, p. S 13664.
66. Ibid., July 28, 1973, p. S 14960.
67. Ibid., July 16, 1973, p. S 13565.
68. Letter from Williams to Mondale, March 8, 1973.
69. *Child Abuse Prevention Act*, Hearings, p. 16.
70. A Children's Bureau conference in 1962 proposed mandatory reporting laws with accompanying immunity from civil or criminal legal action for any person reporting suspected abuse. It was widely assumed that, without the immunity, doctors would be unwilling to report. A year later thirteeen states had enacted reporting laws, and by ten years after that all but one state required reporting of suspected abuse and granted immunity to persons required to report. See Brian Fraser, staff attorney, Na-

sonnel a full dozen times with that question in a session that one of the HEW people later described privately as "terrible," the bureaucrats would assert only that the effectiveness of state laws varied widely and that the department lacked information for a definitive response. The senator was clearly skeptical of state programs, more skeptical of HEW's interest in the subject. "Your first recommendation," he told Stephen Kurzman, assistant secretary for legislation, "is you ought to leave it to the states, and your second answer is you do not know what is going on." Kurzman was not intimidated. "Our first position is not to resort immediately to some new federal mechanism to find the answers," he said.[71]

The Office of Child Development bureaucracy and its political superiors wanted to show concern for the problem but also wanted to resist creation of new federal mechanisms, as Kurzman put it. Senator Mondale saw little reason to be sanguine about making progress through what he perceived to be unimaginative state child welfare programs, so his bill directed HEW to establish demonstration programs. House sponsors adopted the administration's position that demonstration programs are not improved by being run through the Washington bureaucracy. Where the House provided for administration within HEW generally and for oversight by an in-house HEW advisory committee, the Senate stipulated administration within the OCD particularly and created a national commission on child abuse and neglect to study the unresolved issues and report on the effectiveness of the federal effort. The Department of Health, Education, and Welfare was opposed to an independent national commission looking over its shoulder, having long before decided that commissions and ad hoc committees charged to evaluate a program invariably find the program wanting. The department made a counter-offer in a letter to Mondale and to Representative John Brademas indicating its intention to assign responsibility for child abuse to the OCD by administrative order, and offering assurances that in lieu of an external national commission, an in-house oversight committee would "look to experts in the field of child abuse for advice and counsel."[72]

---

tional Center for the Prevention and Treatment of Child Abuse and Neglect, "Legal and Legislative Status in 50 States"; reprinted in *Child Abuse Prevention Act*, 1973, Hearings before the Subcommittee on Children and Youth of the Senate Labor and Public Welfare Committee, 93:1 (GPO, 1973), p. 251.

71. Ibid., p. 94.

72. Letter from Frank Carlucci to Brademas, Dec. 20, 1973, in *Congressional Record* (daily ed.), Dec. 21, 1973, p. H 11934.

As finally enacted, the bill had something for both sides: a floor but also a ceiling on federal financing of state programs; a requirement that at least half of any money appropriated—but not a fixed dollar amount—be spent on demonstration programs; creation of both a National Center on Child Abuse and Neglect and an HEW advisory board to prod the bureaucracy, but no channel for either of them independent of the department.[73]

So the Office of Child Development finally got a new assignment: coordinating HEW's efforts in the child-abuse field. It receives applications for grants, approves some, and makes grants to a fraction of the approved applicants. The size of the fraction depends more on money available than on qualitative differences among proposals. In its first experience with the activity—an experience based on an administrative order from the secretary allocating a total of $4 million to child abuse in hopes of discouraging congressional action on legislation—the OCD found that the applications did not differ much. Virtually any proposal ranked in the upper third could be substituted for any other proposal. This is not to say that the proposals are without merit. The point, rather, is that the OCD role is more ministerial than discretionary, that the office simply allocates funds in response to proposals like one that brought a grant early in 1975 to Children's Hospital of the District of Columbia. The director of the hospital's child-abuse team says that the award allows the hospital to have a full-time child-abuse staff including two social workers, two nurses, one full-time and one part-time pediatrician, a psychologist, a part-time psychiatrist, and four or five paraprofessionals. "We will now have a means that will allow us not only to evaluate and treat, but to follow up each case on an individual basis," she explained when the grant was announced.[74]

Federal money is spent for less worthy purposes than to support multidisciplinary teams that work with abusing parents and abused children. But it is not clear either that the Office of Child Development is uniquely well equipped to dole out that money, or that doing so is much of a job. In child abuse, as in the OCD's credentials program for child development associates, and in its Home Start–Health Start efforts, the bureaucratization of child development is obvious, but important benefits for the children's cause are not.

73. For a public question-and-answer sheet summarizing the scope and provisions of the Child Abuse Prevention and Treatment Act, see *Congressional Record* (daily ed.), May 12, 1975, p. S 7862.
74. *Washington Post*, Jan. 22, 1975.

# 5

# The Politics
# of Comprehensive Legislation

In the initial absence of organized opposition and with help from a coalition of groups interested in day care, early education, and community change, sponsors once maneuvered a comprehensive child development bill through Congress. But after that bill was vetoed late in 1971, supporters found it difficult to command public attention and impossible to maintain legislative momentum. The child development coalition lost strength as differences among its three components became clear. While the Senate went through the motions of passing a weaker bill in 1972, neither sponsors nor skeptics had any illusions about prospects for House consideration. Supporters of comprehensive legislation then let two years pass before even introducing a further scaled-down version of the original proposal. With President Ford and economic reality barring the way to new federal programs in 1975, a renewed congressional initiative in child development that year was admittedly half-hearted.

Though child development has been relegated to what Senator Edward Brooke (Republican of Massachusetts) describes as "a holding action—both in authorizing legislation and in appropriations bills"[1]—its legislative sponsors nevertheless insist they will some day fight again. None of them, however, disputes Brooke's assessment. A holding action in this context means maintaining Head Start without growth while waiting for a political climate more favorable to new legislation. But proponents should understand that the bill passed by both houses in 1971 moved through the congressional process under an advantageous combination of circumstances not likely to obtain again. That combination of circumstances included prolonged uncertainty at high administrative levels, allowing a bipartisan group of congressional sponsors to take the initiative and sus-

1. Speech delivered to the Greater New Brunswick Day Care Council graduating class, New Brunswick, N.J., May 17, 1974 (processed).

tain it over a two-year period; efficient and enthusiastic lobbying by a coalition group successful in bringing supporters of differing approaches into a common camp; a legislative situation that provided a chance for the bill to piggyback on a related bill supported by the administration.

## Congressional Initiative, Departmental Uncertainty

Both the appearance and the apparent disappearance of comprehensive child development from the congressional agenda came abruptly. Unlike national health insurance, medical care for the aged, federal aid to education, and other compelling social issues—in which determined congressional sponsors and interest group supporters assumed that success might ultimately take a decade and that interim failures were not final—child development had a quick fling and was gone. Its legislative success in 1971 resulted, in part, from the interaction of congressional initiative and HEW bungling. Comparable opportunities for the effective use of congressional initiative in child development are not readily foreseeable, one reason that future legislative success will be harder to accomplish.

Democrats in both Senate and House were delighted to take advantage of President Nixon's stated commitment, in his February 1969 message, to the first five years of life. The President was then unsure how his commitment would be discharged. But led by Walter Mondale, twenty-three Democratic senators offered a bill to provide for an expanded Head Start child development program. Over a five-year period, it would have authorized appropriations starting at $1.2 billion for 1970 and increasing steadily to $5 billion by 1974. Mondale's proposal limited itself to assisting children from low-income families or poverty areas. On the House side, Representative John Brademas sponsored a preschool education bill that, while allocating federal money to favor states with relatively large numbers of poor families, did not make children of low-income parents the sole potential beneficiaries. The stated purpose of Brademas's bill was "to provide comprehensive preschool educational programs which will assist children of preschool age to attain their full potential."[2]

The Nixon administration at first responded cautiously to the Mondale-Brademas effort. On the one hand, the new administration was not going to embrace a bill initiated by a liberal Democrat—whether a senator from

2. H.R. 13520, 91:1 (1969).

Minnesota or a representative from Indiana—as part of its own program. On the other hand, the President was moving toward accepting the arguments of his preinaugural welfare task force and of Daniel P. Moynihan, then his White House social policy specialist, in favor of major changes in the welfare system. The changes would inevitably require support for child-care programs for the working poor and for children in single-parent households. Politically, the problem was how to accomplish that end without casting ambitious Democrats as heroes.

An obvious initial course was to encourage delay while the administration worked out its strategy. The Department of Health, Education, and Welfare suggested it be given an opportunity to study the problem. The case for delay was certainly plausible. Developmental services for children was a concept with the briefest of histories; its relationship to traditional protective services like foster care was not clear. It was not yet known what the magnitude of child-care needs might be under the work incentive program for welfare recipients enacted in 1967, but just getting under way in 1969. The leaders of HEW had shown good faith in announcing creation of the Office of Child Development, and in designating a Johnson holdover, Jule Sugarman, as its acting director. After the President committed himself to a concern for the first five years of life, HEW and the White House should be entitled to some time to take stock.

Committees in House and Senate were each assured that Secretary Robert Finch had directed the OCD to undertake a comprehensive study of existing and potential approaches to early childhood programs. The investigation was to consider the relative effectiveness of various types of programs and methods for improving their impact, the numbers of children in need of services and relative priorities of need, and alternative methods for managing, delivering, and financing services.[3] Jule Sugarman explained to a House subcommittee the administration's reluctance to devote energies and funds to a vast expansion of early childhood educational or developmental programs "until we have a more solid base of information."[4] Sugarman's statement was a valid assessment of the state of knowledge in child development. It was also a rationalization for steering clear of the Mondale-Brademas proposals until family assistance—the distinc-

3. *Headstart Child Development Act*, Hearings before the Subcommittee on Employment, Manpower, and Poverty of the Senate Committee on Labor and Public Welfare, 91:1 (Government Printing Office, 1970), pt. 1, p. 109.

4. *Comprehensive Preschool Education and Child Day Care Act of 1969*, Hearings before the Select Subcommittee on Education of the House Committee on Education and Labor, 91:1 and 2 (GPO, 1970), p. 101.

tive Nixon program—was well launched. Support for family assistance, including its child-care component, was not to be diluted by simultaneous consideration of comprehensive child development.

Child development was not reported out of House or Senate committees in 1969–70 because proponents knew there would be more votes in 1971, not because they agreed on the need for an HEW study. In Congress, the administration's posture was suspect. Since the clock was ticking away on those presumably critical first five years of life for millions of children, to wait for a study to suggest what the HEW spokesmen termed "the priority of need for future expansion" seemed unconscionable.[5] Mondale said he would have none of it: "The standard opposition to any human program around here is that we should study it, until we know exactly what to do. It is my impression that we know more than enough to justify a substantial new effort and, presumably, the President felt that way when he asked for a national commitment in this field."[6] Brademas was similarly impatient. In explaining his decision to proceed to hearings late in 1969 on his comprehensive preschool education bill, Brademas dismissed the argument that not enough was known to justify it. "I suppose you never know enough," he said, "and the problem there would be that if we had operated on [that] presupposition, we wouldn't have had a Project Head Start program." If there had been no Head Start, Brademas said, "nobody would care a tinker's dam about preschool programs, anyway, and we wouldn't have had an Elementary and Secondary Education Act, and we wouldn't have had anything."[7]

All of the work that is a necessary preliminary to bringing a piece of legislation to the floor of Congress proceeded despite the HEW argument. House and Senate hearings stretched out between August 1969 and March 1970. Scholars, practitioners, and politicians endorsed the legislation. Bruno Bettelheim of the University of Chicago came to talk about his observations in Israel and report that the earlier the impact of education and other measures on an individual, the greater the difference in his later function. Bettye Caldwell came to talk about her Center for Early Development and Education at the University of Arkansas and to emphasize the importance of linking preschool programs with elementary school programs. Urie Bronfenbrenner, Cornell's child development sage, came to talk of the fundamental importance of focusing attention on the "truly

5. *Headstart Child Development Act*, Hearings, pt. 1, p. 110.
6. Ibid., p. 131.
7. *Comprehensive Preschool Education . . . Act of 1969*, Hearings, p. 215.

forgotten segment of American society—its children—[so] we may yet reverse the present destructive trend and, in the process, rediscover our moral identity as a society and as a nation."[8] The confident eloquence of the psychologists was matched by the day-care spokesmen. For example, President Sadie Ginsberg of the National Committee for the Day Care of Children found the Brademas proposal "an extremely timely and useful bill. . . . The evidence is pervasive that we must reaffirm our concern for life in order to save our young. This bill may be a small step in Congress, but it is a giant step for the children it may serve."[9]

At that stage, there were substantial differences among legislative proponents, but it was not necessary to accommodate those differences. Brademas viewed child development as an educational issue. He put the compensatory early education purpose ahead of any community change considerations. He also put child development as a day-care mechanism ahead of any civil rights objectives that might also be served by comprehensive legislation. Mondale's interest was especially in community change, and in the opportunities that child development programs afforded local community groups to reach directly for federal money. In the main, Mondale's view coincided with the view of child development held by his colleague, Gaylord Nelson (Democrat of Wisconsin), whose subcommittee controlled the Senate bill. Brademas's interest in the educational side was shared by many of his principal cosponsors in the House, both Republican and Democrat, although Representative Patsy Mink (Democrat of Hawaii) insists that her interest grew out of concern for children of working mothers, and the chairman of the full Education and Labor Committee, Carl Perkins, later focused on community organization. There was no urgent need to resolve those differences before passage by both houses. Until that happened, an illusion of untroubled legislative progress would be maintained, and the adherents of community change quietly went to work to move House sponsors closer to the Senate position.

The groundwork was being laid for a major effort on behalf of child development in 1971, when Head Start authorization would be up for renewal. That effort would rest on a full and fresh hearings record. Moreover, endorsement of child development legislation was likely to be provided by the White House Conference on Children scheduled for 1970. Things fell into place nicely. So, before the conference convened, Brademas's subcommittee published a hearings record that ran more than a thousand pages and covered fifteen days of testimony in Washington and

8. Ibid., pp. 154–55.
9. Ibid., pp. 124–25.

two in Chicago. On the Senate side, a comparable drive for Mondale's bill was undertaken by the Labor Committee's Subcommittee on Employment, Manpower, and Poverty. Hearings before that group began in August, then recessed while the first Brademas hearings proceeded in November and December. In February 1970, hearings were going on in both chambers. Because the administration had difficulty in gearing up for the Children's Conference, the hearings were actually completed nine months before the conference met in December. Having done his part to provide them a data base and a receptive congressional environment, Mondale had some advice for the delegates a few days before the conference began. In essence, he told them to seize the moment:

Specifically, insist that a representative group from the Conference be formed to call on the President personally while the Conference is still in session and seek his public support for implementation.... let this be the first White House Conference ever to focus on creating a legislative strategy for implementing its findings.[10]

As for himself, the senator explained, regardless of the administration response, he planned to introduce the constructive proposals of the conference in legislative form and he planned to organize a bipartisan congressional group to work on behalf of children. It was an invitation to the conferees to support enactment of legislation comparable to that Mondale had already sponsored.

Without an HEW and a White House position, the Mondale-Brademas bills, with White House Conference endorsement, were likely to preempt the children's policy field. Whether or not that fact had already occurred to Senator Mondale and Representative Brademas, it finally dawned on HEW's leaders just as the White House Conference assembled. The study they had said they would make during the preceding eighteen months, but had not made, now became an emergency need. The department's internal Board of Advisers on Child Development met for the first time since its creation eighteen months earlier. A day later Secretary Richardson appointed an interagency task force composed of twenty HEW senior staff members knowledgeable about programs affecting children. Paper began to flow. Thirteen reactors reviewed the task force's position papers, needs statements, and alternative draft bills before a report was transmitted. But the comments of both task force members and reactors disclosed that there was little in-house agreement on such basic questions as which children should get services, what kinds of services they should get, or how they should get them.

10. *Congressional Record*, vol. 116, pt. 30 (1970), p. 40507.

The interagency task force, chaired by Director Edward Zigler of the Office of Child Development, assumed an urgent need for the department to develop a strategy on child care and development. It assumed as well that day-care programs in support of family assistance were a federal concern; that federally supported child care should be "developmental" as opposed to "purely custodial"; that direct operation of programs by the federal government at the local level was neither administratively nor politically feasible; and that child development programs would give priority to the poor.[11] The task force did not analyze or document either its assumptions, or the rationale for federal involvement in child development, or the goals of child development programs.

The emphasis on techniques and the failure to attend to theory and philosophy left the department taking a good deal for granted. A careful study of rationale and of goals might have given the HEW leadership cause to wonder just how clear-cut the issue was. To be sure, Zigler's "action memorandum" to Richardson, submitted with the task force documents, noted that the secretary's options included asking for an in-depth analysis of child care and development assumptions and issues, "if you feel that there needs to be a more detailed analysis of the basic assumptions and justifications for the alternatives."[12] Even in offering Richardson that option, however, Zigler discouraged accepting it. Zigler warned that "we may be overcome" by the expiration of Head Start authority; by the likelihood that a bill with extensive bipartisan support would be offered in the House promptly; by the pressure from the Children's Lobby, the Joint Commission on Mental Health of Children, and the Day Care Council to take a position on child development programs; or by the fall-out from the recommendations made by the White House Children's Conference.

So Zigler's message to Richardson was that congressional sponsors had the upper hand. Federal involvement in child care was being pushed from within and without the administration by a variety of groups none of whom could be ignored. The secretary could order continued study, but delay would be a dangerous course. He could initiate fresh legislation under administration auspices, but in the end would have a bill differing from the House subcommittee bill more in detail than in intent.

The sponsors . . . have indicated a willingness to change the Bill in conformance with the Department's recommendations. We may have difficulty in getting

11. "Interagency Task Force on Child Care and Development—Action Memorandum," from Edward Zigler to Elliot Richardson (January 1971), pp. 1–2.
12. Ibid., p. 6.

Committee support for an Administration Bill which differs from the bipartisan Bill because of the extensive and careful efforts the Committee members have already devoted to the Bill over the last year.

If we are to have any credibility with the Congress and the public vis à vis the Administration's concern for effective children's programs, our best route may be that of working with the Committee's Bill.[13]

Richardson accepted the argument too readily. Zigler was new to Washington and new to dealing with Congress. He both wanted a bill and wanted to be involved in fixing its terms. Had the secretary dug beneath the surface, Richardson might have been disposed to set aside the "we may be overcome by events" caution. Expiration of Head Start obviously posed no serious problem. Temporary extension of a program pending completion of administration consideration of its future is a common occurrence. Such an arrangement could readily have been made for Head Start. The possibility that legislation with "extensive bipartisan support" might be offered and moved to passage had validity only if the administration either stood mute or let it be known that it would favor a child development bill. Indeed, such legislation was offered and did pass both houses only after Richardson indicated HEW support. Passage in the House, at least, was inconceivable if the department indicated honest uncertainty about the concept but showed goodwill by reconvening its internal task force.

As for Zigler's suggestion that interest group strength could be important, Zigler was a political novice. Richardson ignored that aspect of the memorandum. None of the groups cited by Zigler was consequential: the Joint Commission on Mental Health was a sad joke in professional circles; the Day Care Council suffered from administrative chaos; the White House Conference had no postconference organizational strength; Sugarman's Children's Lobby was a paper panda.

In any event, around the end of February 1971, the secretary belatedly decided that the department would support a modified version of the bill that had been developed in the Brademas subcommittee during the Ninety-first Congress (1969–70).[14] Following that decision, a departmental work group was able to draft language reflecting the secretary's judgments on substantive items and reflecting the consensus of the Board of Advisors on Child Development. The work group could not cope, how-

13. Ibid., p. 7.
14. The HEW memorandum consistently referred to the modified version of the bill developed in the Brademas subcommittee as the Dellenback-Brademas bill. John Dellenback, an Oregon Republican, was cosponsor. Presumably, it was beyond the pale for the department to support legislation bearing the name of a liberal Democrat.

ever, with unresolved issues relating to the delivery system. Those issues were further complicated by the appearance of the 1971 version of the Brademas bill. The latter was a new model for the new Congress, but HEW was still testing, examining, and preparing to bargain over the old model.


## The Child Development Coalition as Lobbyist

The 1971 version of the House subcommittee's child development bill differed from the subcommittee's earlier version and from the HEW plan in a critically important particular: it did not require child development money and power to flow through a general-purpose government. Representatives Brademas and Dellenback (along with their cosponsors Ogden Reid, Republican of New York, and Patsy Mink) had moved toward the position of civil rights spokesmen and others who emphasized the community change aspects of child development. Although these groups were not entirely satisfied with the details of the Brademas bill, the new approach in the House meant major trouble for HEW. It was no longer true that the differences between the department and the subcommittee were differences of detail rather than of intent as Zigler had earlier characterized them. Those differences had become differences of intent, while the differences between the House and the Senate bills had been transformed into differences of detail.

In view of the high competence of both House and Senate sponsors, achieving the near-accommodation was an impressive accomplishment. This was no case of a lobbyist handing a bill to a member who bumbled along as best he could, garnering votes by virtue of seniority, friendship, or party ties rather than by virtue of an understanding and an ability to communicate the substance of the issue. John Brademas and his House cosponsors all understood very well that a choice of care, cognition, or community change was at issue. Indeed, Brademas never abandoned cognitive development as his primary motivation. The key was to avoid confronting that question while authorizing delivery by units smaller than states. On the Senate side, Walter Mondale, who also knew what he was about, accepted child development under local community control as the issue from the first. House sponsors tilted toward community control—albeit there were differences about size—because supporters of that position put together the only child-care lobby in town. Even if House sponsors on both sides of the aisle had been willing to follow the administration on state control, HEW failed for so long to make a basic response to child development legislation that it lost any chance to influence the House. The OCD's Zigler was for supporting any bill at all, and worrying later about how to implement it. His superiors, however, felt they had complex problems of political philosophy to resolve, to say nothing of practical political problems associated with perpetuating community action groups. Indecision controlled, a remarkably common situation at HEW.

An important factor in the events leading to congressional agreement on child development legislation was Marian Edelman's Washington Research Project Action Council. No organized group with sure leadership capacity was in a position to coordinate the activities of the numerous groups interested in the subject. Some of the interested groups knew what was involved in Washington lobbying, others knew the substantive issues and how to prepare supporting materials for particular positions, still others represented or seemed to represent sizable constituencies concerned about the child development problem. But child development was not central enough to the concerns of the skilled lobbyists that proponents could count on those organizations to monitor legislative developments and to assign high priority to this legislative cause. The Washington Research Project had been established to "run a monitoring operation at the federal level,"[15] and while Edelman really had the monitoring of federal administrative agencies in mind, the project's Action Council, its lobbying arm, was well suited to monitor the legislative path of child development.

In fact, Edelman was able to hold together a coalition of groups interested in child care, child development, and community change at a time when they were not yet ready to fight over which emphasis would control the terms of legislation. Edelman's emphasis was on child development as an instrument of community change. There was never any secret about that, but perhaps because she had thought through the issues more thoroughly than had some others, Edelman could put together a coalition that included the National Association for the Education of Young Children, the League of Women Voters, the AFL-CIO, the Day Care and Child Development Council of America, the National Council of Negro Women, the National League of Cities–U.S. Conference of Mayors, the National Welfare Rights Organization, and a dozen other organizations.

15. "The New Public Interest Lawyers," *Yale Law Journal*, vol. 79 (May 1970), p. 1081.

In later years, some organizations in the coalition would find that community control through prime sponsors composed of groups of only five thousand population was more troublesome a concept than it seemed earlier to be. No reservations on either the community control principle or the minimum population for prime sponsors seriously unsettled the original coalition.

The coalition's real strength was derived from the appearance of support from organized labor. Lobbying work was handled chiefly by Richard Warden, once a staff member in the HEW Office for Civil Rights with which the Washington Research Project maintained close ties. Warden subsequently went on to lobby for the AFL-CIO's United Automobile Workers (UAW), but oscillated between the Research Project Action Council and the UAW. The combination of good luck and good sense that made him the child development coalition's lobbyist meant that community change would not be displaced as a major aspect of the child development effort. Significantly, when members of Congress later assessed the impact of organized groups in the child development field, the organized labor lobby loomed largest in their minds. And Warden—his dedication unaffected by whose payroll he was on at a particular moment —not only served as a catalyst in getting and keeping other labor people interested, but was, in large part, the continuing labor presence on the issue.

Emphasizing publicly the participation of all the members, keeping them all informed through periodic status reports, soliciting their views and their help in frequent meetings, Edelman maximized the value of the coalition approach without having to sacrifice principle in order to keep it together. The key principle, for her, was community control. Marian Edelman saw child development as the Child Development Group of Mississippi where the Head Start program had been, in her words, "perhaps *the* most important social catalyst for change in the state. It helped poor parents understand new ways of having an effect on their children's education."[16] Child-care legislation turning control of services over to the states would have meant, she feared, control by the public schools. "In Mississippi and other southern states this action would have meant the end of parental involvement for the poor."[17] Because she deemed that outcome intolerable, Edelman undertook to mobilize support on behalf

16. Rochelle Beck and John Butler, "An Interview with Marian Wright Edelman," *Harvard Educational Review*, vol. 44 (February 1974), p. 68.
17. Ibid.

of community control. Discovering that it had never occurred to the day-care establishment to draft their own legislation, she proceeded to lead the drafting of what became the Mondale bill.

For some groups, then, where responsibility for the delivery of child development services would be lodged became the most important test by which to judge proposed legislation. Mondale's Senate bill, unlike Brademas's, had been an Edelman-inspired community-control bill all along. That approach was not only preferred by most poverty, civil rights, and organized labor groups; for them, it was not debatable. For example, organization of local community groups to work for community change independent of repressive or indifferent state and local government was a primary concern of the Black Child Development Institute. The institute's Maurine McKinley is explicit on the subject:

We believe that child development centers can be the catalyst for total community development. . . .

It is to the advantage of the entire nation to view the provision of day care/child development services within the context of the need for a readjustment of societal power relationships. . . . As day care centers are utilized to catalyze development in black and other communities, the enhanced political and economic power that results can provide effective leverage for the improvement of the overall social and economic condition of the Nation.[18]

Marian Edelman never left any doubt about how crucial local control was from her point of view: "The heart of this bill, however, is the delivery mechanism. Those of us who have worked with the poor, the uneducated, the hungry, the disenfranchised, have had long and bitter experience in how legislative intent is thwarted in the process of implementation. . . . We think this [local community administration] essential and those concerned with equal opportunity and civil rights will oppose any control of this child legislation to the States."[19] By persuading Brademas and Dellenback to move to community rather than state control, Edelman's people deprived HEW of an easy base from which to negotiate on other disputed matters.

Until the emergence of the Edelman coalition, HEW's new federalists who emphasized the role of state and local governments in child development felt there was a receptive ear for their position in the House subcom-

18. *Comprehensive Child Development Act of 1971*, Joint Hearings before the Subcommittees on Employment, Manpower, and Poverty and on Children and Youth of the Senate Labor and Public Welfare Committee, 92:1 (GPO, 1971), pt. 1, pp. 367–68.

19. Ibid., pt. 2, p. 523.

mittee. Differences between Representative Brademas and Senator Mondale had, of course, existed from the very beginning of the legislative drive in 1969. Both emphasized the comprehensive character of the program; both were concerned about actual supervisory care of children, about children's cognitive development, and about child development as a way of improving the self-image of parents in depressed communities just as other community action programs had had a comparable effect on other population groups. If it became necessary to tilt, however, Mondale would tilt toward child development as a social instrument, Brademas toward the educational side. For Mondale, the probability of child development having a bearing on community change would diminish drastically as community groups and smaller governmental units were precluded from assuming responsibility. Mondale agreed with Marian Edelman's judgment that state control meant that consideration for minorities and socioeconomic diversity would be given up, that the program would be in the hands of state bureaucracies where the poor and the blacks are least influential. Brademas, more concerned about cognitive development, was also more receptive to a role for organized governmental entities in delivering the educational service. The Brademas position might have been acceptable to HEW; the Mondale position was not. When the former began to look more like the latter, the department had something to worry about.

Within a couple of days of the 1971 bill's appearance, HEW's deputy under secretary for policy coordination wrote the secretary in a formal memorandum that the pending bill differed "significantly" from the HEW proposal and from the previous Brademas-Dellenback bill. Should the administration take the initiative and try to work with the Congress to draft a compromise bill, a route "still quite possible, if we move quickly"?[20] Or, should the administration wait until the bill was reported out of committee before deciding on strategy? The question hardly needed an answer because the Office of Management and Budget had already indicated reluctance to approve additional federal responsibility for day care and child development other than that connected with work training of welfare mothers. The OMB was not prepared to clear any version of the comprehensive child development approach under discussion in the department.

20. "Child Care Legislation—Action Memorandum," from the deputy under secretary for policy coordination to the secretary of the Department of Health, Education, and Welfare (n.d.), p. 1.

So HEW could not move quickly because it could not move at all. There were troubles everywhere. The department's own assistant secretary for planning and evaluation, Lewis Butler, rejected full-day developmental day care as unjustified by the economic benefits gained from having a mother work, and unjustified also by "its few unique child development benefits."[21] Butler argued instead for a strategy of part-day child development for poor children, with supplementary day care (defined as "mostly babysitting for working mothers") as part of welfare reform. Accordingly, when Zigler succeeded in getting Richardson's decision to support "some" legislation, it was assumed around the department that the Dellenback-Brademas bill of 1971 would lend itself to a compromise on the issue of a full-day versus a part-day program and on income limits for eligibility. It was also assumed, however, that a child-care bill could be moved along that would avoid subsidizing community action groups in the guise of prime sponsors of child development programs. Although Brademas's 1971 bill put the latter assumption in doubt, HEW could not move to initiate an administration alternative because OMB would not clear any bill on the subject. Nor could department personnel negotiate with Brademas over differences on income limits for eligibility without leaving the now-false impression that such details represented the only impediment to HEW support. In fact, the means of delivering child development services was a far more serious impediment. Income limits were negotiable, but local community groups as prime sponsors were not. That idea had been set aside in HEW at the time that it was embraced by legislative sponsors.

The unresolved issues were put to the secretary for decision, but no consideration was given to wholesale expansion of the number of potential prime sponsors. Options offered Richardson were to limit prime sponsors to states only, to extend eligibility to states and to cities over 500,000 population, or to extend eligibility to states and to cities of some other size, larger or smaller. He chose the 500,000 option on the theory that cities of that size have problems significantly unlike those of smaller cities, and that separating big cities from states would help avoid conflict between rural and urban interest groups. Political strategy also dictated that big cities be authorized to act as prime sponsors. Richardson's advisers pointed out to him in their briefing that large groups of people eligible for the program live in the biggest cities. A bill allowing those political units to

21. "Views on Federal Child Development Strategy," memorandum to the secretary of the Department of Health, Education, and Welfare (Feb. 6, 1971), p. 1.

deal with HEW directly could be expected to attract large numbers of supporters.[22]

Down below, at the OCD level, Zigler was less fussy. His interest was in seeing a bill enacted—any bill. He reasoned that a bill was necessary to give the OCD legitimacy, and that he could work his way around whatever administrative constraints or freedoms were set out in any bill. Without some legislation covering child development and child care, however, there was little reason for Zigler not to be back at Yale. It simply was not his intention to preside over a weakened Children's Bureau and institute small-scale demonstration programs. In addition, there was a question of pride. "What kind of mandate do you have from within the Administration in doing what you want to do?" an interviewer had asked when Zigler first arrived to take over the OCD. "I have every indication that the Administration has faith in my judgment in this area," was the answer.[23] His judgment now, Zigler wrote to Richardson, was to move forward:

The analyses that could reasonably be done have been done; the proposal of the work group has taken political reality and intra-departmental differences into account as well as I can imagine such a balancing being accomplished. In my opinion, it would be nothing less than shameful to neglect this opportunity to significantly improve the lives of the nation's children and their families.[24]

Ten weeks later, after Senator Mondale had moved his bill through four days of hearings on the Senate side, and Brademas had held three days of hearings on his bill, Richardson sent each of them what he described as "a statement of the Administration's position on day care and child development legislation pending before your Subcommittee." While the letter called it "the Administration's position," either the secretary went beyond his authority, or "the Administration's position" subsequently changed. The letter extended an invitation to cooperate in framing child development legislation. It carried no hint of firm opposition on principle to further involvement in the child development field, but spoke instead of the "various child care programs now in place and soon to be enacted by the Congress."[25] But if "the Administration's position" was giving Elliot Richardson trouble, neither House nor Senate proponents were sympathetic to his problem.

22. "Child Care and Development Legislative Strategy—Action Memorandum," from the deputy under secretary for policy coordination to the secretary of the Department of Health, Education, and Welfare (n.d.).

23. Press conference, June 26, 1970 (transcript prepared by Ace-Federal Reporters; processed), p. 26.

24. "Child Care Legislation—Information Memorandum" (April 2, 1971), p. 2.

25. Letter from Elliot Richardson to John Brademas, June 8, 1971.

## By Piggyback to the Senate Floor

Child development came to the Senate floor in 1971 because the Senate Labor and Public Welfare Committee, responding to its own instincts and to the administration's request, recommended a two-year extension of the antipoverty program. The bill providing for that extension served also as the vehicle for moving child development, improved legal services for the poor, and improved rural and urban economic development programs. Child development supporters found the package convenient, perhaps indispensable to their chances for success. With administration and committee support, the poverty bill extension was assured of being called up in both houses. The director of the Office of Economic Opportunity, Frank Carlucci, had urged such extension in March, telling the House Education and Labor Committee that failure to do so would undo much of the progress made in the effort to eradicate poverty.[26] Thus, by rational political calculation, child development would fare better tied to the still-popular Head Start program which was in turn tied to the economic opportunity extender than child development would fare alone.

If the poverty program extender offered a strategically advantageous receptacle for child development, whether it was an appropriate receptacle troubled at least one committee member. Senator Robert Taft (Republican of Ohio) raised that question in executive session, chose not to pursue it there, joined in the unanimous committee vote to report the bill with the child development title attached, then led an effort on the Senate floor to separate child development from the rest of the poverty program legislation. Taft argued later that the committee had marked up the bill in great haste and had not given child development the thorough review it deserved.[27]

That judgment irritated both Walter Mondale and Gaylord Nelson, chairmen respectively of the subcommittees on Children and Youth and on Employment, Manpower, and Poverty which had held joint hearings on child development. "We have had, I think, as much consideration of this proposal as of any proposal the Senate has acted on since I came to the Senate," was Mondale's testy comment, and he added that essentially the same measure had been introduced in the previous Congress with ex-

26. *Economic Opportunity Amendments of 1971*, Hearings before the Subcommittee on Employment, Manpower, and Poverty of the Senate Labor and Public Welfare Committee, 92:1 (GPO, 1971), p. 127.

27. *Congressional Record* (daily ed.), Sept. 9, 1971, p. S 14008.

tensive hearings held on both occasions. "This proposal," said Mondale with a further touch of hyperbole, "is as fully considered as any proposal in the social reform field to come before the Senate in a long time, and perhaps even at all."[28] Nelson, for his part, recalled that child development took more time in the mark-up sessions than any other issue in the bill, and that whether it should be separated from the poverty program legislation was carefully and thoroughly discussed before the unanimous vote to report.[29]

Taft now was acting as Senate spear-carrier for HEW on legislative problems that Secretary Richardson had been slow in facing. In fact, HEW was consistently a step behind outside proponents and congressional sponsors. The department found itself responding to congressional activity that had already achieved significant momentum. For example, the departmental task force's work was still under internal consideration when the Brademas-Dellenback bill was offered in the House although there were numerous signals that the latter was forthcoming. Again, the HEW objections to the Senate version of the child development legislation had barely been thought through when the poverty program bill was being marked up. Richardson did not get around to submitting what he continued to call "administration specifications" to Mondale until mid-June. Yet, a Bayh-Mondale bill sponsored by Mondale and Birch Bayh (Democrat of Indiana) had been introduced on February 2; a bill sponsored by Jacob Javits, Clifford Case (Republican of New Jersey), Fred Harris (Democrat of Oklahoma), and William B. Saxbe (Republican of Ohio), on February 10; and a bipartisan bill bearing the names of thirty senators led by Mondale on April 5.

Richardson and his department simply pulled themselves together too late to face the child development legislative drive effectively. When Taft argued the case for limiting prime sponsors to states and big cities, or argued more generally on behalf of separate consideration of child development in order to further study and refine the issues of delivery, eligibility, and the concept of child advocacy, his position was that of a lawyer raising issues on appeal that should have been raised at the trial level. Preoccupied with what appeared to be a great drive for welfare reform, HEW's top leadership did not even stake out a detailed child development position until the hearings process was almost at an end. Before the belated appearance of Assistant Secretary (for Legislation)

28. Ibid., p. S 14009.
29. Ibid., p. S 14008.

Stephen Kurzman,[30] the argument on the cutoff size for a prime sponsor's population had been advanced only by Jule Sugarman, by then out of HEW and, in essence, a Mondale witness rather than an HEW witness. Moreover, Sugarman's espousal of a minimum population size for eligibility rested on its utility as an administrative device.[31] Where the so-called administration specifications included a cutoff figure first of 500,000 and later, as amended by Richardson, of 100,000 as an alternative to exclusive use of state government, Sugarman's case for 100,000 assumed both the organization of groups of communities and nongovernmental prime sponsors. In the end, if passage of a bill depended on the minimum population specified for eligibility as prime sponsor, Sugarman would readily give in on the population issue. The HEW position, on the other hand, was to stand firm on states and relatively large general-purpose governments; neither private organizations nor community action groups were within the pale.

The HEW case for holding the line on behalf of states and large cities did not prevail. The Senate committee again accepted the "everybody can play" approach to eligibility for prime sponsors. While the bill it reported left ultimate authority in the secretary to decide between competing prime sponsorship plans that might be submitted by states, general-purpose local governments, and public or private nonprofit agencies including community action agencies, the bill also carried a statement of congressional purpose that was plainly indicative of where the sponsors stood: "It is the purpose of this title . . . to provide that decisions on the nature and funding of such [child development] programs be made at the community level with the direct participation of parents of the children and other individuals and organizations in the community interested in child development served in the development, conduct, and overall direction of programs at the community level."[32] Five of the committee's seven Republican members filed supplemental views making the case for limiting prime sponsors to states and general-purpose governments with a 100,000 population minimum. But they were not "dissenting views" and all joined in the unanimous committee vote to report the bill.

Senator Taft was unwilling to turn what in July had been his mild

30. *Comprehensive Child Development Act of 1971*, Hearings, pt. 3, p. 761.

31. See both Sugarman's testimony in *Comprehensive Child Development Act of 1971*, Hearings, pt. 1, especially p. 165, and his letter to Mondale of June 11, 1971, in ibid., pt. 3, p. 920.

32. S. 2007, Calendar no. 328, reported by the Labor and Public Welfare Committee, 92:1 (1971), p. 12.

reservation about the prime sponsor provision into an all-out opposition in September. Taft was willing to make the HEW case on the floor. He got a formal letter from Richardson proposing in particular an amendment to the prime sponsor provision as reported, offered and argued the case for what Richardson was continuing to call the administration's position, lost, and proceeded himself to vote for the bill on passage. Throughout, Taft insisted that a child development title should be enacted. Nor did any other member of the Senate committee oppose passage of the child development bill. It passed handily (49–12) in early September 1971.

The principal opposition came from a different Senate source, and was never alleged to represent either HEW or White House attitudes. Nevertheless, New York's Conservative Senator James Buckley reflected far more accurately the views later expressed by the President than did either the secretary of HEW or HEW's Senate spokesman, Robert Taft. The bill, said Buckley, would commit Congress and the nation "to a social policy that threatens to destroy parental authority and the institution of the family."[33] Buckley later explained his conviction that comprehensive child development should have been as controversial as any piece of legislation in recent memory, yet "a working majority of the Senate was unaware of what was really in it."[34]

There is no mechanism for testing whether or not a working majority of either house is ever aware of what is in bills on which they vote. In most cases, members depend on ideological bedfellows on the appropriate committee to provide whatever warning signals may be necessary. Buckley's dismay resulted from the absence of such warnings. (The "supplemental views" of five Republicans had been on questions of delivery, not of philosophy.) He complained that the bill "was simply there as the pending business when the Senate returned from its summer recess."[35] While the senator continued to characterize the bill, even after Senate passage, as one of the most deeply radical pieces of social legislation ever considered in Congress, Buckley directed his complaints about the absence of warning away from his colleagues and to the failure of the working press to publicize the issue. President Nixon's subsequent veto message adopted Buckley's characterization of the child development title as deeply radical, and also embraced the Buckley argument that a great

33. *Congressional Record* (daily ed.), Sept. 9, 1971, p. S 14010.
34. Ibid., Nov. 12, 1971, p. E 12164.
35. Ibid.

national debate must precede enactment of child development legislation. Neither of these problems had seemed to trouble Secretary Richardson. Neither problem was raised in Richardson's statement of "administration specifications."

## House, Conference, and Veto

No veto hints or threats came from the White House as child development legislation continued to be handled deftly by its congressional sponsors. The bill was maneuvered through the House by John Brademas with an elegant display of parliamentary skill. Most differences between proponents were resolved in the conference committee. While opponents of the final version could not agree to the permissible level of community control, even they were unprepared for the tone of the subsequent veto message.

Whether or not comprehensive child development legislation was an appropriate subject for congressional action was not an issue in the Select Subcommittee on Education or in the full House Education and Labor Committee. The divisive issue was how to do it rather than whether to do it. Some members of the committee favored setting a prime-sponsor population limitation at 500,000; others wanted to go to zero. Brademas characterizes the prime-sponsor population limitation as "without question" the most difficult issue considered in committee deliberations on the bill.[36] The 100,000 figure was the compromise outcome to which HEW reluctantly subscribed. Brademas and John Dellenback, whose bill Richardson had first agreed to support, were equally comfortable with the idea of a 100,000 population minimum for prime sponsorship. They did not see such a stipulation as impairing the cognitive development purposes of the bill which had been their central interest from the first.

Brademas and Dellenback thought 100,000 to be a universally acceptable compromise on the delivery issue but they were wrong in believing they had satisfied the chairman of the full Education and Labor Committee, Carl Perkins. It was a misunderstanding of some significance. Perkins favored the local-community approach and was not disposed, as Dellenback later put it, to give an inch, let alone 100,000 population.[37] Perkins thought he could win by making judicious use of his prerogative

36. Ibid., Sept. 30, 1971, p. H 8879.
37. Interview, Oct. 2, 1973.

as chairman to control the movement of the bill out of the committee. As it turned out, he was outmaneuvered by Brademas on the parliamentary score; but Perkins won on the substantive issue anyway.

The Perkins plan was to deal seriatim with the bills extending the life of the Office of Economic Opportunity and establishing a comprehensive child development program. In the Senate, the two had been packaged together. Brademas, however, was not confident that the House Rules Committee would clear child development. And even if that could be accomplished, he was concerned about the possibility of losing the child development legislation entirely in a parliamentary wrangle. If the House were to pass legislation extending the poverty program without a child development title, the Senate-House conference committee on the poverty bill was making its way and could subsequently become a vehicle for congressional action on child development. But Brademas and his allies were not really confident they could maintain control of the bill under those conditions. They preferred a package approach and decided to bypass Perkins to accomplish it. Accordingly, Brademas introduced as a new measure the child development bill that had been reported out of committee but not yet called up by Perkins. Brademas then offered his new bill as an amendment from the floor to the poverty program legislation, explaining that he believed it important to have a House version as well as a Senate version in conference.

Pressure from Perkins's Appalachian constituency and his own instincts precluded his accepting the Brademas-HEW compromise solution on the prime-sponsor issue. Nor was Perkins happy about Brademas's breach of legislative etiquette in seeking to effect the package arrangement. Perkins first pushed through an amendment to Brademas's proposal. The Perkins amendment reduced the 100,000 population requirement to 10,000, and thereby lost the support of the Republican cosponsors. Later, after House passage of the package—accomplished before a committee report on child development was ever filed—Perkins further countered Brademas's irregular behavior with some of his own by not naming Brademas to the conference committee, a decision Brademas believes Perkins later was "ashamed of."[38] Generally overlooked at the time, it was an indication of the in-fighting that took place within as well as across party lines.

Brademas's parliamentary maneuvering eventuated in House passage,

38. Interview, Oct. 15, 1973.

although by a close 186–183 on the crucial vote. For HEW the long period of uncertainty and of foot-dragging on the child development question now gave promise of being terribly costly. Congressional enactment seemed inevitable since Senate support was never in doubt. The department foresaw trouble over prime sponsorship and over income limits for free child development services. Both House and Senate made it possible for prime sponsors of child development programs to be units other than states or very large general-purpose local governments, a situation the department deplored as an administrative nightmare. Richardson had speculated that there could be as many as 40,000 grantees under the Senate bill.[39] In addition, the Senate bill fixed an income limit on free service that could have adverse consequences for welfare reform, still the administration's most prized domestic effort.

The bill that Mondale took through the Senate stipulated free child development services for children in families with incomes below the Bureau of Labor Statistics' low-budget level, then $6,960 annually for a four-person family in an urban area. Brademas's bill had come out of committee with a comparable provision. Late in the game, HEW realized that a $6,960 level for free services under child development legislation would mean that child-care costs under welfare reform would escalate in accord with that ceiling, or that a double standard would be created: under one bill, free child care up to $6,960 income; under the other, up to $4,320 income. Welfare reform could be made impossible by prior enactment of an overly generous child development bill. The House figure was amended down to an effective $4,320 cutoff after two strenuous efforts on the floor stimulated by an emergency message from Richardson to Gerald Ford, then House Republican leader. When Richardson wrote Ford that "these matters . . . I assure you, are of deepest concern to the Administration," it was not just boilerplate language.[40]

The results of a few simple arithmetic calculations are not flattering to either the House or Senate sponsors of what both called landmark legislation. In the case of families with incomes under $7,000, there would be 6.8 million children below age six and 11.9 million between six and fourteen. Using HEW's (too low) cost figures of $1,300 per child for preschool services and $700 per child for after-school services, the annual cost of the proposed child development program could amount to $17 billion. The

39. *Child Care*, Hearings before the Senate Committee on Finance, 92:1 (GPO, 1971), p. 97.
40. *Congressional Record* (daily ed.), Sept. 30, 1971, p. H 8887.

comparable figure if eligibility for free service were held to an income of $4,320 is $9 billion for 3.6 million preschool children and 6.3 million school-aged children. Even a 50 percent participation rate would have meant $8.5 billion at $6,960 and $4.5 billion at $4,320. No one came close to those amounts in suggesting expenditure authorizations. Richardson, in seeking to hold the line at $4,320, wrote Ford that the anticipated spending level was $1.2 billion, made up of existing Head Start and Social Security Act financing augmented by money earmarked for child care under the welfare reform proposal.[41] The gap between potential costs and planned spending could have been almost $8 billion in the Richardson-approved plan. Brademas's ideas about spending left an even larger gap. He supported the $6,960 cutoff and estimated the cost of the legislation at $350 million a year. Mondale, who also supported the $6,960 cutoff for free service, first included an ultimate authorization of $7 billion in his bill, still leaving a gap of $1.5 billion at a 50 percent participation rate. As passed by the Senate, the bill authorized only $2 billion. Every version of the child development legislation promised more than the money it authorized could buy.

Since it was inconceivable that there would be enough money authorized, let alone appropriated, to provide the promised child development services even to the very lowest income groups, the conference committee's agreement on a $4,320 income cutoff for free service together with a controlled fee schedule for families with incomes up to $6,960 was closer to reality than the Senate bill had been. So was the agreement on an ultimate authorization of $2 billion with set-asides for Head Start and for other purposes. Few members probably believed that any sum approaching $2 billion would actually be appropriated. Although Elliot Richardson later told a questioner that he opposed legislating $20 billion programs with $2 billion authorizations, Senator Nelson said the agreement on these counts was pronounced acceptable to the administration.[42]

No comparable claim was ever made that the sticky question of prime sponsors had been resolved in a manner acceptable to the administration. With a Senate bill providing no minimum population for eligibility as prime sponsor and a House bill providing a minimum population of 10,000, compromise on 5,000 was inevitable. Less clear was whether the conferees would show preference to state governments, with local communities and nonprofit agencies as an allowable fallback, or would estab-

41. Ibid., p. H 8886.
42. Ibid., Dec. 2, 1971, p. S 20270.

lish the latter as preferred prime sponsors. When the conference committee came down on behalf of local rather than state control coupled with
the 5,000 population figure, most House Republicans were ready to follow
their colleagues on the conference committee, all but one of whom would
not sign the conference report. In HEW, the equivocation continued.
Richardson had persistently favored a state-control approach to prime
sponsorship, had accepted the initial 100,000 population compromise
reluctantly, and had given no sign that he could agree to anything less.
Yet Richardson now said that the conference agreement was close to a
workable arrangement and allowed at least one Republican senator to
believe that he would urge President Nixon to sign it.

Many House Republicans with whom Richardson tended to be most
compatible outspokenly opposed the conference agreement. John Anderson of Illinois, for example, called it an "administrative monstrosity" guar-
anteeing a proliferation of prime sponsors each having the least available
expertise and resources and the most unfavorable cost-benefit ratio.[43]
Dellenback called it an irresponsible promise that would set up expectations that could not be fulfilled.[44] Albert Quie (of Minnesota), who had
led the fight against the bill since Perkins's successful amendment to reduce the minimum population for prime sponsors to 10,000, continued to
analogize the arrangement to that of every one-room schoolhouse functioning also as a school district.[45] Each of these rational, moderate, and
thoughtful Republicans might have written a defensible veto message
that would have led to subsequent passage of a new bill giving states
preference as prime sponsors.

The actual veto message took a different tack. Its tone and impact
qualify it as among the most controversial veto messages of the Nixon
presidency. On top of perfunctory objections to the way Congress resolved the issue of prime sponsorship, the President complained de novo
that "for the Federal Government to plunge headlong financially into
supporting child development would commit the vast moral authority of
the National Government to the side of communal approaches to child
rearing over [and] against the family-centered approach."[46] Supporters
could not have been more outraged. Senator Nelson and others took the

43. Ibid., Dec. 7, 1971, p. H 11934.
44. Ibid., p. H 11922.
45. Ibid., Dec. 1, 1971, p. H 11625.
46. The text of the President's veto message (H. Doc. 92-48) is contained in *Congressional Record* (daily ed.), Dec. 10, 1971, pp. S 21129–30.

choice of language as deliberately inflammatory, and as designed to suggest something faintly subversive about the position of the bill's sponsors. Still smarting a few months later, Nelson let it be known that after the veto he had received apologies from administration people within HEW as well as from Republican members of Congress. Willing to concede that Richardson "would have written a message that would have made more sense," Nelson explained both what he thought had transpired and the consequences of the President's language:

Not once during these discussions [with Richardson] was there a philosophical attack made on the fundamental proposition of the child development program, so we didn't know we were going to be sandbagged by somebody and neither did the Secretary. Somebody in the White House decided, after reading attacks on child development by the rightwing in this country, "We are going to have to call it 'communal living.'". . . .

. . . However, we are in a political atmosphere and when the President of the United States charges communal living, bringing up the specter of some kind of communism or something else, we are all adults here, we know what that means. We know it means violent outbursts by people, and I can show you my mail, and so this creates a very tough problem.[47]

The senator was right on all counts. The "communal" question had never been raised during the long period of negotiations over income levels for free service or over the question of prime sponsors. Acknowledging that no administration spokesman had earlier objected to communal approaches to child rearing, HEW's assistant secretary for legislation could only explain, "I think that is the President's feeling and he, after all, is presented with a different question in facing the legislation as a whole after enactment."[48]

In an informal discussion eight months after his celebrated resignation from the administration in the Nixon "Saturday night massacre," Elliot Richardson said that he "went to the mat" in fighting to delete the "communal approaches" phrase from the message vetoing child development, but President Nixon was personally insistent on retaining it. Richardson describes himself as "morally certain" that a judgment made at the time of the veto by Representative Brademas is correct: its tone and conclusion

47. *Establishing Priorities Among Programs Aiding the Poor,* Hearing before the Senate Committee on Finance, 92:2 (GPO, 1972), pp. 68 and 86.

48. Office of the White House Press Secretary, "Press Conference of Frank Carlucci, Acting Director, Office of Economic Opportunity, and Stephen Kurzman, Assistant Secretary for Legislative Affairs, Department of Health, Education, and Welfare," Dec. 9, 1971 (processed), p. 4.

stemmed directly from the President's wish to appease right-wing critics of his China policy. Richardson calls the veto a "fish" thrown to opponents of the Nixon China policy. Three major changes in policy toward Communist China had been announced in 1971: end of the trade embargo (June 10); announcement of a planned presidential trip to China (July 15); support for seating Communist China in the United Nations (August 2). Child development came along before the actual trip to China at a moment, Richardson believes, when Nixon was looking for a way to disarm his most conservative critics. One of the latter, Representative John Ashbrook, who was then being urged to oppose Nixon in the 1972 presidential primaries, termed the veto "a signal that a lot of people have been looking for."[49]

If Richardson correctly analyzes the Nixon motive, the President succeeded in his objective. A widely circulated and extensively quoted column by James J. Kilpatrick, whose work and thoughts are much admired by conservatives, had said of the child development bill: "It is the boldest and most far-reaching scheme ever advanced for the Sovietization of American youth. . . . In the context of a Sovietized society, in which children are regarded as wards of the state and raised in state-controlled communes, the scheme would make beautiful sense. . . . if Richard Nixon signs it, he will have forfeited his last frail claim on Middle America's support."[50] So the "signal" to which Ashbrook referred may have been Nixon's use of "communal approaches" after Kilpatrick's reference to state-controlled communes. In sending the signal to the right, the President let it appear that his secretary of HEW was either incompetent, or without influence, or out of touch. Richardson both believed and said that there is "a great need for child care programs which contribute to the development of the child."[51] That conclusion cannot be reconciled with opposition on principle to the bill passed by Congress. If the veto message had simply dealt with the problem of an administratively manageable delivery system, Richardson would have been covered. But it did not, and he was not. He did not, however, discourage reports about his personal distress. Having turned the other cheek as secretary of HEW, Elliot Richard-

49. John Brademas quotes Ashbrook as making this statement in *Congressional Record* (daily ed.), Dec. 14, 1971, p. H 12504.

50. Kilpatrick's column is reprinted in ibid., Dec. 2, 1971, p. E 12897.

51. *Child Care*, Hearings before the Senate Committee on Finance, 92:1 (GPO, 1971), p. 93.

son was to resign as attorney-general twenty months later over a matter of grander principle. Ironically, the latter also involved a presidential decision to leave Richardson far out on a limb.

Whatever its motivation, Nixon's veto effectively ended the drive for child development legislation. No delivery-system arrangement could overcome the philosophical antipathy inherent in the veto message to further public intervention in child development for any group other than children of AFDC mothers. Quie told an interviewer it was a bill correctly vetoed for incorrect reasons.[52] John Anderson termed "sheer nonsense" the notion that the bill would nationalize or Sovietize America's children.[53] But if those moderates might have supported another bill with different administrative arrangements, too many members were captured by allegiance to the President reenforced by the same kind of mail that upset Senator Nelson. When John Brademas could not begin to count a favorable majority in the House, he went on to other things, while Perkins read the tone of the veto as absolutely precluding child development legislation in the Nixon years.

### How It Happened

The truth is that a seriously flawed bill—ambiguous in what it promised, inadequate in its fiscal authorization, at best inefficient in its administrative specifications—moved through Congress in 1971 under the most advantageous circumstances:

Head Start was still widely regarded, especially in liberal political circles, as having shown the way to overcome social or cognitive or both kinds of deficits among children of the poor.

The decennial White House Conference on Children had adopted child development as its preferred goal, thereby appearing to give professional and popular endorsement to the idea.

The national administration was emphasizing public support for child care as part of its welfare reform program, thereby lending visibility and respectability to government-financed day care.

A new bureau in the federal administrative structure had been created with a charge to focus on the issue of child development.

Equally dedicated—and not yet competing—House and Senate spon-

52. Interview, Oct. 5, 1973.
53. *Congressional Record* (daily ed.), Dec. 7, 1971, p. H 11935.

sors of child development legislation took maximum advantage of favorable workloads and timetables in both houses of Congress to advance that rare occurrence, a congressionally initiated idea for public policy.

A coalition of labor and public-interest groups, some interested simply in child care, some in cognitive development of children, some in civil rights and community change, was assembled and held together, although the three goals are not identical.

The women's liberation movement, full employment, and general economic prosperity made it realistic to assume that millions of mothers would be able to make a free choice between mothering and working if child care became widely available.

There is little prospect that those circumstances can be replicated.

# 6

# Policy Advice
# by Commission, Committee, and Conference

During ten years of high receptivity to enhanced social intervention on behalf of children, social altruists and child development professionals were offered three formal opportunities—all federally financed—to construct a policy agenda. One, the Joint Commission on Mental Health of Children, resulted in a compendium covering everything and emphasizing nothing; a second, the 1970 White House Conference on Children, resulted in a near miss; the third, a National Academy of Sciences–National Research Council Advisory Committee on Child Development, ended in shambles with participants squabbling over nonsubstantive issues and incapable even of producing a report two years after its target date. In addition, a Senate Subcommitee on Children and Youth, which was ostensibly created in order to help implement the recommendations of the 1970 White House Conference on Children, has been hard-pressed to find an agenda.

The clearest general lesson from these activities is that children's policy is not successfully nurtured in official conferences, commissions, or advisory committees. Participants subsume their special concerns under a call for public action that is so vague as to be useless and dilute their individual causes by throwing them into a single basket. Yet the temptation to join an official advisory body, whether an exclusive group of a dozen or a nonexclusive mass of six thousand, seems irresistible. The advisory bodies follow one on another, participants dreaming of achieving policy successes comparable to royal commissions in England and Canada. If those invited were to review the activities and accomplishments of sponsored advisers on children's policy, however, they might conclude that it would be more socially profitable for them to make other use of their time.

118

### The White House Conference on Children

Public resources, press attention, and the numerous perquisites that come to persons and groups who can identify their efforts as "from the White House" all help in creating an atmosphere conducive both to legislation and to voluntary action by concerned citizens. Proponents of one or another kind of public policy therefore regard White House interest as a major breakthrough. The decision to hold a conference that will be labeled "White House conference" is considered a triumph for most social causes, as it was in the 1960s for civil rights and for nutrition. Yet the assumption that a decennial White House conference will be the watershed between limited, protective public policy and enlightened, developmental policy seems badly taken in the area of children's policy.

By many tests, however, the White House Conference on Children is a going concern. Over the years, conferences have grown in size, the period of preconference planning has been lengthened, appropriations to sustain planning and the conference itself have increased, conference reports and related products have become more voluminous, the demand for invitations has intensified. For all of this, the importance of the conference has diminished as a focal point for mobilizing anything on behalf of children. Between 1909, when it began, and the latest experience in 1970 the decennial White House Conference on Children has changed from an expert, advisory body dealing with general principles to an oversized assembly with an unrealistic mandate, and changed again to a potential confrontation between government and its critics. By the time the 1970 conferences—one on children and a separate conference in June 1971 on youth—dragged themselves to an end, their chairman found it "a distasteful experience," and so did many participants and a substantial number of the interest groups the conferences were expected to satisfy.

The conference idea is so firmly established that it would take forthright action to forestall subsequent conferences. Six decades of precedent make it unnecessary for child development proponents to lobby on behalf of convening a White House Conference on Children. No statute required such a conference in 1970, but there was a clear positive presumption stemming from the years of precedent. Unless the White House specifically decided against it, bureaucrats in the Department of Health, Education, and Welfare would take steps to start a conference in motion.

Nor could such steps be considered an abuse of bureaucratic authority; elected officials depend on the bureaucracy to provide precisely this kind of continuity. In the case of the Nixon administration, the issue of a conference that would not take place, in any event, until two years after Nixon's first inauguration could not rationally be put on a list of high priority decisions to be made personally by the new President or his White House assistants.

So, with Head Start riding high, and research on the benefits of early childhood intervention programs in full swing, and day care appealing to welfare reform planners, a White House conference—especially without having to beg or fight for it—seemed an attractive opportunity to put everything together. The first low-keyed sign that the bureaucratic system was fulfilling its responsibilities came from Mary Switzer, held over by the new administration as administrator of the Social and Rehabilitation Service, in April 1969. Switzer noted that the conference would likely not be held until late in 1970, but that it was time for formal planning to begin. Of the conference itself, she told some friendly congressmen that it had been held every decade since 1909, had been "most significant in leading the way to improved children's services . . . [had] become a tradition in American life . . . and [had] been the focal point for mobilizing public understanding and support for the needs of children."[1]

### From Involved Specialists to Open Assembly: 1909–1960

A search for evidence to support Switzer's claim that the conference has led the way to improved children's services yields results only in the case of the first conference in 1909.

When nine social workers and social reformers wrote President Theodore Roosevelt in December 1908 proposing a conference "under your auspices, in Washington," asserting even a marginal federal responsibility for the welfare of needy children was a radical idea. The stated concern of the writers was with children who make no trouble but are simply unfortunate:

The State has dealt generously with her troublesome children; but what is she doing for those who make no trouble but are simply unfortunate? There are

1. *Departments of Labor and Health, Education, and Welfare Appropriations for 1970*, Hearings before a Subcommittee of the House Committee on Appropriations, 91:1 (Government Printing Office, 1969), pt. 6, pp. 8 and 18.

a large number of these children for whom there is need of special activity and interest. . . . They are not delinquents; they are accused of no fault; they are simply destitute or neglected.[2]

Within three days, Roosevelt invited over two hundred child welfare workers to a conference which met only one month later. Then it took just two days of conferring for the Conference on the Care of Dependent Children to reach and transmit fifteen conclusions and recommendations to the President. The first of them spoke to the question of child care, public and private charity, and the maintenance of the parent-child relationship:

Home life is the highest and finest product of civilization. It is the great molding force of mind and of character. Children should not be deprived of it except for urgent and compelling reasons. Children of parents of worthy character, suffering from temporary misfortune, and children of reasonably efficient and deserving mothers who are without the support of the normal breadwinner, should as a rule be kept with their parents, such aid being given as may be necessary to maintain suitable homes for the rearing of the children. This aid should be given by such methods and from such sources as may be determined by the general relief policy of each community, preferably in the form of private charity rather than of public relief. Except in unusual circumstances, the home should not be broken up for reasons of poverty, but only for considerations of inefficiency or immorality.[3]

The first conference did have a real impact on child care because the principle of public responsibility for child welfare was novel and consequently benefited from the repetition. The 1909 White House conference is properly credited with giving strong impetus to the movement for mothers' pensions, the precursor of aid to dependent children. In addition, both the drive to establish a federal Children's Bureau and the drive to establish a national voluntary child welfare organization were accelerated. Thus, in 1911, Illinois enacted the first state mothers' aid law; in 1912 the Children's Bureau was created; and in 1915 the Bureau for the Exchange of Information Among Child-Helping Organizations was founded, in 1920 being incorporated as the Child Welfare League of America. The 1909 conference also encouraged the growth of adoption agencies and development of higher standards on the part of child-care agencies. By any test, the first White House conference had both a raison d'être and an impact justifying the conclusion by the Children's Bureau that the 1909

2. *Proceedings of the Conference on the Care of Dependent Children Held at Washington, D.C., January 25, 26, 1909* (GPO, 1909), pp. 17–18.

3. Ibid., p. 192.

meeting "had far-reaching effects on child care in the United States for many decades."[4]

The ideas and philosophy expressed at the 1909 conference were then new and provocative. But the friendly analysis provided by the Children's Bureau indicates that postconference developments were the results of "osmosis" rather than direct political follow-up. Political action to further conference aims was limited to a letter from President Roosevelt to the various state governors stating: "I heartily endorse the declarations of the Conference and bespeak your cooperation in getting the same before the people in your State directly interested in the subject matter thereof."[5] Roosevelt was already a lame duck when the conference idea was first broached. His ability to secure cooperation only declined as his remaining days in office dwindled.

The idea of a regularly scheduled decennial conference—albeit not yet a regular "White House conference"—took hold in 1919. In form and substance, that meeting was a replay of the first: a small group of some two hundred specialists, a few laymen, and a few foreign visitors reaffirmed the resolutions of the 1909 conferees favoring home care and, where home care is not possible, high standards of institutional or substitute care that would approximate home life as nearly as possible. The principal importance of the second conference is its existence rather than its product. The first conference responded to an unmet, unrecognized human need. The second regularized the conference idea, and implied that persons preoccupied with problems of children would have a periodic outlet for their concerns and their energies. For that benefit, there is a cost. With a regularized decennial conference, politicians and federal agencies respond to children's issues as convenient without real fear of constant harassment. Interest in children follows a predictable cycle. While every conference after the second vowed to maintain a determined follow-up effort, each conference is itself the high point. The crowd left to follow up has neither resources nor political bargaining power. The ten years between conferences, moreover, is enough time for disenchantment with the last effort to be obscured by the enthusiasm and high hopes of those preparing for the next conference.

President Hoover called the third conference in the summer of 1929 to

4. U.S. Department of Health, Education, and Welfare, Social and Rehabilitation Service, Children's Bureau, *The Story of the White House Conferences on Children and Youth* (1967), p. 5.
5. Ibid., p. 6.

"study the present status of the health and well-being of the children of the United States and its possessions; to report what is being done; to recommend what ought to be done; and how to do it."[6] In providing the conference planners with that charge and with a grant of $500,000—a great deal of money in 1930—Hoover transformed the conference from a visible outlet for a small group of highly involved specialists to a mammoth research project cum oversized, unfocused discussion group. For sixteen months prior to the Washington meeting, twelve hundred persons were involved in information-gathering and research, a far cry from the one-month lead time and two hundred participants of the original conference. This conference's opening session was attended by three thousand people. So, the 1930 conference had much to say, too much, about the needs and rights of children, the proper approaches to children with special needs, the importance of child welfare services and the like. Final reports which appeared over the course of several years comprised thirty-two volumes and over ten thousand printed pages. One product that survived was the Children's Charter which the conference endorsed—an idealistic nineteen-point statement of aims for all American children, "regardless of race, or color, or situation."[7] Forty years later, Senator Walter Mondale would call the charter "a fine agenda for action today."[8]

Subsequent conferences assembled in response to calls from Presidents Roosevelt (1940), Truman (1950), Eisenhower (1960), and Nixon (1970), no one of whom chose to be the president responsible for ending the "tradition." Focus was never achieved. Consider the product of the Midcentury (1950) Conference: sixty-seven recommendations, a pledge to children, and two books on healthy personality. The pledge, a set of sixteen vows taken by conference participants, is indicative of the degree of specificity of this conference's product. Among the vows (in abbreviated form): "we give you our love"; "we will recognize your worth as a person"; "we will encourage you always to seek the truth"; "we will work to lift the standard of living"; "we will protect you against exploitation and undue hazards."[9]

By 1960 the conference style had become ludicrous, the logistics staggering. Seventy-six hundred participants were distributed among five daily concurrent theme assemblies. Two hundred and ten workgroups produced

6. Ibid., p. 8.
7. Ibid., p. 12.
8. *Congressional Record*, vol. 116, pt. 30 (1970), p. 40506.
9. *The Story of the White House Conferences*, pp. 20–21.

six hundred and seventy recommendations. Incorporated in a composite report of findings, each recommendation was apparently equal to every other. Rather than establish priorities among the recommendations, the President's national committee expressed the hope that the growth and development of children and youth would be fostered as policies and practices were "molded from this cauldron of ideas."[10]

It was, however, more catch basin than cauldron. For example, recommendation number 483 endorsed the Supreme Court decision on school desegregation, number 586 "commended" parent and lay groups for their leadership and effort on behalf of the mentally handicapped, and number 628 supported a preventive program that would include "identification of youngsters most likely to become unmarried parents." Even the Children's Bureau, which helped organize the conference, itself had difficulty coming to grips with the number and tenor of the recommendations: "In their eagerness not to ignore a single facet of the lives of children, today and tomorrow, the participants had gone 'overboard' in assuring that their beliefs were represented—and in expressing their faith in the essential dignity and worth of each individual."[11] Not much was molded out of all this except, perhaps, the groundwork for a conference in 1970. The last three of the six hundred and seventy recommendations dealt with that subject, including one proposal that the 1970 conference be conceived as a prelude to a world conference on children and youth.

Among those who had seen a few, the conventional wisdom about the White House conference as "significant," as "a tradition," and as "a focal point" had doubters even before 1970. One of them, for example, is Mike Gorman, executive director of the National Committee Against Mental Illness and among the most effective of all Washington social policy lobbyists. A full year before the 1970 children's conference, Gorman predicted the impact of that long-in-the-future conference:

We are going to have a White House conference in 1970 on [children and] youth. We have had one every 10 years. I can write the resolutions for them now, because they will be the same ones as passed in 1909. . . .

You can roll eggs on the White House lawn and it will have the same effect on legislation.[12]

10. *Recommendations: Composite Report of Forum Findings—Golden Anniversary White House Conference on Children and Youth, March 27–April 2, 1960, Washington, D.C.* (GPO, 1960), p. vii.

11. *The Story of the White House Conferences*, p. 26.

12. *Community Mental Health Centers Act Extension*, Hearings before the Subcommittee on Public Health and Welfare of the House Committee on Interstate and Foreign Commerce, 91:1 (GPO, 1969), p. 232.

A comparable skepticism was expressed a few years ago by another participant-critic, William Carr, executive director of the National Education Association. "In retrospect," said Carr, who participated in four White House conferences, "it seems to me that each successive meeting has set a new record for the profundity of the principles uttered, for the eloquence of the sentiments expressed, for the solemnity of the vows pledged and for the number of pages of documents produced." Noting that the failure of the 1960 conference to concentrate on a single area meant that nothing was excluded that had any relevance to the well-being of children and youth, Carr went on to suggest that inasmuch as the 1960 conference was concerned with children in a "changing world," the 1970 conference might deal with children in "a changing solar system."[13] Carr even managed to test and confirm the validity of his cynicism about making progress through the White House conference technique. He proposed a set of resolutions to the 1960 conference, listened as most of them were severely disputed and attacked, then explained that the resolutions had in fact been offered and passed at the White House conference in 1930.[14]

## A Political Event: 1970

President Nixon named a White House assistant as chairman of the 1970 conference. The President thereby implicitly rejected the traditional separation of the White House Conference on Children from political reality, and inter alia rejected the Children's Bureau. Since the administration had made plain its reservations about the bureau when the Office of Child Development was established a few months earlier, it was not surprising that the bureau should be bypassed. What was surprising in the selection of Stephen Hess, however, was that all of the professional child welfare world was bypassed, in favor of a chairman whose experience and ambition lay outside the social policy sphere. The Hess appointment indicated that the 1970 conference was to be run with appropriate regard for the real problems and sensitivities of the sponsor—the White House—rather than as an invitation to child welfare specialists simply to reassert their belief that a big and rich government showed insufficient compassion for little children.

Originally brought into government service during the Eisenhower ad-

13. *Washington Post*, March 31, 1960.
14. *Community Mental Health Centers*, Hearings, p. 232.

ministration, Hess spent part of the intervening Democratic years writing a Nixon biography. He was one of the small group who had remained loyal to Nixon during the bad years after his loss of the California gubernatorial election in 1962. In the good year, 1969, Hess had been Daniel P. Moynihan's deputy in the White House Urban Affairs Council. Hess later explained to an interviewer that, coincident with the liquidation of the Urban Affairs Council, he was told that he was needed to help shore up HEW Secretary Finch. The latter was already showing signs of the inability to cope with HEW's complexities and pressures that would drive him into the sanctuary of an appointment as White House counselor. Hess would have preferred a more consequential assignment in HEW or elsewhere than the conference chairmanship, but he took it. The conference would pass, and new opportunities would then be at hand for a politically sensitive administrator.

The possibility that the conference could have political consequences was spelled out for Hess within a day or two of his appointment when he was moved out of his White House office to preclude the appearance of presidential responsibility for conference activity. A memorandum to Hess from Presidential Assistant John D. Ehrlichman a couple of weeks later provided a further reminder.

The White House Conference on Children and Youth may have some direct relationship to the 1970 Congressional elections.

I assume that the Conference is scheduled for December of 1970 and that in the various preliminary meetings and publicity handouts you will have clearly in mind the possible effect of Conference activities on the outcome of the 1970 election.[15]

Ehrlichman was probably reassured by a subsequent report on conference staffing from Hess addressed to the vice president, Ehrlichman, and half a dozen other White House officials. The stated purpose of the report was to identify some thirteen key conference executives by title and occupation, and by prior Republican connection. And later on, another Hess memorandum called White House attention to the care taken to speak out on behalf of the President's program as he met with regional groups preparing for the conference.[16]

Too much should not be inferred from Hess's willingness to run a conference that would at least avoid antagonizing if not please the sponsor. Doing so involved him in no basic compromises with principle, and there

15. Memorandum, Dec. 29, 1969.
16. Memorandum from Stephen Hess, March 30, 1970.

is no evidence that the conference would have been any more useful had the chairman been nonpolitical, like some of his predecessors in the job during previous conferences. Indeed, on one major conference issue where Hess made a politically oriented decision, there was a respectable nonpolitical case for it as well. The issue was ostensibly procedural—whether or not to authorize a plenary session of the conference. Even before the conference convened, a caucus of the Council of National Organizations for Children and Youth (CNOCY) met and passed two resolutions— one demanding a plenary session at which issues of national social policy could be dealt with, and one condemning the conference leadership for its failure to invite active citizen participation. The CNOCY demand for a plenary session was introduced by Lawrence Feldman, then executive director of the Day Care and Child Development Council of America (DCCDCA). Having reported to his constituency three months earlier that "the atmosphere surrounding the Conference is now probably irretrievably stained with suspicion of political motivation,"[17] Feldman now declared a willingness to "move outside the conference" for a plenary session if Hess did not call one.[18]

What Feldman had in mind is evident from an editorial in the December 1970 Voice for Children, the monthly DCCDCA publication. Complaining that the "design of the 1970 Conference substitutes smooth evenings of entertainment for hard encounter with critical issues of national policy," the editorial declared that the conference had the potential for formulating "a substantial national policy regarding the rights of children and parents." Such a policy was said to involve the inevitable "reordering of federal priorities" in favor of children and to include, in the DCCDCA view, the right of every child, parent, and community to "quality child care services."

There was no danger that grandiose goals of this sort would have any more impact than they had had after previous conferences. Partly, however, out of interest in getting a more substantive body of recommendations, and partly to forestall a resolution denouncing the Vietnam war, Hess decided against a plenary session. He was trying to avoid "another situation where we come out of here endorsing motherhood." Instead, Hess approved a procedure by which delegates could rate, by ballot, issues of overriding concern. This would be done by the delegates in their individual forums, with the final formulation of recommendations made by

17. Voice for Children, vol. 3 (September 1970), p. 2.
18. Washington Post, Dec. 14, 1970.

the six cluster chairmen. Hess told a press conference that he wanted specific proposals that could be dropped into federal and state legislative hoppers.[19] It was also true, if unsaid, that he did not want to preside over a runaway White House conference likely to attack the President's program.

Hess wanted the conference to be characterized by political realism, originality in style, and fun for the participants. He also wanted it to help children, and not to be merely a meeting at which the old crowd could socialize and reinforce each other's well-known positions. To accomplish these objectives, two-thirds of the thirty-seven hundred voting delegates were chosen by governors, congressmen, and the conference staff. Forum topics and forum chairmen were chosen by Hess and his staff. Discussion chairmen included few of the child welfare, labor, or civil rights figures prominent in past conferences, while the program arranged by the conference staff left little to chance. Delegates were to spend the majority of their time in group discussions of the topics developed in the working papers, and the nondiscussion time in pursuing "special events": film showings, workshops with artists, musical events, field trips, sensitivity training sessions, role-playing exercises, puppet shows.

When it came to substance, delegates to the 1970 conference, like delegates to every other conference soberly assured by the President of the United States that their recommendations would receive "the most careful consideration," played out their roles. They proceeded to reach conclusions. The President's opening statement had hinted at the conclusions that would be most warmly welcomed. In its consequences for children, Nixon said, his family assistance plan (for which the administration then still held high hopes) was "the most important piece of social legislation in the history of this nation." He cited other government initiatives on behalf of children: the Right to Read program, the Office of Child Development, education reform, and food and nutrition efforts. The President said he would like his legacy to children to include peace, a strong economy, providing families with children an income floor, and "the best education, the best health, the best housing that any children have ever had, anywhere, any time."[20]

Conferees matched the President in platitudes. Following Hess's procedures for reaching conclusions, delegates produced sixteen "overriding

19. *Washington Post*, Dec. 17, 1970.
20. "Remarks at the Opening Session of the White House Conference on Children —December 13, 1970," *A New Road for America: Major Policy Statements, March 1970–October 1971* (Doubleday, 1972), pp. 454–62, especially 456, 459, and 460.

concerns" and twenty-five specific recommendations. The substantive distinction between concerns and recommendations is less clear than is the parliamentary path to inclusion on each list. Ten of the overriding concerns were selected by cluster chairmen from lists of recommendations presented by the forum chairmen. The remaining six grew out of petitions signed by at least two hundred persons. The sixteen concerns were ranked by delegates in order of importance by a weighted-vote system. "Comprehensive family-oriented child development programs" wound up at the top of the list of overriding concerns. Each of the twenty-five forums produced one of the twenty-five recommendations which were ranked simply on the basis of the number of votes cast for each. The lead recommendation was to "provide opportunities for every child to learn, grow, and live creatively by reordering national priorities."

In their own critical reviews of the 1970 conference, a striking number of participating groups focused on procedure and style rather than on product.[21] How a conference arrives at vague conclusions is as important as the conclusions themselves. But the product of the 1970 conference is no better nor worse than that of the earlier conferences. The ninety-nine associations included in the technical assistance committee objected to being ignored by conference managers, not to the conclusions of the conference. In the present case, Hess's style did not please professional groups accustomed to being involved and consulted. The American Public Welfare Association's journal, for example, subsequently complained that the conference "had been cast in a new mold—ignoring the 'establishment' and fragmenting the accustomed ways at [sic] arriving at consensus." According to the Public Welfare editorial, the 1970 conference was "stratified and rigid, its leaders' talents and energies used on forms and structures rather than purposes and goals."[22] Association leaders also disliked Hess's bypassing of state organizations on children and youth which had grown out of the 1950 and 1960 conferences. An AFL-CIO spokesman was of the same mind. Leo Perlis, director of the AFL-CIO's Department of Community Services and a conference delegate, complained that citizens' organizations were rejected by the people running the conference. He named a number of such rejectees: the Child Welfare League of America, the Family Service Association, and agencies connected with the National Assembly for Social Policy and Development.[23]

Devotees of the White House conference technique would probably

21. "Children Can't Wait," Public Welfare, vol. 29 (Spring 1971), pp. 160–66.
22. Ibid., p. 120.
23. Congressional Record (daily ed.), Feb. 18, 1971, p. E 837.

point to institutionalized child advocacy as a major achievement of the 1970 meeting. A National Center for Child Advocacy was created within the OCD's Children's Bureau "to identify and promote improvements in conditions which adversely affect the growth and development of children." And six Parent and Child Centers around the country also became child advocacy centers—by and large doing what the centers had already been doing. The advocacy idea did not originate at the conference—where it rated sixth in specific recommendations—but was inherited, with all its vagueness, from the Joint Commission on Mental Health of Children. If invention of as amorphous a concept as child advocacy must stand as the principal contribution of either the joint commission or the conference, neither can expect immortality.

The truth is that the 1970 children's conference has had little consequential impact on either Congress, the White House, or anybody else. Neither private nor public programs have resulted. No legislation has been enacted. Congress did pass a child development bill late in 1971, but that bill was the inevitable climax of the Head Start experience rather than a conference product. Moreover, President Nixon vetoed it in a message at odds with the prevailing consensus of the conference which had formally voted child development programs its number one concern. Within two years, it was as if they had given a million dollar conference and no one had come. The limits of public responsibility for children and how to discharge that responsibility are no more clear after the conference than they were before. But that result is no more attributable to the political leadership of the 1970 conference than the comparable result is attributable to the nonpolitical leadership of earlier conferences. The White House conference is a better technique for bolstering the ego of many of its participants than for formulating a workable policy program.


## An Ongoing Watchdog

Senator Walter Mondale reviewed the record of White House children's conferences just before the 1970 conference and reached a correct conclusion about consequences although he misread the character of the reports. The record, Mondale said, is of conferences making "strong, sweeping, perceptive reports which ultimately do nothing but gather dust." Actually, the reports are too vague to be strong and too emotion-ridden to be perceptive, but they do gather dust. To preclude that outcome, he advised the delegates to let this White House Conference be the first ever to focus on creating a strategy for the legislative implementation of its findings.[24]

For his part, the senator decided that legislative follow-up on the White House conference was one important justification for a Senate Subcommittee on Children and Youth. But that subcommittee, created in 1971 at Mondale's instigation, has not found the product of the 1970 conference to be a practical agenda. Instead of pointing the way to new directions and objectives for congressional implementation, the conference's highest priority recommendation built on legislation that Mondale —as well as sundry members of the House—had already offered in 1969 and had considered "ready for enactment" months before the conference met. Since the full Labor and Public Welfare Committee was already cut up into a collection of independent subcommittees—a "condominium" is David Price's apt characterization—the Children and Youth Subcommittee has found it hard to develop a work plan, and has had troubles defining its jurisdiction. With the condominium almost fully occupied, Children and Youth had to take a basement apartment. Less and less rather than more and more attractive to ambitious, socially concerned members of the Senate, the subcommittee's prestige and influence are not high.

Beyond the conference follow-up, indicators of just what Mondale hoped for from a subcommittee are laid out in the proposal he made to Senator Harrison A. Williams just as Williams became chairman of the Senate Committee on Labor and Public Welfare. The letter to Williams is substantially different in tone and in particulars from Mondale's pre-conference speech. The speech complained of "a certain lack of immediacy" in the reports prepared for the conference, and suggested "a very hard and tough look at the results of school desegregation and . . . the continued ravages of hunger and malnutrition,"[25] as well as a focus on the need for smaller institutions, regulation, program accountability, outside advocacy, participation, innovation, and legal rights. In the letter to Williams, Mondale, appreciably more cautious, twice offered assurances that the subcommittee's responsibility would be primarily nonlegislative. The idea of a "very hard and tough look" at school desegregation and at hunger and malnutrition does not reappear. Instead, the case for the subcommittee rests on the "need to establish a forum in the Senate to focus in a coordinated way on the problems of children and youth," and on a "probe [of] the more pervasive issues concerning children and youth [for] which existing subcommittees with their numerous legislative responsibilities often simply do not have time."[26]

Standing subcommittees come easy in the Senate Labor Committee, and only a month later Williams announced the formation of the Subcommittee on Children and Youth. Williams reflected more of Mondale's cautious letter than of Mondale's aggressive speech, explaining "we must ... find a way to talk directly with ... young Americans," and "we need to talk together and to learn from one another."[27] Seven of the full committee's ten Democrats and five of its seven Republicans were named to the new subcommittee. Mondale pledged to Williams that the subcommittee would not undertake to report bills for some indefinite period of time, and that it would steer clear of child-related issues—particularly Head Start—falling in the jurisdiction of existing Labor and Public Welfare subcommittees. Unfortunately, at least from Senator Mondale's point of view, the latter limitation covered most things.

The subcommittee has had trouble finding an appropriate role within the constraints agreed to. In the life of the Ninety-second Congress, for example, with the White House conferences on children and on youth, and the child development bill left over from 1969–70, as ready take-off points, Mondale's subcommittee ran just twelve days of hearings, seven of them jointly with another subcommittee. Of the six topics covered, only two—sudden infant death and youth crisis services—dealt with new matter rather than with reviews of the conferences or reruns of the child development proposal. Among the generality of Labor and Public Welfare subcommittees, hearings ranged from two to seventy-seven days. Only three of the committee's subcommittees were less active than Children and Youth, and their jurisdictions are significantly more limited: railroad retirement, the handicapped, migratory labor. In the Ninety-third Congress the subcommittee held hearings and reported its first bill, child abuse. Ironically, Child Welfare League spokesmen disapproved, finding it ill-advised to emphasize abuse out of the whole cluster of problems of neglected children.

Early in the life of the subcommittee, Mondale spoke of it as an instrument to provoke congressional responsiveness to expressed needs. "The professionals and the parents have been speaking without the kind of

26. Letter of Jan. 28, 1971.
27. *Congressional Record*, vol. 117, pt. 3 (1971), p. 3997.

response that society must have," he said. "There has to be a way of giving them rising visibility and rising support. That is one of the reasons that the Subcommittee on Children and Youth was created, to try to make Congress respond, institutionally, to these needs."[28] After President Nixon's devastating veto of the Child Development Act of 1971, however, a different view appeared to take hold. Sidney Johnson, who was the subcommittee's staff director until 1976, interpreted that experience to require a less aggressive subcommittee posture. "America has to be convinced there is a major problem before it will support legislation," he told an interviewer. "We offered a solution before most Americans realized there was a problem." The subcommittee did then turn its attention to noncontroversial yet dramatic issues like sudden infant death and child abuse.

By the time the Ninety-third Congress convened in 1973, the bloom was already gone. Richard Schweiker, a liberal Republican member from Pennsylvania, made a "pragmatic move" off the subcommittee, convinced that it had little future.[29] Edward Kennedy continued as a member, but his expression of concern about the needs of children was most actively displayed through his work as chairman of the Labor Committee's Health Subcommittee and his participation in the Select Committee on Nutrition and Human Needs rather than through the Children and Youth Subcommittee.[30] Jennings Randolph (Democrat of West Virginia) found it hard to pinpoint a unique subcommittee product, and reached a conclusion simultaneously apologetic and optimistic: "Naturally, the problems of establishing a new subcommittee and defining its jurisdiction delayed considerably the activities of the Subcommittee. . . . The impact of work to be done by the Subcommittee will have a beneficial effect on future generations of American children."[31]

But there is a problem in determining just what work is to be done. "We're an ongoing watchdog and resource for dealing with children's problems like the White House Conference is, except we don't meet every ten years," Sidney Johnson explained while he was staff director. "We're

28. *Comprehensive Child Development Act of 1971*, Joint Hearings before the Subcommittees on Employment, Manpower, and Poverty and on Children and Youth of the Senate Labor and Public Welfare Committee, 92:1 (GPO, 1971), pt. 1, p. 233.

29. As reported by Kathleen Casey, then staff assistant to Senator Schweiker, in an interview, Aug. 7, 1973.

30. Letter to Gilbert Steiner from Edward Martin, administrative assistant to Senator Kennedy, July 26, 1973.

31. Letter to Gilbert Steiner from Senator Randolph, July 22, 1973.

here. . . . We attempt to do what can be done in the present circumstances."[32] The comparison with the children's conference is apt. Mondale's subcommittee has trouble finding a course that is at once specific, universally appealing, politically practical, and grand-scale. "I'm becoming convinced that one of the revolutions under way, which is perhaps the most damaging thing going on in this country, is the growing pressure on and destruction of the American family," Mondale told an interviewer.[33] Yet legislation to arrest that destruction, if it can be arrested by legislation, cannot be framed in Mondale's Children and Youth Subcommittee with its three-member professional staff and restricted jurisdiction. So the subcommittee turns to the sudden infant death syndrome and to the issue of battered and abused children, fragments of the larger concern. With a real need to show results, the subcommittee will continue to bite off fragments, all worth pursuing, but a far cry from the probe of "the more pervasive issues" proposed by the chairman a few years ago.

### Proposing a Shift in Strategy

One special problem of the White House conference is the attention it generates by virtue of its name and visibility. Perhaps, the argument goes, the conference could be more successful in producing specific proposals to meet specific needs if it could have the financial and other support given recent conferences but could organize differently and could avoid the pressures generated by the White House label. The Joint Commission on Mental Health of Children (JCMHC), an undertaking of the latter half of the 1960s, met those conditions. Like the 1970 White House Conference on Children, JCMHC was formally sponsored by the federal government, was sustained with federal money, was in the works for several years, and did involve hundreds of people inside and outside the government—in many instances, the same people as were involved in the conference. Again like the conference, the JCMHC found a dedicated spokesman in the Senate: Abraham Ribicoff, once secretary of HEW, played for JCMHC the role Walter Mondale played for the White House conference, providing visibility and sponsoring its recommendations. The final similarity between the enterprises is that neither made much differ-

32. Interview, May 29, 1975.
33. "A Reporter at Large: Conversation with a Senator," *New Yorker*, May 19, 1973, pp. 125–26.

ence in the substance of federal policy affecting children or in the way the issue is perceived.

Ribicoff's interest in the joint commission idea stemmed directly from the observation in the Warren Commission report on the assassination of President Kennedy that Lee Harvey Oswald's mental problems had been recognized when he was thirteen but had never been treated. Specifically mentioning that point, Ribicoff has said that the Joint Commission on Mental Health of Children "grew out of the terrible tragedy of the Kennedy assassination, the tragedy which made us conscious of many things that are weak in our society."[34] Not everyone in Washington saw the value of a child mental health study group. In particular, Ribicoff's proposal to spend $500,000 annually in 1966 and 1967 for a joint commission had to overcome the Bureau of the Budget's reluctance. At one point, the Budget Bureau dropped from a supplemental bill the $500,000 included for the JCMHC's first year, but at Ribicoff's urging the appropriations committees provided the money.

Preparation of the joint commission report ultimately took three years instead of two and cost the federal government about $1.5 million. Numerous units within the Department of Health, Education, and Welfare and over forty private organizations were involved. More than five hundred scholars and practitioners in the children's field were somehow associated with the project. Even the commission's board of directors was large—fifty-four persons, most of them doctors.

Released in draft form at a May 1969 meeting of the American Psychiatric Association, and published between hard covers a year later, the 578-page *Crisis in Child Mental Health: Challenge for the 1970's* examined conditions within American society, including poverty and racism, that contribute to mental illness in children, and detailed the inadequacy of preventive and remedial measures.[35] Calling the country's lack of commitment to its children "a national tragedy," the commission recommended a systematic program beginning with the prenatal period and continuing to age twenty-four to guarantee every American an opportunity to develop to his full potential. The commission described its proposals as "a shift in strategy for human development in this nation." In addition to many specific proposals, the commission made three broad recommendations which it gave equal weight: comprehensive services, a broad range of re-

34. *Congressional Record*, vol. 111, pt. 20 (1965), p. 27571.
35. *Crisis in Child Mental Health: Challenge for the 1970's, Report of the Joint Commission on Mental Health of Children* (Harper and Row, 1970).

medial and mental health services, and an advocacy system to help achieve the first two objectives. As a part of the child advocacy system the commission called for the creation of a President's advisory council on children and for the establishment of a hundred child development councils throughout the country. The latter were to ensure that "complete diagnostic, treatment, and preventive services are made available to all children and youth."[36]

Response to the report within the professional community was positive, but not uncritical. Many important groups in the field, including the American Psychiatric Association, the American Psychological Association, the American Academy of Child Psychiatry, the American Association of Psychiatric Services for Children, and the National Association of Mental Health, recorded themselves in support of the commission's findings in principle if not in all detail.[37] Some of the supporters, however, had reservations. A five-member committee of the prestigious Group for the Advancement of Psychiatry, whose membership is limited to about two hundred of psychiatry's elite, criticized the commission for its broad-brush approach to mental health and its resultant lack of clinical emphasis.[38] The American Academy of Child Psychiatry said in its endorsement that the advocacy system would be meaningless without the proposed network of clinical services. The American Psychological Association agreed that children's interests should be represented at the highest levels of government, but hoped that such representation would "not result in a mere proliferation and duplication of agencies with little substantive power."[39]

Politically, the commission's report was simply out of phase by half a decade. The Great Society was over; less rather than more social intervention was the controlling philosophy in Washington. The Westinghouse report on Head Start put a brake on planning new children's programs. For all of the distinguished names associated with it, the JCMHC work drew no response at all from the White House. President Nixon never referred to it publicly. The commission's chairman, Reginald Lourie, M.D., told an interviewer that it was as though the report "never

36. Ibid., p. 11.
37. "Psychiatrists Clarify Joint Commission Report on Children," *Roche Report: Frontiers of Hospital Psychiatry*, vol. 7 (July 1, 1970), p. 1.
38. Ad Hoc Committee, "Crisis in Child Mental Health: A Critical Assessment," Group for the Advancement of Psychiatry Series, vol. 8, no. 82 (New York, February 1972; processed). For a discussion of the report, see review by Donald J. Cohen, M.D., in *Children Today*, vol. 1 (July–August 1972), pp. 34–36.
39. "Statement on the Report of the Joint Commission on Mental Health of Children Approved by the Board of Professional Affairs, American Psychological Association" (November 1970; processed).

existed as far as the White House was concerned."[40] As for media reaction, the *New York Times* and the *Washington Post* carried a story or two on the inside pages in 1969 about the commission's findings and recommendations. Only the *Times* mentioned it, again briefly, when it reappeared in 1970. Joint commission leaders who had hoped for a response comparable to that accorded the hunger issue a few years earlier were admittedly disappointed.

Bothered especially by the absence of a White House response, a delegation from the American Psychiatric Association, the professional organization with which the JCMHC had closest ties, called on Peter Flanigan, an assistant to the President, in December 1970. It was the first time in the association's history that it had had direct contact with the White House. The group "pleaded for some material gesture of support for implementation of the report of the Joint Commission on Mental Health of Children," specifically the financing of at least twenty child development councils throughout the country.[41] That visit got no results. When it became clear that the joint commission report had never reached official attention in the White House or HEW, the commission's executive committee decided to call it to the attention of HEW Secretary Richardson, and did so in a meeting with him about a year after the call on Flanigan. Richardson, Lourie told an interviewer, "was grabbed by the Commission's recommendation for a strategy and planning body in the child health and mental health field." The secretary was said to have seen this second-order commission proposal as a possible basis for an integration of social services approach, one of Richardson's causes.

Richardson's response grew in importance as joint commission leaders came to realize they could point to precious few accomplishments despite the bulk of their report. The commission had some bearing on the 1970 amendments to the Community Mental Health Centers Act which authorized children's units in the health centers. Because many conference participants had been involved in the joint commission project, JCMHC could be said to have contributed to the interest in child advocacy pressed by the 1970 White House Children's Conference. Puny enough to begin with, these achievements grew even thinner as time passed. The 1970 authorizations for children's services in community mental health centers were not backed with consequential amounts of money. For the three years between 1970 and 1973, only $18 million of an authorized $62 mil-

40. Interview, April 4, 1973.
41. "APA Presses White House on Mental Health Needs," *Psychiatric News*, Dec. 16, 1970.

lion was appropriated. Later, President Nixon suggested that the entire program be turned over to the states. Similarly, the National Center for Child Advocacy in the Office of Child Development has had little money and little impact. Nor was its cause helped by a 1973 study showing that child advocacy, particularly as it was defined by the joint commission—a planning, coordinating, and monitoring system on all levels of government—is hard to find.[42] Even JCMHC's Reginald Lourie acknowledges that programs financed by child advocacy demonstration grants are "flops," although Lourie insists that they were "set up for failure."[43]

Neither the indifferent response to the joint commission's total product nor the limited success of particular pieces discouraged Lourie and his associates. Clearly, the commission did not want to go out of business. It has shown impressive staying power. Elliot Richardson's positive reaction to a fragment of the report became a lifeline. No matter that the JCMHC proposal dealt with child health and mental health while Richardson was interested in integration of services without the emphasis on children. Joint commission spokesmen could be very flexible. If the resources were behind human services integration, so be it. A planning grant from HEW made it possible to explore the idea of a human services institute.

The grant eventuated in a proposal to HEW for the formal establishment of a "Human Services Institute for Children and Families." The proposal was emphatic in its support for integration of services. In seeking support from HEW for a three-year period, the joint commission explained the need for a Human Services Institute (HSI):

Categorical grant programs have been expanded and supported with some predictability, but the effectiveness of some of these human services programs is now subject to increasing scrutiny. There is sufficient evidence to indicate that fragmented and compartmentalized approaches, highly specialized vertical service systems, agency "turf protection" and professional isolation have combined to prevent the development of effective approaches to aiding those who require assistance. Fiscal and manpower resources are not being used efficiently.[44]

Quoting President Nixon, Richardson, and the JCMHC itself on the need for new and comprehensive approaches to service delivery, citing

42. Alfred Kahn, Sheila Kamerman, and Brenda McGowan, *Child Advocacy: Report of a National Baseline Study* (Columbia University School of Social Work, 1972), see especially p. 13.

43. Interview, April 4, 1973.

44. "Human Services Institute for Children and Families: Application for Project Grant to Social and Rehabilitation Service" (Dec. 12, 1972; processed), p. 2. On Jan. 15, 1973, the institute was awarded SRS grant no 87-P-80075/3-01.

revenue sharing and the proposed allied services legislation, the project proposal argued the importance of systematic analysis of such strategies. But the argument was characteristically vague: "Comprehensive programs require a comprehensive planning effort dedicated to understanding the environments in which the programs are to work."[45] Functions outlined for the institute included policy analysis and development, policy implementation, study of manpower development and training, and information collection and dissemination.

Three HEW agencies combined to make the Human Services Institute a grant totaling well over half a million dollars. But by the time its board of directors got organized, Elliot Richardson had left HEW, and integration of services was no longer an especially fashionable HEW slogan. And when the institute's board members finally sat down together in early 1974, a number of them were found to be unhappy with the services integration approach, thus depriving the institute of even the fuzzy objectives it was born with.

By the beginning of 1975, six years after completion of the JCMHC report and nine years after its creation, the commission, now an institute, was just hanging on. Over the previous twenty months, it had hired an executive director and a staff, several of whom came from HEW, allowed them to espouse integration of services, then fired the director, and after a long search that became a joke in the children's policy field hired another director. No agreement was reached on a program. On the other hand, there could hardly be room for disagreement over specifics in view of HSI's research and policy development committee report that "nothing human is alien to HSI." The prospects for the future seemed grim, however, as HEW officials gave evidence that the grant would soon end, and a succession of HSI board members indicated disenchantment, maybe even disaffection. The HEW agencies put money into a Human Services Institute in the first place in order to learn whether the authors of the integration of services concept would take it past the verbal level. The answer to that question, at least, seems clear.


## A Most Prestigious Failure

As befits a group formed under the aegis of a Washington policy-research group always characterized as "prestigious," the Advisory Committee on Child Development established by the National Academy of

45. Ibid., p. 5.

Sciences–National Research Council drew its membership from the upper crust of the child development field.[46] Its failure even to file a report is ascribed by various members to bad staffing, bad interpersonal relations, and bad timing. All of these explanations are less compelling than the suggestion that the committee's problem lay in its conception, that no committee so charged and so constituted could succeed.

When Edward Zigler decided in the spring of 1971 to provide about $200,000 of Office of Child Development money to support an advisory committee on policy, he anticipated a committee product that would balance specialized knowledge and general wisdom. The wandering style of the Joint Commission on Mental Health of Children would be avoided. A practical document would be produced suitable for transmission to the secretary of HEW, perhaps to the President, and even to the nation.

To implement this plan, the OCD contracted with the National Academy of Sciences–National Research Council where Henry David, executive secretary of its Division of Behavioral Sciences, became the man in charge. For David, who is part humanist, part historian, part research administrator, and who had served briefly as president of New York's New School for Social Research, it was just another task. For the committee chairman, Professor Harold Stevenson of the University of Michigan's Center for Human Growth and Development, it was more significant. Stevenson's appointment as chairman seems to have been preordained: he was a one-time teacher of Zigler's at the University of Texas; he proposed to Zigler that NAS-NRC be the home for an advisory committee; he served on the executive committee of NRC. Nevertheless, final selection of members fell to David. While David's selections did not coincide with his own nominees for membership as closely as Stevenson would have liked, Stevenson saw no reason to quarrel over the choices made—all persons of "excellent reputations" in child care, child health, psychological aspects of child development, and welfare dependency.

From the beginning, however, Stevenson and David differed over most things, including staffing of the committee. By the third meeting, they were fighting openly. Stevenson was prepared to use NAS-NRC as a housekeeping convenience, a mere conduit for OCD support since he was persuaded that the arrangements David had made for NAS-NRC staff

46. This discussion of the NAS-NRC Advisory Committee is based on steady observation of committee meetings, discussions with all members of the committee, and exchanges of correspondence with most of them. The members of the committee and its staff knew that this book was in preparation.

help to the committee were inappropriate—a physiological psychologist for executive secretary and a former day-care licensing staff member as resource person. Stevenson wanted a full-time staff person who could serve as coordinator between the chairman and several subcommittees established at a previous meeting, and among the subcommittees themselves. He wanted someone with both a working knowledge of the field and an ability to move around the federal agencies. It was also clear that Stevenson preferred that this person be based in Michigan. David resisted the appointment of an independent, high-powered staff member, holding out for short-term consultants and regular NAS-NRC personnel.

Over time, the David-Stevenson battle became very personal and very intense, so much so that several members attribute the committee's failure to "the staffing problem" or to what they euphemistically term the "unwise choice of a chairman." Stevenson, on the other hand, came to believe that for some mysterious reason "the staff of the agency involved was actively engaged in trying to insure our failure." Rather than that absurd conclusion, it is more likely that David, an intellectual who could not readily adjust to a formal downgrading of his role, was simply trying to justify his own participation.

The committee suffered from staffing problems but it did not fail because of staffing problems. In the absence of professional help, members did most of the work themselves. No staff-developed product would have been superior in quality to any of several drafts actually prepared by committee members. Nor did the committee fail because of the Stevenson-David problem. Ultimately, the committee held its meetings without Stevenson, who finally resigned. A little later David retired from NAS-NRC. Neither separation was the key to success, nor would either separation have mattered had it occurred much earlier. The problems of the committee were more fundamental.

Within the individual subcommittees and in the full committee, differing perceptions of role split those who believed a large-scale research effort to be warranted from those who felt that the task should not be made to seem overcomplicated, that ex cathedra statements would be adequate. So, for example, at an early meeting of the child care subcommittee one member urged a ringing proclamation on behalf of more extensive and more carefully defined standards for public day care; a second member insisted that the job was to assemble extensive data dealing with the size and shape of the problems of care of disadvantaged children; and a third member suggested the focus of the care issue should be on retarded and handicapped children in institutions. Understandably, the subcommittee concluded that it would not progress without instruction from the parent committee about the shape of the document to be made available to the OCD. But the full committee could not provide those instructions because it could not agree on a work program, could not agree on how its product should look, and could not agree on the scope of its responsibilities. The viewpoints of members were too dissimilar ever to permit agreement on how to divide the subject into manageable pieces.

To put it differently, the strength of the committee was in the reputations of its members; understandably, those members came to the project to teach, not to be taught. Their separate views of what constitutes first-order problems in child development could not have been accommodated even by a chairman and an executive officer who were compatible. Mary Keyserling was not prepared to abandon a featured role for day care any more than Harold Watts, who had presided over the study of New Jersey's negative income tax experiment, was prepared to let income redistribution be downgraded. The psychologists and the health specialists took no less serious a view of the areas of their concern. The former disagreed among themselves. Urie Bronfenbrenner, for example, worked to push the cognitive development theme in a direction that Stevenson would not abide. And Dorothy Height of the National Council of Negro Women characterized a late draft as "kind of a white report" that failed to confront the problem of institutional racism.

Eighteen months after its report was due, a committee majority finally reached an informal agreement on Judge David Bazelon's judgment that they faced "a stale record." With the grant money spent, Stevenson resigned, David retired, Zigler long since gone from the OCD, and the national interest in child development muted, the advisory committee simply faded away. David Goslin, who came from the Russell Sage Foundation to be Henry David's successor at the National Academy of Sciences, took on the task of issuing some kind of report, but Goslin had no illusions about its merits or its practical value. In the NAS-NRC committee, the challenge of setting a national agenda for children's policy claimed its most prestigious and probably its easiest victim.

# 7

# Lobbyists for Children

Neither the traditional nor more recent styles of political action are available to children. They cannot vote, make political contributions, organize themselves to lobby in Congress or the administrative agencies, or write and speak on behalf of parties and candidates. They are of little use to protest organizations. As political actors, children are useless and dependent. If children are to be either advantaged or simply protected, other groups must speak and act on their behalf. Some such groups, like the White House conferences and the Office of Child Development, are sustained by the national government. A substantial number of private associations also devote themselves to the children's cause, but the model for a lobby on behalf of children is not clearly evident.

Since parents do have a potential for political activity and have interests complementary to children's interests, they might logically be expected to constitute a lobby of surrogates. That expectation often is borne out in the area affecting the largest number of families, public education, although all parents do not lobby on the same side of all educational issues. Few public programs other than education seem to be regarded as of comparable importance by a comparable number of parents. Aside from school food service workers and from teachers concerned about their jobs, most children's advocates tend to be motivated by altruism, not self-interest. They constitute a lobby of surrogates, pure in purpose, but with a different order of concern than that shown by the teachers and the school feeding workers.

After the depression and before the stimulus of the women's, civil rights, and poverty movements of the sixties, there was surprisingly little exhortation on behalf of the children's cause. Since then, surrogate lobbyists for children have been heard more frequently. Torn between the pursuit of limited goals for relatively small numbers of unlucky children and broader, inexact goals on behalf of the universe of children, they often sound more hortatory than precise. There is a good deal of telling congressmen, for example, that people must be brought back into the lives of children and children must be brought back into the lives of people, that a nation that can go to the moon can care for its unlucky children, that services must be provided to all children who need them. There is less disposition to narrow in on a specific proposal and on program priorities. So, rather than facing a backlog of issue areas, the Senate's Children and Youth Subcommittee has had trouble keeping its agenda full and its members interested.

Nor is it unknown for respected spokesmen for children to push massive and expensive public policy activity without bothering to document their case or with a less than thorough knowledge of the evidence they do present. One instance of the latter involved the late Milton Akers, director of the National Association for the Education of Young Children, who not only embraced a 1969 proposal for child development legislation, but urged on the House subcommittee the idea that comprehensive services anticipated under the bill be provided from the prenatal period:

In fact, some rather startling discoveries ... would strongly suggest that the scope of our efforts should be extended to the time of conception. I am referring to the Scrimshaw studies done first on animals and then in Africa, which have dramatic possibilities.[1]

Representative John Brademas, sponsor of the legislation, asked for a further discourse on "certain Scrimshaw studies. Maybe you can tell us what you mean by that?" Akers could not because "I have to confess to you I have not read his materials; I have only heard references to them."[2] While Brademas turned to another subject, the exchange left others cautious about accepting lobbyists' assertions of scientific bases for policy proposals in this field.

Two years later, the president-elect of the Day Care and Child Development Council, another eminent leader of the early childhood field, testified at Senate Labor subcommittee hearings on the Comprehensive Child Development Act. It was a $13 billion bill that would affect millions of disadvantaged preschool children immediately and that had the potential to affect all preschool children. The bill had been introduced five

---

1. *Comprehensive Preschool Education and Child Day-Care Act of 1969*, Hearings before the Select Subcommittee on Education of the House Committee on Education and Labor, 91:1 and 2 (Government Printing Office, 1970), p. 11.

2. Ibid., p. 17.

weeks earlier, its thrust had been known to the professional community at least since 1969. This professional leader said he was all for it. Yet he had not taken the time to prepare a short written statement explaining his interest in the bill.[3]

Albeit some proponents are overzealous and others are underorganized, a variety of voices speak on behalf of the children's cause in the lobbies of Congress or in the federal administrative agencies. One of them is a byproduct of the drive for equal rights for women. Another stems from the support provided by philanthropic foundations for associations and activities concerned with problems of the disadvantaged. On the other hand, one effort to create a children's lobby without tax-exempt status was virtually stillborn. Several other surrogates, recently resurrected from various stages of inactivity, found their new leases on life in jeopardy within a couple of years. And even where there would seem to be a high degree of self-interest—as in women's concern with day care—lobbyists show little unity. And perhaps the most firmly established organization concerned with public policy affecting children does little lobbying and has little effect on social policy even in foster care and adoption—the limited segment of children's affairs it regards as its unique concern.

## A Lobby with Limited Goals

In the quiet time, from the end of World War II until the Great Society period two decades later, child welfare services meant services to a relatively small group of children who were neglected or who were living outside their own homes. Since the Social Security Act separated cash relief for dependent children from other child welfare services, the dominant concerns in the welfare community became preventive services designed to keep a child's home intact, and foster care and adoption work. Throughout this quiet time, only one national voluntary organization —the Child Welfare League of America (CWLA)—took as its primary purpose promoting the welfare of children as expressed in those services. Founded in 1920 as a league of voluntary associations, none of which espoused massive change in the style or intensity of intervention, the

3. *Comprehensive Child Development Act of 1971*, Joint Hearings before the Subcommittees on Employment, Manpower, and Poverty and on Children and Youth of the Senate Committee on Labor and Public Welfare, 92:1 (GPO, 1971), pt. 1, p. 154.

CWLA contented itself for most of its first fifty years with studies of arrangements made for children in need of parents, with specifying standards for various child welfare services, and with disseminating an endless list of publications. Made up of nearly four hundred child-serving agencies, the Child Welfare League of America continues to keep its distance from both "child development" and aid to dependent children. Meeting the needs of its constituents, the foster care and adoption agencies, remains the organization's principal business. Even-handed service to its members, whether public or private agencies, with sectarian or nonsectarian interests, guides day-to-day staff activity.

Although the league has shown more diversity of interest in the 1970s than during its first half century of life, there is no claim to even-handedness between membership service and social policy development. To survive, CWLA Executive Director Joseph Reid explains, it is necessary to serve the membership.[4] League activities are patterned by its membership base which is largely inseparable from its financial base. The financial base rests in roughly equal proportions on income from membership dues, earnings and gifts, and foundation grants. Private agencies' dues range from a minimum of $500 to a maximum of $5,000. The comparable figures for public agencies are $300 and $1,000. Total dues income is around $750,000, total league annual revenue around $2 million. But both gifts and grants tend to be related to the confidence of the donor or the foundation in the capacity of the league to work effectively with and through its member agencies. Consequently, membership dues have something of a multiplier effect. It is possible to conceive of membership dues without gifts and grants as supplementary financing; it is not conceivable that the kinds of gifts and grants that come to the league would come if it did not rest on four hundred child-serving agencies. A basic law of survival for the league, therefore, is to maintain a program that is attractive to its dues-paying members.

Most of those dues payers provide highly specialized services, and the league's administrative managers know it. Neither the Cunningham Children's Home of Urbana, Illinois, nor the Methodist Children's Home of Missouri, to take two examples from the membership list, pursues an interest in children generally. Rather, their interest is in children who cannot be cared for in their own homes. It is important to these agencies to be accredited by the league, because such accreditation helps them com-

4. Interview, Sept. 26, 1972.

mand public and professional confidence. If the Child Welfare League were less sober and traditional an organization, accreditation would have less value. It is not important to most agency members for the league to take on a social reform mission on behalf of children who can be and are served in their own homes no matter what the special problems of such children may be. Joseph Reid thinks pursuing broad social policy issues would expend the greater part of CWLA membership. And having survived since 1953 as executive director, Reid has reason to believe that he knows how to satisfy the greater part of the membership.

Its history, the composition of its membership, and its financing all point the league toward a conservative definition of child welfare and of its own role. It keeps a steady eye on foster care issues, it fights against the overshadowing of foster care problems by public assistance, and it systematically avoids a leadership position on any children's issue that is not directly related either to foster care or to adoption. That approach, however, does not leave the league administration entirely comfortable. Since the league is the oldest, the best-known, and the most elaborately organized association working in the children's field, operating officials cannot avoid participation in discussions of the substance and strategy of programs for children. Reid explained to an inquiring senator a few years ago that the league's "basic purpose" is to "raise standards in the child welfare field, and particularly to improve conditions for those children who are outside their own homes." Apparently dissatisfied with his own answer, however, Reid went on to add, "We are interested in children generally."[5]

That ambivalence between a broad and a narrow concern is reflected in the league's formal reports. "The Child Welfare League of America is concerned with the well-being of the 71 million children in our country," its statement of full agency information begins. But immediately following comes a description of what the agency does, and there the league is said to be "striving for improvement of services to deprived, neglected and dependent children in the United States."[6] The latter is formidable enough an undertaking to require no apology, yet there is a substantial difference between a concern for the well-being of 71 million children and a concern for that fraction of the total who can be characterized as deprived, neglected, and dependent. Again, the league's fiftieth anniversary

5. *Social Security Amendments of 1971*, Hearings before the Senate Committee on Finance, 92:1 and 2 (GPO, 1972), pt. 4, p. 2030.
6. Child Welfare League of America, Inc., "Full Agency Information for the National Budget and Consultation Committee" (March 1971; processed), p. 1.

brochure terms CWLA "the spokesman for all children"—then proceeds to describe its work in the far narrower field of traditional child welfare services.[7]

With the concurrence of a cosmopolitan group of league officers, Reid has tried to meet the contradiction operationally in much the same manner that it is met in the formal reports, that is, by actually adhering to a nuts-and-bolts-of-foster-care-and-adoption stance while insisting that the league does have broader interests. The league has chosen not to be a central participant in the drives for welfare change and for comprehensive child development legislation. It has kept the appearance at least of interest in those activities by sustaining in Washington a spokesman with a distinct reformist style. William Pierce was first in charge of a two-person Washington outpost, from which he was pursuing a study of the expansion of day care in the United States. Pierce subsequently became "child care consultant," and ultimately acquired a more elegant title: director of policy development in the CWLA Center on Governmental Affairs. Except for a brief period when William Lunsford, formerly a lobbyist for the American Friends Service Committee, shared responsibility for CWLA Washington affairs, Pierce has been the primary CWLA presence in Washington.

Pierce's style and Reid's appear compatible only at a distance of two hundred miles. While some thirty-five administrative and professional staff members under Reid's direction in New York largely emphasized consulting services on foster care to local communities and standards-setting for child welfare services, the league's man in Washington preoccupied himself with the endless round of meetings and discussions that preceded and followed the child development legislation passed by both houses in 1971. Reid's orthodox approach to child welfare issues, and his reluctance to push the league to a leadership position in the emerging day-care policy battles has not restrained his Washington colleague who became the gadfly for the counter-administration day-care effort in Washington. Where Reid and his New York staff seem restrained and nonjudgmental, the same image of the CWLA is not provided by the Washington office.

The Washington office style has its supporters. League leaders in New York know that they are in danger of disaffecting the liveliest part of the actual and potential membership precisely because of the failure to

7. Child Welfare League of America, Inc., *Guarding Children's Rights, Serving Children's Needs* (New York: CWLA, August 1970).

broaden league horizons. The director of a Michigan agency that is experimenting with new approaches in finding adoption opportunities for hard-to-place handicapped and older children has told Reid bluntly: "I have only a small agency out in the middle of Michigan, but my Board isn't so sure it wants to get involved with CWLA because you've got a stodgy reputation."[8]

### Fighting the Child Development Consortium

Maintaining a posture both in and above the child development battles of the post–Head Start period produced some problems for CWLA more troublesome than being termed "stodgy." These problems are well illustrated in the league's effort to keep abreast of the work of the Child Development Associate Consortium without allowing itself to become part of the consortium. When the idea of a child development associate (CDA) was first being discussed, the emphasis was on early childhood education and a set of credentials for early-education workers. Subsequently, the Office of Child Development (OCD) leadership tended to blur the distinction between the education emphasis and the child-care role. Wary of a new credential being established in the children's field that might ultimately have significance in the area of foster care, the CWLA monitored the planning work. After the consortium received its first grant in mid-1972, the league continued to monitor activities of the consortium board, but declined to join. This led to a wasteful and overblown dispute that did no credit to either the CWLA or the consortium.

A succession of league complaints about the composition of the CDA Consortium's board and standing committee structure failed to make clear the extent of the league's interest in the consortium. Nor did the league make a positive proposal. Impatient with the league's posture, the CDA Consortium's executive director distributed a report—widely available in child welfare circles—that said of the Child Welfare League: "Has declined to join the Consortium. Has expressed a generally negative attitude about the CDA concept, the Office of Child Development and the Consortium."[9] That characterization invited a dispute. Its author should have known that the Child Welfare League could hardly abide being pictured as unfriendly to the Office of Child Development. Pierce termed the re-

8. Personal observation, Nov. 1, 1974.
9. C. Ray Williams, "Summary of C.D.A. Consortium, Inc. Organizational Activities to January 15, 1973" (Jan. 22, 1973; processed), p. 6.

port "untrue and misleading." "The Record of the position of the Child Welfare League of America, Inc., in regard to the CDA concept, the Office of Child Development and the Consortium must be set straight."[10] Reid followed up, calling the statements about the league "libelous," and requesting proof that a correction he had drafted was sent to all recipients of the original report.[11] The wordy correction—ten times the length of the original—was ambiguous in regard to the CWLA position on both the consortium itself and the concept of the credential. It was unambiguous, however, in its assertion of support for the OCD from which Reid neither actually wished to be alienated nor to appear alienated.[12] The protest and the elaborate correction were shipped off to the OCD's acting director who, like other nonparticipants in the exchange, wondered why the league did not either make a positive contribution to the consortium or simply withdraw entirely.

Because CWLA leaders allowed themselves to be diverted from the pursuit of basic objectives, the league needlessly squandered some of its goodwill and energy in fights over CDA Consortium organizational and procedural trivia. With the OCD struggling to find programmatic focus, the Child Welfare League might better have occupied itself pushing the OCD to a concentration on improved foster care and adoption services. That possibility had already been explored in the Office of Management and Budget during the early Nixon years. Some external pressure might have moved it along.

### Innovation from Outside

The foster care and adoption lobby took less advantage of ten years of upsurge of interest in children than did welfare, nutrition, or day-care proponents. That state of affairs only began to change when a relatively new philanthropic foundation made children in need of parents a cornerstone of its program, and undertook to marry modern technology and ideas to the Child Welfare League's prestige. An offer in 1974 from the Edna McConnell Clark Foundation of some $800,000 in grants enabled the league to add other new business to the issue of day care and child development with which it had never quite decided how to deal.

10. Letter from William L. Pierce to C. Ray Williams, March 29, 1973.
11. Letter from Joseph H. Reid to C. Roy (sic) Williams, April 9, 1973.
12. Ibid. The correction is included in the body of the letter from Reid to Williams.

The Clark grants offered the league a chance to combine its primary objectives with the kind of innovative activities its leaders felt they should be pursuing. The foundation's goal was to ensure permanent family placement for more children, in particular, children separated from permanent families and waiting for adoption, and children "lost" in the foster care system. If the major objective of the foundation program could be fully accomplished, children would be placed in families much more promptly than heretofore. That much-to-be-desired outcome might require the Child Welfare League to review the continuing validity of its institutional purposes. Any such problem was far enough in the future, however, not to trouble the CWLA when Clark's staff proposed a new national program to bring children awaiting placement together with the "seeking" families. Estimating a national total of such children as high as a hundred thousand, planners hoped to demonstrate that older, handicapped, or disturbed children could be placed.[13]

If the demonstration was compelling, those involved would constitute a strong lobby on behalf of federal support to expand the effort. Clark's in-house judgment was that using the CWLA as the host organization for a special unit dealing with this problem would be a practical way to get the job done and a good way to revitalize a strong but highly traditional organization.[14] But the revitalization of the CWLA and demonstrating success in placement of waiting children were viewed as equally important. The Clark Foundation was building up a surrogate lobby for children awaiting adoption. Without such a lobby, the foundation might hope to help a small fraction of the universe of children involved. With such a lobby and the demonstration program to provide it its cause, a continuing program sustained by Office of Child Development resources would become a realistic possibility.

The Clark Foundation also provided support for a tracking system that might preclude prolonged placement in foster care. Rapid turnover of caseworkers, heavy case loads, and the absence of a complainant have contributed to an infrequently aired but well-known scandal in child welfare. Children simply become lost in the system. Placed in foster care situations that bring no complaints from foster parents as long as fees are paid and no complaints from natural parents because of their indifference or in-

13. Child Welfare League of America, Inc., "The National Adoption Institute: A Special Action Project to Find Homes for the Waiting Child" (May 13, 1974; processed), p. 1.

14. Peter W. Forsythe, "Child Welfare League of America, Inc." (May 22, 1974).

capacity, children may go for years without a systematic review of their situation. Horror stories are told from time to time of false entries dictated into the record in order to simplify the problems of an unskilled, overworked caseworker, or of lost case files resulting in "lost" children. Again using the league as the corporate leader, the foundation has led in developing a national prototype for a management-information system for children's services. The ultimate goal of the system is standardization of basic case information and improved management practices on a nationwide scale. Here as in the demonstration involving the waiting child, the dual strategy involves demonstrating what might be achieved and strengthening the capacity of the Child Welfare League to serve as an effective and informed lobby on behalf of a particular group of unlucky children.

So by 1975 the Child Welfare League had been linked by grants to the program of a big-spending foundation that analyzed the league's strengths and weaknesses better than the league had for itself. Clark combined foundation goals with legitimate but underdeveloped league interests. Before Clark, the CWLA gave too little attention to what its role should be in the dramatic new emphasis on child development and day care as the children's issues of the Johnson and early Nixon years. Although in Washington William Pierce argued persistently against proprietary day care, that opposition by itself did not constitute a CWLA policy agenda on behalf of children. League members are child welfare agencies, yet CWLA has often seemed less than clear about what it would do for them either by way of service or by way of leading in the development of public policy. Given an opportunity to emphasize what it knows best, and given some conditions that make it necessary to reexamine its traditional standards, the Child Welfare League is likely to be successful as a surrogate lobby on behalf of a relatively small but especially depressed group of children. It is not likely to become a wide-ranging lobby, intervening at various levels and with various techniques on behalf of various groups of unlucky children.


### New Feminists, and Old

It is an open secret that unrelieved responsibilities of motherhood do not satisfy millions of women. Large numbers have made a conscious decision not to bear children. Others have favored some kind of day-care arrangement that frees them for out-of-home employment. Still others have tried to effect basic change in the traditional distribution of child-care responsibilities between men and women.

Implementing either the day-care or the shared-responsibility decision poses complicated problems. In the real world, day-care services that are conveniently located, reasonably priced, and quality oriented are scarcely more common than are share-the-care fathers. The day-care decision may be put into effect through private arrangements, but governmental participation will inevitably be necessary to accomplish it on a routine basis. Shared responsibility has its own difficulties. "Leave the baby in Daddy's office," Karen de Crow advises in her *Young Woman's Guide to Liberation*.[15] Those who press for a network of publicly sponsored group-care and family day-care facilities come closer to the mainstream. Even among the new feminists, only a few groups emphasize sharing, either as a substitute for or pending the creation of readily available day-care services. Most women's groups insist that day-care service rather than shared parental responsibility is the goal of the women's movement, and that that goal is also in the best interests of child development. So, if organized women's groups are likely to serve as surrogate lobbyists for children, day-care legislation would seem to be an appropriate subject to pursue. Demands for publicly supported child-care services commonly do appear on the "must" lists of liberated women's groups, but the issue gets less attention than those causes affecting women only: the equal rights amendment; equal employment opportunity; abortion.

While each will insist that, in this context at least, there is a coincidence of interests, important differences in style and technique exist between those groups taking children as the principal point of departure and those groups taking women as the principal point of departure. Women-oriented groups do more lobbying in the traditional sense, threatening political retribution, trying to maintain continuing contact with friendly legislators. Child-oriented groups behave more like educational institutions, reporting findings and conclusions and hoping that the product will trickle down to and affect legislative committees. In the child-care field, if recent substantive work of the child-oriented organizations could be grafted on to the aggressive style of the new feminists, prospects for an effective surrogate lobby would be improved.

Consider, first, the women who interest themselves in public responsibility for children purely as a matter of social altruism. Compared to the

15. *Young Woman's Guide to Liberation: Alternatives to a Half-Life While the Choice Is Still Yours* (Pegasus, 1971), pp. 193 and 196.

new feminists, the social altruists are older, richer, and more apt to be interested in particular groups of disadvantaged children. The social altruists are disposed to review existing programs and to deplore the gaps between program goals and what their members observe of programs in operation. These socially concerned women—some of whom have practiced women's liberation for decades without asserting it as a cause—report and urge in the style of early twentieth century reformers like Lillian Wald and Florence Kelley who first persuaded Theodore Roosevelt of the desirability of a Children's Bureau. Leaders of these groups are not likely to be heard complaining about their own lot as women, but are likely to pick out areas of concern that affect other women and other women's children. Their emphasis is on the children of deprivation, as it has always been.

The archetype is Mary Dublin Keyserling, a well-to-do consulting economist who served as director of the Women's Bureau of the Department of Labor from 1964 to 1969 and in various other federal posts during the previous three decades. In the early and mid-1970s Mrs. Keyserling was at once an active member of the National Academy of Sciences–National Research Council's Advisory Committee on Child Development, chairman of the NAS-NRC group to evaluate HEW's Community Coordinated Child Care program, and director of a national study of day-care conditions to which seventy-seven local sections of the National Council of Jewish Women (NCJW) contributed. Immediately upon conclusion of the NCJW project, Mrs. Keyserling directed a project designed to put in place a continuing National Council of Organizations for Children and Youth. Next, she undertook a study of New York City's child-care facilities on the invitation of Mayor Beame. Even discounting the customary compliments paid to a witness known to be friendly to the sponsor's bill, Senator Walter Mondale's reference to Mrs. Keyserling's "pioneering work" in day-care evaluation is apt.[16]

Mrs. Keyserling's approach to lobbying for the children's cause is based on empirical evidence she has assembled about child care. It is seen most clearly in the NCJW's 1972 report, *Windows on Day Care*, the most recent detailed inquiry into the extent and nature of child-care services being provided for children of working mothers and for children of mothers who do not work and are in poverty. Unlike the documents produced by the new feminist groups, the preoccupation of *Windows on Day*

16. *Comprehensive Child Development Act of 1971*, Hearings, pt. 2, p. 651.

*Care* is not with women but with the care given children. Its strength is in the first-hand accounts of actual day-care programs; its approach to what is needed is derived from an image of what is good for children. The Keyserling-NCJW work says, in effect, that if children could cast protest votes, picket, or riot, they would have cause to do so. "Children in day-care cannot lobby the Congress in their own self-interest and protest these abominable circumstances," Mrs. Keyserling explained to an interviewer. "They cannot complain. We must do it for them."[17]

Differing from Mrs. Keyserling's pragmatism, the feminist approach to lobbying for child care is derived from theory, from feminist ideas of what a woman's role ought not to be.[18] According to feminists, society has fostered the idea that a woman who wishes to avoid her destiny and take on a career must choose between motherhood and a career. But one should not have to preclude the other. Pointing out that men are not asked to choose between fatherhood and a career, the analogy between the choices presented to women and men is used to show that parenthood is only one role in a full life composed of many roles.

The next step is to argue explicitly that motherhood is not a full-time role, and that for society to view it as such is degrading to women. "Perhaps the greatest cause of women's second-class status is the traditional belief that anatomy is destiny," asserts a position statement of the twenty-thousand-member National Organization for Women (NOW).[19] Varying degrees of involvement in motherhood, as if on a continuum, ranging from the complete involvement of the full-time mother to the noninvolvement of the childless single woman, should be possible. For women who do choose to have children, child bearing should not be inextricably linked to child rearing. The fact that a woman gives birth to a child does not mean that she has to have total responsibility for the care and raising of the child. To claim that she does have the sole responsibility is to deny her opportunities for other roles. "Some*one* does not have to take care of the children; some*two* will share them," one feminist has put it.[20] Greater equality between the sexes would make new child-care institutions necessary. Shared parental child-rearing responsibility, day-care centers, and group child-rearing are the obvious suggestions.

17. Interview, Jan. 4, 1973.
18. This discussion of the feminist approach to public and private responsibility for child care borrows from a research memorandum prepared by Joy Silver.
19. *Comprehensive Child Development Act of 1971*, Hearings, pt. 3, p. 751.
20. Jane O'Reilly, "The Housewife's Moment of Truth," *Ms.* insert in *New York*, Dec. 20, 1971, p. 58.

At least one NOW spokeswoman explicitly denies that the persistent arguments for child-care programs advanced by the movement should be interpreted to emphasize freeing women from child care. That emphasis, according to Vicki Lathom, coordinator of NOW's child-care task force, is a distortion of the feminist position. Women's needs, Lathom explains, are simply inseparable from children's needs. The emphasis on how child care benefits the mother is overdone by the press, "and, perhaps, by those looking for ways to discredit the women's rights movement."[21] Acknowledging that it is committed to work for universally available, publicly supported child care, NOW finds the demand for child-care services is the most misunderstood of all women's rights demands. It is not true that feminists "simply want warehouses to drop off their children." What they do want is a way to break the one-to-one twenty-four-hour relationship of mother and child which they claim can be as stifling to the child's growth as to the mother's. Although spokeswomen for the movement do speak of a center as "more than merely custodial," nonsexist, integrated, and staffed by males and females, neither the literature of the women's equality movement nor its spokeswomen deal with operational questions bearing on workable plans for policy development—locations, earliest entering age, adult-child ratios, length of time a child should stay. It is the general principles about women that come through. Women should be free to develop their capacities to the fullest. Full-time responsibility for the care of children can hamper a woman's development. Child-care centers should ease the burden for women so they can develop freely.[22] If the attention paid to child-care legislation is at all attributable to women's liberation, it is because child care rode on the coattails of the extensive attention given to all aspects of the liberation movement.

The new feminists are persistent lobbyists but they are not persistent on behalf of child-care goals. A principal reason is that meager resources can be spread only so far: the equal rights amendment and legalized abortion are dominant concerns. Tall talk is no substitute for a showing that sanctions can be imposed on unresponsive politicians, and no political campaigns have turned on attitudes toward child-care legislation. To be sure, when a group of women who had been successful in helping to push the equal rights amendment through Congress incorporated in November 1972 as Women's Lobby, Inc., their newsletter described child care as "a

21. *Comprehensive Child Development Act of 1971*, Hearings, pt. 3, p. 751.
22. Ibid., p. 753.

primary legislative goal."[23] But two years later, an interviewer concluded that Women's Lobby President Carol Burris showed "no particular interest" in day-care legislation. Burris even failed to mention the subject spontaneously in a recital of issues being pursued by the lobby. Asked specifically about day care, Burris noted the "overload" on legislators asked to meet feminist demands for universal free child care and minority demands for separate cultural facilities for black and other minority children.[24] The Women's Lobby, it appears, had confronted the dilemma of care versus community change and, temporarily, had been stymied by it. In her own mind, Burris pushed the day-care issue off until a later year.

Similarly, the National Women's Political Caucus emphasized its interest in child care in 1972. Support for comprehensive child-care legislation became a "nonnegotiable" condition for caucus endorsement of any candidate for office that year. It was a brave front in view of the state of the caucus in the fall of 1972: broke and disorganized, in arrears on salary payments to its staff members, torn by disagreement among its policy council members over whether to remain multipartisan or to set up two separate political arms, one Democratic, one Republican. No "condition" was imposed by the still-struggling yet still-living caucus in 1974. Its child-care program was then not clear, but the caucus continued to sound tough in other areas.

In sum, the new feminists and more traditional women's groups have different weaknesses as surrogate lobbyists for children. While the feminist groups lack internal unity and lack a primary focus on children, so the weakness of the surrogate lobby exemplified by Mary Keyserling's activities is its episodic nature. She will make her argument and document it with pertinent field data, but having done so is not likely either to threaten or to nag. She will go on to the next specialized activity. One or another report has its impact, then fades from attention, and there simply cannot be enough dramatic reports constantly to keep children's issues and interests before policymakers. Mrs. Keyserling is not a lobbyist who will roam the halls of Congress or badger White House or HEW officials. The new feminist spokeswomen are more disposed to do so, but there is no certainty they will narrow in on the children's cause. The consequence is that neither old nor new feminists constitute a continuing surrogate lobby for children.

23. "The Woman Activist: An Action Bulletin for Women's Rights," vol. 2, no. 11 (November 1972; processed), p. 1.
24. Interview, Dec. 3, 1974.

## Surrogates of the Seventies

Three systematic efforts have been set in motion since 1970 to create a continuing presence in Washington working on behalf of children. One, the National Council of Organizations for Children and Youth is alive, but certainly not a powerhouse. A second, the Children's Lobby, which aspired to be a powerhouse, had few members, few dollars, and much discord from the outset. It has not survived. If there is a viable children's lobby on the scene, it is the result of the evolution of the Washington Research Project into the Children's Defense Fund of the Washington Research Project. An examination of the life cycle of each of the three efforts defines the status of lobbying for children as a general cause.

### A Modest Style

The most modest of several recent attempts to create a continuing lobby for the children's cause—a lobby that would by whatever means call the problems of unlucky children to the attention of men and women of power—is Mary Keyserling's creation, the National Council of Organizations for Children and Youth (NCOCY). Mrs. Keyserling wrote the specifications for transforming a moribund Council of National Organizations into a National Council of Organizations. Having performed the plastic surgery, she withdrew from the case. But it is likely to take more than a cosmetic change to make an effective lobby out of a weak organization of organizations. In a few years, when its general support grants expire, the NCOCY is likely to confront skeptical philanthropists. And it is not clear how the organization will frame the case for its permanence. Because the NCOCY is driven neither by ideological fervor nor by self-interest nor by a sense of mission, it could quietly fade away. Because it reflects the ideologies and missions of many groups, their conflicting priorities may also pose problems for an organization that undertakes to do more than simply service its constituents.[25] Finally, the NCOCY quickly

25. Some of the "founding member" organizations of the NCOCY are the AFL-CIO, American Academy of Pediatrics, American Association of Sex Educators and Counselors, American Home Economics Association, American Podiatry Association, Arrow, Inc., Camp Fire Girls, Child Development Associate Consortium, Future Farmers of America, National Urban League, Institute of Life Insurance, and the Volunteers of America.

showed that its action goals are adjustable according to the interests of philanthropic foundations willing to provide financial support. Against these deficiencies, there are strengths: an exclusive but broadly conceived emphasis on children; continuity of activity; concern with policy; knowledgeable leadership.

The new group is the successor to the Council of National Organizations for Children and Youth (CNOCY) founded in 1949 as an advisory council on participation of national organizations for the Midcentury (1950) White House Children's Conference. The 1950 conference's follow-up committee incorporated the council, but the latter survived as an independent entity when the follow-up committee dissolved in 1953. In the following five or six years, the council's primary activity, according to Robert Bondy, its chairman, was to participate in conferences "for stocktaking and coordinated planning."[26] A live entity, however, when President Eisenhower's planning committee assembled to organize a 1960 White House conference, the Council of National Organizations was invited to serve an advisory function in 1960 comparable to that of 1950. Despite a membership of five hundred and fifty organizations in 1960, and the production of a book-length "Report of the Council" for that year's White House conference, the CNOCY again went into hibernation thereafter. By the 1970 conference, its role was uncertain, its participation of no consequence other than to record itself as a caucus in favor of post-conference follow-up. A few council leaders subsequently decided to consider the possible formation of a new organization with more effective "action-oriented approaches."[27]

In the spring of 1972, dispirited officials in HEW's Office of Child Development who were having trouble understanding their own mission provided the CNOCY with a $50,000 grant (matched with $25,000 in private funds) to finance a study of the organization's mission. Mary Keyserling directed this effort, called Project—Action Now, to define goals, structure, and financing of a new organization. Her report proposed four functions for a new organization, three of them such routine activities as providing a clearing house service, sponsoring conferences, and

26. Robert Bondy, "The Council of National Organizations on Children and Youth," in *Focus on Children and Youth*, a report of the Golden Anniversary White House Conference on Children and Youth (1960), p. vii.

27. "Background Information with Respect to Project—Action Now for Children and Youth and the Proposed Establishment of the National Council of Organizations for Children and Youth" (March 1973; processed), p. 1.

undertaking special projects. The heart of the proposal called for the organization of cluster groups—in day care, health, and juvenile justice—to develop and support legislation, influence the administration of programs, and improve citizen involvement.[28] Put another way, the National Council of Organizations for Children and Youth which took shape along the lines proposed by Mrs. Keyserling was set up by nearly two hundred organizations to be a children's advocacy group under color of a research and educational organization's tax-exempt status.

The decision to go the tax-exempt route was a critically important one as other surrogate lobbyists for children were learning around the same time. It made possible an $80,000 two-year general support grant from Carnegie Corporation supplementing annual dues payments of $100 by the member organizations. Then, with its well-organized health cluster able to claim participation in the effort to increase federal appropriations for maternal and child health, the NCOCY moved to expand. One opportunity came with the interest of the Edna McConnell Clark Foundation in foster care programs. Foster care had not been on the original list of action goals, but for $25,000 of Clark Foundation money the NCOCY identified thirty-seven organizations reasonably expected to have an interest in the subject and agreed to convene and service a foster care cluster. Clark expected the cluster to bring together a broad range of "potentially powerful national organizations" to disseminate information about the needs of parentless children, and to specify action programs through policy statements or comparable products.[29]

At the same time, Clark was putting massive amounts of money into the Child Welfare League of America, the focal point of the foundation's work in foster care. Accordingly, the CWLA could take calmly the diversion of $25,000 to the NCOCY in 1974. The grant, however, does foreshadow some possible troubles that the NCOCY will have to overcome or avoid in the future if it is to survive. Inevitably, its search for financing will put the council in competition with its own constituent organizations. The more successful that search, the greater the potential for ill will from part of its own membership. Aside from competing with itself, so to speak, for financial resources, the NCOCY will have to show that it can consistently provide expert information not available elsewhere. With only a director, an assistant to the director, an editor, a secretary,

28. Ibid., p. 2.
29. Peter W. Forsythe, "National Council of Organizations for Children and Youth" (May 22, 1974; processed).

and an intern for staff, that will become very difficult to accomplish across a large number of cluster areas. It will also become difficult to persuade congressional committee staff to brief cluster groups as the latter grow in number and as they issue critical policy statements.

A superficially safe alternative is to emphasize maximum effectiveness rather than maximum growth, by concentrating staff specialization in a few areas; holding cluster-group activities to a small number; avoiding extensive fund raising. But such a strategy ultimately will cause member organizations with interests outside the areas of concentration to fall away. Moreover, the more specialized the cluster-group concentration, the greater the likelihood that the NCOCY will be less knowledgeable than one of its constituents, and the more certain the competition for money and for recognition. Judith Helms, the council's executive director, told an interviewer that a division of responsibility will let the NCOCY do organizational work and let "others" provide technical assistance. The veterans elsewhere who are the "others" are not likely to see things quite that way. For example, it was a few months after the Clark Foundation provided the NCOCY a grant to create a foster-care cluster that the Child Welfare League of America quietly transformed its Washington office into a CWLA Center on Governmental Affairs and renamed its Washington-based child-care consultant as director of policy development. The reorganization was not necessarily a warning or a challenge to the NCOCY. The Child Welfare League is itself an organization of organizations, however, and it has had fifty years of experience in keeping its guard up.

In the meantime, the National Council of Organizations for Children and Youth is embarked on a modest effort to educate its members in the belief that they will galvanize an otherwise uninterested policymaking apparatus. The whole effort is too modest. The council brings nothing new qualitatively to any of its cluster areas. Mrs. Keyserling, the founding mother, envisioned a powerful leader who might become a dynamic advocate for children in Washington. That the NCOCY and its executive have no strong following is not surprising given the council's dependence on foundation support and its need to avoid moving out in front of its members. An interest in children, per se, and an orderly organizational arrangement are not much on which to mount a specific program. The advantages that the NCOCY enjoys are only comparative. Unlike the Children's Lobby, a former competitor with a sharply different style, the NCOCY is alive. Modest goals, financial realism, and avoiding even the appearance of a "cult of personality" all help the NCOCY to survive, but there is more to social altruism than the ability of an organization to survive. The NCOCY's pleasant low-keyed activity makes so little difference in the public effort expended on behalf of unlucky children that one may ask whether it is worth the exertion.

### A Lobby That Never Lobbied

At the very beginning of the 1970s, with an administration-sponsored family assistance plan under active consideration in Congress, with comprehensive child-development legislation also receiving serious attention, and with interest in social policy to benefit children generally at a very high level, it was reasonable for a national leader in the field to conclude that the moment was at hand to organize a national lobby for children. Jule Sugarman, by then New York City human resources administrator, was the leader. No neophyte to national activity, Sugarman earlier had run the Head Start program both in the Office of Economic Opportunity and in HEW, and had attempted to redirect and restructure the federal Children's Bureau. In the course of that activity, he worried the elite of the child welfare profession, and was defeated by them as he reached for the top job in the new Office of Child Development. Sugarman went on to New York, but he was persuaded that children's interests were much too narrowly represented in Washington. His case was impressive: the effective lobbyists in Washington had only peripheral interest in children's causes and gave their principal energy to other questions; groups working on behalf of children were limited both by their separate categorical interests and by their tax-exempt status which inhibited lobbying activity. The Children's Lobby was invented to overcome these limiting conditions.

At one point the Children's Lobby claimed over a thousand members. Few of them, however, paid the annual dues, which ranged from $15 (or less for low-income persons) to $150. It had a forty-six-member board of directors, about one-third parents and two-thirds special interest and general representatives. Few board members in any of the three categories showed continuing interest. Its twenty-member executive committee included Sugarman; George Wiley, founder of the National Welfare Rights Organization; William Pierce, CWLA's "man in Washington"; Evelyn Moore, executive director of the Black Child Development Institute; Greg Coler, executive director of the Minneapolis Day Care Association; Robert Pauley, president of the California Children's Lobby, a group that claimed almost a thousand members, a $40,000 annual budget, and a registered lobbyist on the payroll; Joyce Black, president of the New York Day Care Council; P. F. DelliQuadri, a social work administrator who had served briefly as chief of the Children's Bureau before the changes made in 1969 to make room for Sugarman. Yet, after three years the Children's Lobby had little to show for its elaborate structure—no office, no paid staff, no legislative program. Its board of directors did not meet after the lobby's first (and only) annual meeting in April 1972. While the executive committee continued to meet periodically thereafter, a quorum rarely was present at any of the meetings. George Wiley, the lobby's treasurer and most experienced organizer on behalf of a depressed group, did not attend a meeting between the April 1972 session and his death in the summer of 1973. Six months after Wiley died, Jule Sugarman moved from New York to Atlanta, Georgia, where he became city administrator. Just before his departure for Atlanta, Sugarman was asked by an acquaintance what was to happen to the Children's Lobby. "I am taking it to Atlanta with me," he answered. "It's right here in my breast pocket."

Conceived as the political arm of the child services movement, the lobby's brief and discordant life illuminated the internal political problems of that movement, but accomplished nothing for the children's cause. The Children's Lobby was a Sugarman creation; it collapsed because most of its putative leaders, who included some of the country's best-known child advocates, had trouble adjusting to Sugarman himself and could not adjust to the principal proposal he pushed: a children's trust fund.

Neither the idea of a trust fund nor any other substantive question occupied as much of the Children's Lobby's time and energy after its creation in 1970 as did its own internal politics. The dominant issue from its beginning to its fading away just three years later was how the lobby should support itself. Should the organization be only a registered lobby supported entirely from membership fees and contributions that are not tax deductible, or should it seek in addition tax-exempt foundation funds that could be used for research purposes but not lobbying activities? While paying consistent lip service to the lobby idea, Sugarman never gave up the possibility of foundation support. Most of the other lobby activists had their hands full raising foundation money to support their own organizations. Jule Sugarman was viewed as unwelcome competition.

Sugarman's effort to set up the Children's Lobby began in November 1970 with a "Dear Friend" invitation to an organizational meeting at the following month's White House Children's Conference. It was good timing. Many delegates were unhappy with the conference set-up before it ever began, discontented over having been excluded from the planning, suspicious of the political connections of the conference chairman. Their distress was not alleviated by the controlled style with which the conference was run. So, a Children's Lobby with its promise of a continuing commitment to the children's cause, not managed by the White House, was an especially attractive idea at that point. Little commitment was really required of the two-hundred-odd delegates who attended the organizational meeting. They voted "aye" to the formation of the lobby and went home feeling, perhaps, that the Children's Lobby they had approved would do for children what the National Welfare Rights Organization had done for welfare mothers or what the Southern Christian Leadership Conference had done for blacks. In fact, however, the unanimity and the impact of the Children's Lobby peaked at the moment of the vote for its creation.

The lobby, as Sugarman described it, would be "frankly and openly a lobbyist for the interests of children, youth and families," concentrating "its entire energies on efforts to enact legislation, secure appropriations and promote effective administration." Sugarman said that the efforts of some organizations in this direction had been hampered by their tax-exempt status. The Children's Lobby would not be so constrained because it would be supported entirely by membership dues and nondeductible contributions. Existing organizations were assured that the lobby would not compete with their activities—and by implication for their funds. "In fact," Sugarman stated, "we see the Lobby as an action arm to press for the adoption of ideas which have been developed by those organizations."[30] But the potential for trouble was there: Sugarman offered an idea of his own—a federal children's trust fund—"which could become the first legislative objective of the Children's Lobby." The *Washington Post* reported the trust fund to be "one of the lobby's specific goals," yet it was clear that the idea was Sugarman's alone.[31] While the trust fund was not pursued during the small-group sessions held in December 1971 and in January 1972 to plan for the annual meeting, Sugarman did raise the possibility of a tax-exempt research arm for the lobby. That did not go well. Sugarman was told first that such activity would duplicate the

30. "Dear Friend" letter dated November 1970, headed "Temporary Committee for the Children's Lobby" and signed by Jule M. Sugarman (processed).

31. *Washington Post*, Dec. 14, 1970.

work of the numerous organizations already doing research. An additional warning came from California Children's Lobby President Robert Pauley, whose organization had decided against such a set-up because of the difficulty of keeping the two activities legally separate.[32] Sugarman apparently decided to let the matter ride. His memorandum to members of the interim steering committee reported, "A decision has been made to use Lobby funds only for those activities which could not be conducted on a tax exempt basis."[33]

The trust fund and the tax-exempt research unit could be left on the back burners. However, no Children's Lobby in the process of organizing in the fall of 1971 could avoid the challenge posed by President Nixon's veto of the child development bill that December—particularly after the lobby had bought a half-page ad in the *Washington Post* to urge enactment of the bill.[34] Sugarman told a January 1972 session of the annual meeting planning committee that the lobby had "decided to spend some time working for the passage of the Comprehensive Child Development Bill." This activity, he reasoned, "would help build the Lobby's reputation."[35] In fact, it was a major factor in the lobby's instant failure, because there were important differences between Sugarman and his associates in regard to the child development legislation, differences about whether to support child development as child care or child development as community change. First evident when the child development bill was making its way through Congress, those differences hardened when Sugarman later began to push his pet project, the children's trust fund.

Unwilling to reject participation in a children's lobby out-of-hand, yet unable to agree on what they would lobby for, planners of the Children's Lobby undertook to constrain the lobby's founder and interim president. The liberal wing of the child-care movement (such groups as the Washington Research Project Action Council, the Black Child Development Institute, the AFL-CIO, the Children's Foundation, at times the Day Care and Child Development Council of America, and the Child Welfare League's Washington arm) had little use for Sugarman's ties to the states and the governors. These groups had not forgotten Sugarman's support during the 1970 congressional hearings of a minimum population

32. Minutes of the meeting of the Annual Meeting Committee of the Children's Lobby, Dec. 20, 1971, Shoreham Hotel, Washington, D.C. (processed), p. 1.
33. "Review of Actions to Date," Jan. 20, 1972 (processed).
34. *Washington Post*, Nov. 9, 1971.
35. Minutes of meeting of the Annual Meeting Committee of the Children's Lobby, Jan. 8, 1972, Shoreham Hotel, Washington, D.C. (processed), p. 1.

of 100,000 for prime sponsors of child development programs and they had not forgiven him for it. Nor were they happy about the work he was doing at the time for the child-development task force of the Education Commission of the States. In discussing reactions to Nixon's child development veto, Sugarman said that he had been in touch with the various interested parties and had drafted "some ideas which could be a possible meeting ground."[36] The compromise talk was irritating to the liberals. They did not want to be identified with it. Richard Warden, who lobbied at various times for the Washington Research Project Action Council and for the United Automobile Workers, but whose participation in the Children's Lobby was "personal and private" and temporary, pointed out that there would be a number of child development bills to consider, that the state role would be an obvious point of controversy. The CWLA's William Pierce—the lobby's secretary—wanted assurances that the lobby would be bound by membership opinion—not simply Sugarman's. The Day Care and Child Development Council's Theodore Taylor denounced "small elitist groups who go around community people and parents."[37] If the lobby was an extension of other groups that support state control, Taylor would have none of it. The AFL-CIO's Mary Logan, who was not a member of the board of directors, sought to delay lobby decisions until after the April 1972 annual meeting because she hoped to insure representation of groups of consumers—parents, community group leaders, labor people—"rather than those solely oriented to the interests of state and local governments." Logan reported to her boss, Bert Seidman, that one aspect of her involvement with the lobby was to get together a list of people "we would like to see elected to the permanent board."[38]

Eighteen months after Jule Sugarman sent out his invitation to participate in organizing a Children's Lobby, the first annual meeting of that lobby took place in Washington. (By way of contrast, eighteen months after its creation, the National Welfare Rights Organization had mobilized protest marches in more than fifty cities across the country. It claimed affiliates in thirty-five states involving nearly two hundred local groups with a dues-paying membership reasonably calculated at over six thousand family heads.[39]) Small group sessions discussed the issues these same people had been discussing for years and expressed concern about the

36. Ibid., p. 2.
37. Ibid.
38. Memorandum, Feb. 22, 1972.
39. Gilbert Y. Steiner, *The State of Welfare* (Brookings Institution, 1971), p. 285.

problems they had always been concerned about. The plenary session neither inspired participants nor stimulated policymakers. Opposition was voted to the then-pending welfare-change legislation with its emphasis on work incentives and work training for young mothers. But for its positive goals the meeting could only agree that the lobby play "an active and positive role" at all governmental levels and in coalition with other groups "to develop and promote legislation that is in the best interest of children and their families."[40]

Organizational games and ways to limit the authority of the lobby's president preoccupied the lobby's board of directors during the three meetings it managed to sandwich around the plenary session. With a president, a secretary, and a treasurer, nine vice-presidents, and forty-six board members, from which twenty executive committee members were drawn, the Children's Lobby did not lack for chiefs. Some of them took pains not only to discourage interest in a tax-free research arm, but also to proscribe thinking about it:

Any consideration of a 501-c-3 [tax-exempt research] arm is only to be undertaken after a reasonable period of time, *i.e.*, at least a year, and then only after polling the Board and reporting the results of that poll to the Executive Committee for their further Study and Consideration to then be reported back to the full Board for its approval or disapproval.[41]

In the unlikely event that Sugarman failed to appreciate the import of that plain language, the board spelled out its distrust by adopting another constraining resolution that could hardly be misunderstood: "It is the will of the Board that the Board shall be polled before any changes shall be made in the non-negotiable positions of the Board."[42]

With their business done, the lobbyists adjourned to await a promised inclusion in the *Congressional Record* of the various resolutions adopted in small group sessions. Upon publication, copies were to be sent to all members of the lobby. This technique was designed to serve a dual purpose: offprints of the appropriate pages of the *Record* would be an economical yet dignified way of reproducing the material, and appearance under those auspices would signify easy access to policymakers. That sign, in turn, was expected to stimulate membership. As it developed, the reverse obtained. For months and months there was no insertion in the

---

40. Minutes of the First Annual Meeting of the Children's Lobby, April 8–9, 1972, Shoreham Hotel, Washington, D.C. (processed), p. 5.

41. Ibid., p. 3.

42. Ibid., p. 2.

*Record,* consequently no offprints, no demonstration of easy access, no chance to claim any credit for influencing Senate passage of child development legislation, and no stimulation to membership growth. Although the material had gone to the staff director of his Subcommittee on Children and Youth before the end of April, Senator Walter Mondale did not make the insertion until August 17, and then in a heavily edited version. Referring to the first annual meeting as having been held "recently," Mondale also added a good word for Sugarman and for Greg Coler,[43] a lobby vice-president and one of Sugarman's few allies in the lobby's leadership. While Coler, director of the Minneapolis Day Care Association, was singled out because he shared a state affiliation with Mondale, this recognition of Sugarman and Coler alone did not help the already troubled relationships among the few active leaders of the Children's Lobby.

From the end of the first annual meeting to Sugarman's departure for Atlanta with the lobby in his breast pocket, the Children's Lobby was characterized principally by emergency appeals from Sugarman for money to maintain the lobby, and by formal unveiling of Sugarman's proposal for a children's trust fund.[44] Instead of enthusiastic support, the latter provoked needling letters to Sugarman from Pierce, the lobby's secretary, who made no secret of his deep suspicion of the motives behind Sugarman's willingness to do business with state governors and Sugarman's interest in creating a tax-exempt research arm of the lobby. Pierce raised a series of questions about Sugarman's failure to provide minutes, secure publicity, command attention at the White House, call another board meeting, and raise money. The severity of the money problem was evidenced by a series of pitiful calls from Sugarman for a campaign wherein each board member would recruit five or six new lobby members each month. Board members disposed to cooperate might have first looked inward. A substantial number were not themselves paying members of the lobby.

A report from the office director to Sugarman projected the resources of the Children's Lobby as of July 1, 1972, at a sickly $188.29.[45] Sugarman told his executive committee that because of financial difficulties and because August was a slow month, the one-person New York office of the lobby would be closed. Still waiting for Mondale to make the insertion,

43. *Congressional Record* (daily ed.), Aug. 17, 1972, pp. S 13822–26.
44. The proposal is described in ibid., July 26, 1973, p. S 14750.
45. Memorandum from Lanie Puharich to Gregory L. Coler and Jule M. Sugarman, June 6, 1972.

he coupled assurances that the resolutions of the annual meeting would be distributed as *Congressional Record* reprints with one more appeal that each member find three new members.[46] Two sparsely attended executive committee meetings were held in Washington late in 1972 just as the National Council of Organizations for Children and Youth was emerging as a proponent of children's causes, a proponent, moreover, that could pay its bills. Pierce's minutes of the last of these Children's Lobby executive committee meetings note that a major part of the meeting was devoted to discussion of reorganization of the lobby, failure of board members to attend meetings, and "general lack of responsiveness."[47] While Pierce did not include it in his minutes, Greg Coler did report to Sugarman, who had not been present, Pierce's observation that the structure of the lobby was excessively influenced by Jule Sugarman whose dual role as lobby president and New York City human resources administrator never left Pierce comfortable.[48]

Most of the bickering and most of the dreaming about new ways to raise money were of interest only to the half dozen or so stalwarts who met in Washington. When Sugarman moved on his own, however, early in 1973, to publicize "A Children's Trust Fund and Revenue Sharing Act" some activists who had not bothered themselves with the lobby's internal politicking took a hand. Sugarman had been biding his time to publicize the trust fund idea. He recognized that the children's cause was armed with a small stick at best, and that the battling within the lobby served only to fracture the stick. He had concluded months before the executive committee's final meetings that the future of the lobby was doubtful because of its inability to match stated interest with money. Uncertain about his own career plans when the Lindsay administration ended in New York City, Sugarman decided that he had to present the case for the trust fund while he could still speak as administrator of an important human services program and while there was still a Children's Lobby that could furnish the proposal an organizational tie.

The trust fund issue renewed the dispute between those like Sugarman who considered it unrealistic if not undesirable to bypass state governments indefinitely in the development of social programs and those like Marian Wright Edelman of the Washington Research Project Action

46. Letter from Jule Sugarman to "Lobby Member" (July 6, 1972; processed).
47. Minutes of the executive committee meeting of the Children's Lobby, Dec. 8, 1972 (processed), p. 1.
48. Letter from Coler to Sugarman, Jan. 12, 1973.

Council who saw no hope for social programs under state control. Since the great bulk of the $2.75 billion to be deposited to the trust fund would be specially shared revenue available to the states for new children's programs or program expansion, Marian Edelman foresaw a series of disasters: federal standards, monitoring, and enforcement would be impossible; parent and community involvement would not be assured, nor would compliance with nondiscrimination provisions of the Civil Rights Act; Head Start and other community-based programs targeted at disadvantaged children would end. The effect, in her judgment, would be to disperse limited funds so broadly that few, if any, "real programs for children would emerge."[49]

A few weeks after Edelman dispatched an early warning to Sugarman, an internal Action Council memorandum further detailed objections to the trust fund including a warning that while the proposal paid lip service to continuation of categorical programs, it was so general that those categorical programs would certainly be threatened. The net effect of the trust fund, said Judith Assmus, the Action Council's representative in Washington, would be "few-strings-attached" revenue sharing to the states for children.[50] While Edelman and her colleagues attacked the substantive aspects of the trust fund proposal, William Pierce fired off a complaint about materials that described the trust fund also identifying Sugarman as president of the lobby. Nor did Pierce like the report that had come to him quoting Sugarman as saying he planned "to use the Children's Lobby" to push the trust fund.[51]

Battling as fiercely as if the stakes involved were control of a giant industry or labor union rather than a bankrupt association of social altruists, Sugarman turned his defense into a good offense. He mailed a mimeographed invitation to board members of the Children's Lobby asking each to vacate the seat if he or she could not devote time to development and to fund raising. Failure to respond would be taken as evidence that the member could no longer participate, that is, as a resignation. Had there been something to rule, it would have been akin to dissolving a parliament and ruling by fiat. Pierce, who bothered to reply, expressed his admiration for the leader: "I believe that everyone acknowledges your leadership, Jule, in many of the areas of social concern; you are one of the

49. Letter from Edelman to Sugarman, Jan. 15, 1973.
50. "Sugarman's 'Children's Trust Fund and Revenue Sharing Act,'" memorandum from Assmus to Edelman, Feb. 9, 1973, p. 3.
51. Letter from Pierce to Sugarman, Feb. 16, 1973.

people that has a name when it comes to 'children's programs.' " But, he said, the automatic resignation procedure was "counter-democratic."[52] Counter-democratic or brilliant parry, for all practical purposes it marked the end of the Children's Lobby. There was no money, no office, no staff, no program, no board, no interest, only Jule Sugarman and William Pierce exchanging ripostes.

Although the Children's Lobby expired, there were some satisfactions for Jule Sugarman. He warned from the beginning that a tax-exempt arm would be necessary for financial stability. When the Children's Lobby board was finally willing to discuss the question, the ground had been preempted by the National Council of Organizations for Children and Youth. Sugarman's ally in the councils of the lobby, Greg Coler, became the first director of NCOCY, then went on to other things, but NCOCY lives on as a tax-exempt organization. And Sugarman's proposal for a trust fund was introduced in bill form in July 1973 by Senator Abraham Ribicoff, once secretary of health, education, and welfare. Without mentioning the Children's Lobby, but calling Sugarman the father of the trust fund concept, the senator said Sugarman's efforts on behalf of American children are "unsurpassed and he deserves our gratitude."[53] The text of the bill as well as an explanation of it in the form of questions and answers were all inserted in the *Congressional Record*, thereby providing a convenient source if the trust fund ever attracted political interest. A few months later, right around what would have been the third birthday of the Children's Lobby, Sugarman started the discussions that led to his appointment as chief administrative officer of Atlanta.

## A Viable Strategy

When Jule Sugarman, his Children's Lobby weakened, unveiled a plan for a special revenue-sharing fund for children, the proposal was not taken calmly by those who doubted the commitment of most state governments to meeting the needs of unlucky children. Marian Edelman, for example, was not then prepared to compromise on the issue of community control in child development. In her judgment, she told Sugarman, to advocate special revenue sharing as an alternative to comprehensive child development legislation was to give up, to desert those depressed children already being served and to destroy programs that should be preserved. On top of

52. Letter from Pierce to Sugarman, March 7, 1973.
53. *Congressional Record* (daily ed.), July 26, 1973, pp. S 14749–52.

that, however, the really devastating word for Sugarman was that the sagging Children's Lobby was facing competition. An evolving children's focus would turn the Washington Research Project into the Children's Defense Fund of the Washington Research Project. "It would be too bad," Edelman wrote Sugarman, "if those of us who care about children begin to fight each other, which would be inevitable."[54] And they both knew who would win.

In the world of children's advocacy, Edelman's role was growing and Sugarman's was shrinking. Sugarman could neither attract money nor achieve consensus for the Children's Lobby; Edelman had little trouble on either score. Following on her experiences with the Mississippi Head Start program, her leadership of the Washington Research Project Action Council—the project's lobbying arm—in its successful effort to interest Congress in child development legislation, and a period as director of an Office of Economic Opportunity–financed Center for Law and Education at Harvard, Marian Edelman turned to legal advocacy on behalf of disadvantaged children. She brought with her the Washington Research Project "apparatus"—important congressional contacts; a reputation for activity that was altruistic, not self-serving; good contacts with philanthropic foundations and with well-informed people in Washington who tend to favor community groups over state governments as agencies to carry out social programs. Among "concerned" people, Sugarman had admirers and detractors, friends and enemies. Edelman had admirers even among those who were not allies. An Edelman-directed children's lobby would likely be as dependent on the strength of its directors as would a Sugarman-directed lobby, but the former would less likely be torn by internal conflicts.

As it has developed, the Children's Defense Fund (CDF) is a nonprofit organization of lawyers, researchers, and federal policy monitors dedicated to long-range systematic advocacy and reform on behalf of children served by public and private institutions.[55] Combining the persistence of the women's movement with targeted aspects of children's issues, building on experiences in the civil rights and child development legislative struggles, the fund undertook both to protect good programs already in place, and to work for new programs that would retain the emphasis of the sixties on parent involvement and community change. There

54. Letter, Jan. 15, 1973.
55. "An Introduction to the Children's Defense Fund" (Washington, D.C.: Washington Research Project, n.d.).

was no room in that formulation for a state-dominated revenue-sharing program for children.

While the Children's Lobby was tearing itself apart internally, thus dissipating whatever strength in child advocacy it might have had, and while the National Council of Organizations for Children and Youth was making small plans and also having trouble finding a satisfactory director, the Children's Defense Fund pinpointed areas of program concentration and hired the staff to move the program along. The fund's priority areas included (1) the right to education for children excluded from school; (2) classification and labeling of children; (3) the right to treatment and education for institutionalized children; (4) the care and treatment of children by juvenile justice systems; (5) the right to adequate medical care and the delivery of health services for children; (6) the use of children as subjects for medical and drug research.[56] Within these areas, the CDF has undertaken research, monitors administrative agencies, provides public information, litigates, and offers technical support to local groups working with children. It has no local chapters—"We would go crazy servicing them," Edelman explains—but CDF staff goes out of its way to meet with local groups active in children's issues.[57] Individual staff members speak before groups as disparate as an American Medical Association committee and a plenary session of the National Urban League convention. Comparable invitations were not extended to the Children's Lobby, nor is it likely that either the lobby or the National Council of Organizations for Children and Youth could meet such requests if made.

It is precisely the in-depth strength of the CDF that distinguishes it among surrogate lobbyists for children. The struggling, one-person lobby —whatever the success of Ralph Nader's early days as a one-person consumer advocate—is unlikely to be effective. The appearance of omnipresence, of momentum, makes a difference. Big government is not challenged with a little stick, and the congressman who hears of the Children's Defense Fund from a constituent at home will give it attention when a CDF presentation is made in Washington. The fund consciously set out

56. Ibid. The absence from this list of early childhood development is noteworthy in view of Edelman's role in support of the 1971 bill (see chap. 5, above). Nor does early childhood development appear among the CDF activities listed in Marian Wright Edelman, "Report of Second Year Activities of the Children's Defense Fund of the Washington Research Project, Inc." (October 1974; processed), pp. 7–8.

57. Informal remarks to the Women's Caucus of the Brookings Institution, Jan. 14, 1975.

in its first years to lay a solid factual, public relations, and organizational base for its planned action program.

Edelman's premise is that effective child advocacy is a result of specialized coalition-building. That strategy brought together in support of child development a host of socially oriented groups that split badly on President Nixon's family assistance plan. "The facts and particular politics of individual issues to a large extent dictate the results of that issue," she says.[58] Different groups who may not join a general child-advocacy effort may coalesce around some issues affecting children because their interests are involved. So be it. Edelman sets out to maximize strength around each of several important issues, and those who can in good conscience join in only one pending cause are entirely welcome in that coalition. The CDF's initial program issues were selected not only for their own importance, but with an eye to their potential coalition-building and constituency-building possibilities.

The Defense Fund picks its issues for impact and for what it calls flexible change strategies. It has tried to pick indisputably harmful practices like school exclusion and jail detention of children as entry points into the case for reform of public education and juvenile justice systems. Marian Edelman characterizes the "American assumption that we love children" as a "myth," citing as evidence the absence of a societal priority on ensuring that all children get enough food, clothing, health care, education, and other services.[59] The CDF's first published report, *Children Out of School in America*, found children excluded from school for reasons ranging from pregnancy to the inability of some families to pay for clothes, textbooks, school fees, or transportation charges, to schools' lack of programs for children with many kinds of mental, physical, and language handicaps. It also found "rampant" the use of suspensions and other disciplinary devices to throw children out of school.[60]

Responses to an exposure of such practices are likely to be forthcoming from both social altruists and responsible public officials at all governmental levels who share responsibility for public education, for equal opportunity, and for due process. The Defense Fund views that range of

58. Edelman, "Report of Second Year Activities of the Children's Defense Fund," p. 8.

59. Marian Wright Edelman and others, *Children Out of School in America: A Report by the Children's Defense Fund of the Washington Research Project, Inc.* (Children's Defense Fund, 1974), foreword.

60. Ibid., p. 5.

response as precisely in accord with its objective of provoking broad debate about educational reform. School exclusion, like several other issues pinpointed by the CDF for initial activity, can be attacked in a variety of ways. Rather than total dependence on pressuring a legislative committee, for example, progress can be achieved through litigating, developing and pushing draft legislation, monitoring administrative behavior, organizing local groups. The strategy of the fund is to make the nation aware of the inadequacy of its commitment to children. No other lobby of surrogates defines its role in comparable fashion, and no other lobby of surrogates is as well equipped to do the job.

Yet, it is by no means clear that the Children's Defense Fund can survive. It has chosen a tax-exempt status—presumably as a nonlobbying educational and research organization—and found early success in attracting foundation support. However, Marian Edelman is uneasy about allowing the cause she espouses to depend on the big foundations. And foundations' interests are transitory—today's preoccupation with children in trouble can evaporate in the fashion of yesterday's preoccupation with civil rights or with hunger. The CDF can hardly depend on its constituents for financial support. It can appeal to a broad cross-section of "concerned Americans" in the manner of John Gardner's Common Cause, but that inevitably raises the possibility of overdependence on some narrow section of the broad cross-section.

"It is imperative that people and agencies with whom we seek to deal (and change) understand that we possess the institutional capacity for a long haul fight," says Edelman.[61] The fund does not now possess that capacity. Neither does any other surrogate lobbyist for children, but the Children's Defense Fund is closest to acquiring it.

61. "Report of Second Year Activities of the Children's Defense Fund," p. 10.

# 8

# A Nearly Free Lunch

In the stream of social programs, those pinpointed toward feeding children might be expected to have relatively easy going. Children are neither expected to work before they can eat nor are they liable to be excluded from public benefits on moral grounds. Moreover, where the benefit is food itself rather than cash, there is no reason to fear that it will be diverted to some unwarranted use by an irresponsible caretaker. The ambiguities inherent in comprehensive child development as a discrete, easily understood, policy goal are not inherent in the provision of nutritious meals. The most likely objection to pursuing the latter goal may be the possibility of benefits reaching some nonneedy recipients, but again since the benefit is food and the recipients are children, such an outcome could hardly be characterized as a scandal.

The national school lunch program—extensively and expensively improved in the seventies—is the success story of the children's cause. While comprehensive child development, child-care centers, and child welfare services have floundered, school lunch has flourished. Transformed from a farm bloc preserve that benefited a fraction of the middle class, the subsidized school lunch has become a social benefit that is almost universally available. Federal expenditures have been directed increasingly toward children of poor families. Welfare-oriented congressmen and lobbyists for various nutrition groups who have helped effect this change continue to push for improvements in school feeding. Some would concentrate on reducing to zero the number of schoolchildren to whom the lunch program is unavailable; others believe attention should focus on reaching children who are eligible for free or reduced-price lunches but are not getting them; still others think nutrition education should become a part of the lunch program. And while both the Johnson and the Ford administrations have tried to limit benefits to the poor, a contrary movement

176

has developed in support of a universal feeding program. "I still believe," Senator Hubert Humphrey has said, "that every boy and girl is entitled to at least one nutritious lunch per day as they attend our schools under the laws of compulsory education."[1]

Federal payments to the states in 1976 for child nutrition—school lunch, school breakfast, and nonschool food assistance—exceeded $1.7 billion in cash and $440 million in commodities. Aside from public education itself, no social welfare activity provides public benefits to more children than school lunch. Specifically, so-called type A (nutritionally balanced) lunches were available in 1975 to 87 percent of all schoolchildren.[2] Of these 44 million possible participants, 25.3 million were sometime participants, and 10 million of them were served lunch free or at a reduced price. The total of 10 million beneficiaries of free or reduced-price lunches exceeds by over 2 million the number of children receiving payments under aid to families with dependent children, although the latter encompasses an appreciably wider age range. In addition, a school breakfast program was providing a daily average of 2 million meals, and special food service programs in day-care centers and in summer recreation programs together served a daily average total of 2.25 million participants.[3] While most breakfast beneficiaries were served lunch as well, and some major fraction of the summer recreation meals were served to children who also benefited from school feeding, between 25 million and 26 million individual children were reached by the combined programs.

It was not ever thus. Whatever the anxiety of the "hunger" lobby to go the last mile in school feeding, to provide a universal free lunch, a great many miles were covered while attention was focused on more sweeping public welfare proposals. In the last year of Lyndon Johnson's Great Society, school lunch was available to 38 million children. Only 2.5 million of the 20 million actual participants received a free or reduced-price lunch. School breakfast, a pilot program then authorized for two years

1. *Federal Food Programs—1973*, Hearings before the Senate Select Committee on Nutrition and Human Needs, 93:1 (Government Printing Office, 1973), pt. 4, p. 396.

2. Type A is not necessarily the only kind of lunch service available. So-called à la carte lunches, not federally subsidized, are offered in many schools, sometimes along with, sometimes in lieu of, the type A lunch. The distinguishing characteristic of the type A lunch is that it meets certain nutritional requirements specified by the U.S. Department of Agriculture.

3. *Agriculture and Related Agencies Appropriations for 1976*, Hearings before a Subcommittee of the House Committee on Appropriations, 94:1 (GPO, 1975), pt. 4, p. 931; and *Annual Report of the Council of Economic Advisers, January 1976*, p. 102.

only, served a relative handful of children. Day-care and summer recreation feeding programs were unknown. In 1975 as in 1968, however, the Department of Agriculture and its critics differed over the number of needy children not benefiting from school feeding, and differed as well over the prospects for reaching them whatever the number might be.

### The Transformation of School Lunch

The transformation of school feeding from an outlet for farm surplus to a small convenience for part of the middle class to an important welfare benefit for children of the poor occurred over a span of four decades. The New Deal's Agricultural Adjustment Act, concerned primarily with improving the farmer's purchasing power, included a provision that appropriated annually to the secretary of agriculture an amount equal to 30 percent of the gross receipts from customs revenues. This provision of the 1935 act, which has come to be referred to simply as section 32, was designed to compensate the farmer for the higher purchase costs resulting from the effect of tariffs. The legislation authorized the secretary to spend revenues from section 32 on the development of new uses for farm products, and on benefits, indemnities, and donations to low-income groups in order to divert surplus farm commodities from the normal channels of trade where they could not be consumed. Contributions to school lunches were one of the earliest uses of section 32. The surplus problem disappeared temporarily with World War II, but Congress then chose to permit section 32 money to be diverted to school lunches anyway. Some day the war would end, and the farmer's purchasing power would again need shoring up.

When, early in 1946, Congress considered institutionalizing federal aid for school lunch, not much was said about the farm problem, and what was said exaggerated the importance of school lunch as a farm relief measure. Senator Robert A. Taft, who objected on principle to providing subsidized lunches to children whose parents could afford to pay the full costs, objected to the farm relief argument as invalid, characterizing school lunch as "merely a drop in the bucket . . . wholly unimportant so far as solving the agricultural problem is concerned."[4] While all the farm organizations supported the proposal, so did organized labor, organized religious groups like the National Catholic Welfare Conference, and women's

4. *Congressional Record*, vol. 92, pt. 2 (1946), p. 1612.

organizations typified by the National Council of Jewish Women. "Statism" and "socialism" troubled hard-core conservatives who viewed with alarm the prospect of children discovering that they were fed with federal funds, and who foresaw destruction of the state and local school system by pressure from Washington. But Senator Richard Russell (Democrat of Georgia) offered predictable assurances that a schoolchild "who has a good bowl of hot soup and a glass of sweet milk for his lunch will be much more likely to be able to resist communism or socialism than would one who had for his lunch a hard biscuit which had been baked the day before and which he had brought with him to school in a tin can."[5] With the elimination of a title that would have authorized matching funds for training school lunch supervisors, equipping lunchrooms, and teaching courses in nutrition education, passage was achieved easily. Administration of the basic school lunch program was left with the secretary of agriculture, though not because of congressional anxiety to use the program to benefit the farmer. Congressional predisposition to avoid changing an arrangement with which it was familiar tilted what might otherwise have been an even balance between the Department of Agriculture and the Office of Education in favor of the former. Indeed, had the training and nutrition education title survived, program administration would have been divided.

### "Bite Tax" or "Tax Bite"

The permanent program authorized in 1946 marked a shift in emphasis from farm relief alone to farm relief cum child nutrition. Apportionment of appropriations was to be determined on the basis of the school-aged population of the various states and on relative need as indicated by per capita income of the states. Although the act provided for initial dollar-for-dollar state-federal matching and a gradual increase to three state dollars for each federal dollar, in practice state resources are not involved at that level. Children's payments have counted as part of the state's matching obligation, a situation that once provoked the late Senator Taft to conclude that the "whole thing is not a matching idea. The States are not required to do anything. The [federal] Government does it all, except what individuals contribute."[6] Per capita income as a factor favored the

5. Ibid., p. 1611.
6. Ibid., p. 1612.

poor southern states; school-aged population favored the heavily popu-
lated northern states. Neither criterion narrowed in on the problem of the
very poor child, although the act provided from the outset that lunches
were to be served at a reduced price or free to children who could not pay
the full cost.

Determination of ability to pay for lunch was left to local school officials. Yet, the larger the number of free or reduced-price lunches a school
official authorized, the higher the "regular" price would probably have
to be. Since children's payments for lunch were first set at a level high
enough to cover most of the required state matching, further price increases to cash customers for the benefit of the poor tended to be resisted.
John Perryman, executive director of the American School Food Service
Association, characterized this problem as the "bite tax." Because there
was no special appropriation for free lunches, he claimed that, as a national average, "every tenth bite the paying parent buys is a tax, a tax
being spent to feed someone else's child. . . . In every community, the
paying child is literally taking a part of the food from his mouth to feed
the non-paying."[7] At best, local school authorities were trapped by the
program's ambiguity of purpose. Was school lunch legislated out of compassion for hungry children or out of convenience for middle-class families? As long as the answer was unclear, it was unreasonable to expect
local school administrators to assume responsibility for charging the paying majority to meet the needs of the impoverished minority. It was
equally unreasonable to expect them to turn away from the problem of
the ill-fed child.

Facing a conflict of interests and apparently not caring enough about
this problem to make it a major educational cause, school administrators
avoided the lunch problem whenever they could. And they could avoid
it most of the time. During its first fifteen years of life, the National School
Lunch Act of 1946 provided its benefits selectively and at a leisurely rate
of growth. In 1960 about 13 million children were participating, roughly
7 million more than had participated in 1947. Free or reduced-price meals
did not grow proportionately. The number of such meals served annually
first peaked at 212 million in 1950, declined through most of the next
decade, and did not reach that figure again until 1960. As a percentage of
total meals served, the free or reduced-price segment was significantly
smaller in 1960 (10.1 percent) than it had been in 1950 (16.6 percent).

7. John N. Perryman, "Testimony prepared for delivery before the House Education
and Labor Committee" (May 29, 1968; processed).

School administrators in poor districts who were anxious to meet the nutritional needs of low-income children found the problem insoluble. Others entered the program hoping for the best. They were disappointed. In order to feed the poor, the alternative to raising the cost of lunches to paying children was to increase the local district's contribution. But the larger the number of poor children in a district, the greater the likelihood that local revenues would be severely limited. The decline in the number of free lunches came about because, lacking local tax revenue to swell the lunch "pot," and constrained by a practical ceiling price for paying customers, schools simply dropped out.

Pressures for change were conspicuously absent. None of the six hundred and seventy recommendations of the 1960 White House Conference on Children and Youth dealt with the school lunch program. School supporters had problems they ranked higher. The Eisenhower administration consistently made it clear that it regarded most poor relief as a state and local problem. Special federal benefits to enable local districts to feed poor children never reached the discussion stage in that atmosphere. Neither underfed children nor their parents were organized, and as events a decade later showed, if they had been it is unlikely that they could have been satisfied with a free lunch. Congress showed no particular concern about the limited reach of the lunch program—essentially a benefit for the middle class and particularly attractive in the South. Indeed, southern members with agricultural constituencies were twice blessed: in addition to soaking up agricultural commodities, in the period before the mid-sixties the school lunch program was feeding a larger share of the schoolchildren in the southeastern United States than in any other region of the country. This was due partly to geography. Because many of the children in the South live long distances from schools, schools there were generally built with cafeterias. In the North, children have lived close to school and usually walked home for lunch. Neighborhood schools in northern cities, frequently built without lunchrooms, tended not to participate in the lunch program. As late as 1962, for example, only about 32,000 of Detroit's 300,000 public schoolchildren were participants. In sum, school lunch was no issue at all for big-city liberals, and a well-functioning program for southern and rural conservatives.

Later, it would become commonplace to say that school feeding targeted to poor children was shunted aside by indifferent southerners. But for the period before 1961, the evidence points to a different conclusion, that no particular effort was made by anyone to overcome the built-in impediment to the use of school lunch as a welfare instrument. That impediment, of course, was an apportionment formula that reimbursed schools at a fixed rate whether or not a child paid for his lunch. An effort by the Kennedy administration to mitigate this problem by donating additional amounts of surplus commodities to poor schools might have kept lunch prices down in such schools. It would not, however, have solved the basic problem resulting from the absence of money earmarked for free or reduced-price lunches.

The idea of improving the apportionment formula for the benefit of poor children in poor school districts simply did not surface in legislation until President Kennedy's agriculture message of March 1961. Kennedy had already shown some preoccupation with the problem of making the country's agricultural abundance available to the poor. His first executive order, signed on inauguration day, 1961, liberalized and expanded the system of direct distribution of surplus commodities in accordance with the recommendation of a Kennedy task force on depressed areas. The agricultural message spoke of improving distribution and nutrition at home, affirmed instructions to the secretary of agriculture to increase surplus food distribution to the needy, confirmed the launching of pilot food stamp programs, and recommended "expansion of the school lunch program." Specifically, the President called for increased expenditures to schools providing a high proportion of free lunches, and for a change in the allocation formula. "In this way," Kennedy said, "the best possible nutrition will be made available to every school child, regardless of the economic condition of his family or his local school district." That admirable objective was not so different from the original act's stated intention to serve lunch "without cost or at a reduced cost to children . . . unable to pay the full cost."

The bill that a year later came out of the House Education and Labor Committee[8] and the House Rules Committee—in both cases, unanimously—carried two keys to utilization of the lunch program as more

8. The Legislative Reorganization Act of 1946, passed a few months after the National School Lunch Act, assigned jurisdiction over school lunch to the House Education and Labor and Senate Labor and Public Welfare Committees although funds are controlled by agricultural appropriations subcommittees in both chambers. In the Senate, moreover, legislative matters continue to be assigned, by convention, to the Agriculture Committee. A threat to challenge this arrangement was made by Wayne Morse (Democrat of Oregon) in 1968. Morse clearly meant it as a message to the Agriculture Committee not to junk a liberal objective Morse thought possible to achieve in the Labor and Public Welfare Committee. The message was heard.

than a middle-class convenience. First, building on the head start that southern states already enjoyed in school lunch participation, the proposal substituted actual program participation for school-aged population as one factor determining apportionment of federal money among the states. Relative wealth of the states remained a second factor. The effect of the change was to encourage states to feed more children. By so doing, they would increase their federal payments, a result that under the previous formula was a consequence of the birth rate in past years rather than the participation rate of the moment. The existing formula probably discouraged states from increasing participation because the fewer children fed, the greater the federal reimbursement per meal. Southern congressmen could not view the proposed change as threatening since their states had relatively high participation and relatively low per capita income, the combination that would produce the maximum federal payment for the general lunch program. For northern states that might begin to take school lunch seriously, the more they built up participation, the better off they would be.

Second, the Kennedy administration introduced a mechanism to increase the chances for a free lunch for poor children. The lunch act included a new section 11 authorizing extra funds for poor schools serving a large number of free or reduced-cost lunches. Although by the mid-seventies the cost of section 11 would represent more than half of the $1.4 billion in federal cash payments to the states for child nutrition, no such future was predicted at its birth. "The purpose of section 11 of this bill," explained Representative Cleveland Bailey (Democrat of West Virginia), its House floor manager, "is to try to bring to the 15 or 18 what might be called needy States a little bit of assistance that will help them to see that the children do not go hungry at lunchtime."[9] And, even by the standards of the time, the authorization was for only a little bit of assistance: $10 million in 1963 and open-ended thereafter, with the seemingly generous open-ended authorization for future years implicitly constrained by the specific figure fixed for 1963.

It was not the dollars authorized by section 11 that provoked what little opposition there was to school lunch expansion. For some, who were "wholeheartedly in favor of schoolchildren drinking milk and having enough to eat," the idea of further federal participation in "providing food, clothing, and the other necessities of life" was disturbing.[10] Others

9. *Congressional Record*, vol. 108, pt. 7 (1962), p. 9709.
10. Ibid., p. 9798.

would have been happier if the regulations dealing with free lunches were a matter of state control. In the end, only eleven members of the House would vote against the school lunch amendments, and the Senate never found it necessary to take a recorded vote. Yet ease of passage should not be confused with widespread congressional concern. Fewer than a third of all House members could be rounded up for a crucial teller vote on state versus federal control.

School lunches continued to be less than a compelling cause even for the sponsors of section 11. To begin with, the Kennedy administration preferred to push its experimental food stamp program to the point where a national effort could be urged. Then, Agriculture focused its innovative capacity on the resulting Food Stamp Act of 1964. Expanding the lunch program turned out to be more complicated than it seemed. Additional federal funds to reimburse schools serving free lunches were of no use to schools that had no facilities for serving meals. State school lunch supervisors did not perceive themselves either as welfare workers or as salesmen but as administrators. They had come to understand the administrative aspects of the 1946 school lunch act, knew how to deal with the Department of Agriculture under the provisions of that act, and saw no special advantage but a good deal of potential trouble in changing the rules. When both House and Senate agricultural appropriations subcommittees regularly refused to earmark money for section 11, no complaints were heard until Senator Philip Hart (Democrat of Michigan) in 1965 acted on a long-held conviction that school lunch should be a way of helping the poor. Hart's floor amendment providing $2 million for section 11 produced the first federal financing of the lunch program targeted to needy children.

Ten years later, cash payments to the states under section 11 were estimated at $751 million, and satellite child-feeding programs in day-care centers and summer programs—also directed to the poor—generated another $187 million. This massive change stemmed from the anxiety of budget planners first in the Johnson and then in the Nixon administration to respond to the "discovery" of hunger in America by redirecting food subsidies from middle-class beneficiaries—whether farmers or consumers—to the poor only. Of all aspects of the war on poverty, none achieved greater long-run success than food relief. One important reason was the mechanism chosen to accomplish it both for households and for children. Food stamps and school feeding each revert to the pre-Social Security Act style of relief-in-kind rather than in cash. Opposition to the provision of public relief is minimized when that relief takes the form of shelter, clothing, or food to those unable to provide for themselves. The cash relief principle embodied in the Social Security Act was a triumph for social reformers who argued that relief-in-kind stigmatizes its beneficiaries. It should be remembered, however, that the cash relief originally anticipated by that act was limited to the aged, the blind, and the orphaned, groups beyond suspicion of indolence and cheating. Because the war on poverty reached out beyond the old, the sick, and the orphaned, the probability of benefits accruing to some who might more easily "cheat" became a subject for renewed discussion. Assistance through food stamps, rather than their cash equivalent, provided reassurance. So did a free school lunch or breakfast for children of the poor instead of a cash payment of equivalent value to poor families with school-aged children.

### Redirection versus Expansion

Senator Hart's one-man effort that produced $2 million for special assistance in 1965 was given no help by the White House. Nevertheless, it turned out to be the device the administration would use to try to turn the school feeding program into an antipoverty weapon while economizing on the total costs of child nutrition. A Budget Bureau memorandum in December 1965 directed departments and agencies to review existing programs for possible savings in view of escalating Vietnam war costs.[11] Agriculture had offered a few million dollars in its special milk program, asserting that the difference could be picked up by local sources without passing the costs on to the child-consumer. President Johnson saw bigger possibilities. "A compassionate government need not be a profligate government," said his budget message late in January 1966. "I intend to propose legislation to improve the nutrition of needy children." What was left unsaid in the message was that the proposal would also virtually end subsidies for middle-class school feeding. The special value of the Hart amendment to the White House political strategy became clear five weeks later in a presidential message on domestic health and education. In Colorado and in North Carolina, the President said, where demonstration programs were conducted in poverty areas providing school lunches at sharply reduced rates, "the results were amazing." Even Senator Hart

11. *Congressional Quarterly Almanac*, 1966, p. 330.

must have been overwhelmed by the flow of positive findings now reported. "Virtually all the children purchased the school lunch—less than one-third had done so before. The children were more alert and interested in learning. The absentee rate fell by as much as 37 per cent. School dropouts were reduced."

With this glowing account of what had been accomplished in the eight hundred schools involved in the demonstration as evidence, it should have been easy to agree with the President that "too little of the federal assistance in the school lunch program has been directed toward children who need it most." Who would quarrel with "a major redirection of our child nutrition efforts to children who would otherwise grow up hungry, suffer the diseases that come from being ill-nourished, and lack the energy so essential to learning"? To achieve its purpose, the administration proposed a child nutrition act that extended school lunch to more needy children, provided aid for purchase of school food equipment, established a pilot school breakfast program, created demonstration programs for out-of-school child feeding in day-care centers, and extended distribution of "surplus" fluid milk—a program begun in 1954—to schools lacking the lunch program. All of this was to be accomplished with a federal cash outlay of about $100 million less than had been appropriated for school lunch and milk programs in 1966.

Congress may have believed it, but it did not buy it. Some of Johnson's budgeters would suggest later that Congress was never expected to go along. Like an unsuccessful assault on the expensive veterans' hospital program in 1965, the proposal to cut back on middle-class school feeding may have been expected simply to define the limits of federal activity. For school lunch proponents, maintaining the status quo in the general support program became a triumph. By focusing on the plight of poor children, and by presidential assertions to the effect that "it is hard to teach a hungry child," the administration made it impossible for Congress to continue to ignore them.

The explanation is plausible if not provable. What is provable is that Congress showed itself so unwilling to abandon the middle-class subsidy that no sponsor for the administration bill could be found in the Senate, while the House sponsor—Harold Cooley, Democrat of North Carolina—marked the bill "by request." The eventual result was an extension of the benefits of the lunch program to more poor schoolchildren (but not outside the school setting), the creation of additional feeding programs for them, and the continuation of the existing lunch program subsidies for paying customers.

Hearings and debate occasioned by the administration's 1966 proposals provided the first close congressional look at the school lunch program in twenty years, and Congress clearly liked what it saw. By June, the plan to "redirect" school feeding was a memory. Secretary of Agriculture Orville Freeman joined Senate Agriculture Committee Chairman Allen Ellender (Democrat of Louisiana) in drafting an alternate bill "to eliminate language which was raising fears that substantial changes" would be effected in the existing subsidy. Ellender assured his committee that his bill was quite different from the administration's which "would have completely superseded and revised the National School Lunch Act."[12] Nor was he friendly to mixing the lunch program "with the 'Headstart' or 'Head-on' or whatever you might call the programs in the poverty program," a judgment shared by the ranking Republican on the committee, George Aiken of Vermont, who agreed that school feeding programs should not be put under the poverty program "which has not worked at all."[13] Accordingly, the bill that came out of the Senate committee placed no new emphasis on the needy. The accompanying report described the lunch program as "a model of effective Federal-State-and-local cooperation" and stated as its primary aim "to improve child nutrition [although] it also fulfills an additional major objective of increasing the market for American farmers."[14] Two weeks after that report was filed, a letter from President Johnson to Secretary Freeman signaled administration capitulation. Where the earlier presidential message spoke of the demonstration program as a basis for "a major redirection of child nutrition efforts," Johnson now wrote Freeman that the successful demonstration provided a sound basis for administration of the "expanded program" provided for in the Ellender bill.[15] The final irony came later when the agricultural appropriations conferees dropped a Philip Hart-inspired provision earmarking $4.5 million for special assistance. Both "redirection" and "expansion" collapsed under the weight of the status quo.

That most basic principle of economics—there is no such thing as a free lunch—was ignored, not disproved, during the years between enactment of the National School Lunch Act in 1946 and the antihunger crusade of 1967–68. The act stipulated, after all, that children who could not pay were to be served free or at a reduced price. And in some cases,

12. *School Milk and School Breakfast Programs*, Hearings before the Senate Committee on Agriculture and Forestry, 89:2 (GPO, 1966), p. 1.
13. Ibid., p. 11.
14. *Child Nutrition*, S. Rept. 1360, 89:2 (GPO, 1966), pp. 2 and 5.
15. *Congressional Quarterly Almanac*, 1966, p. 331.

John Perryman's "bite tax" was accomplishing that objective. Where the need was greatest, however, the "bite tax" could not support free lunches without driving paying customers out of the lunch program. When the Johnson administration proposed redirecting subsidies to the poor, its motives were suspect—and not without cause. Because the administration had offered no help to Senator Hart when he sought to finance free lunches for the poor, redirection was viewed as a money-saving device rather than a principled decision. If it could not have redirection, the administration—now hard-pressed for money with which to fight in Vietnam—would not urge expansion. Accordingly, Agriculture Secretary Freeman joined the congressional "save the status quo" forces, and helped draft appropriate legislation. Freeman wound up with the President's congratulations on the free lunch demonstration program, President Johnson wound up with an impressive-sounding Child Nutrition Act, Congress wound up with a triumph in preserving existing lunch subsidies, and Senator Hart and the free lunch cause wound up with nothing new.

### Defenders of the Middle-Class Subsidy

The lesson of the skirmishes that eventuated in the Child Nutrition Act is that a middle-class subsidy is not likely to be redirected toward the low-income population even under political circumstances advantageous to the poor. Presidential support coupled with national interest in the antipoverty program could not begin to overcome the reluctance of many state bureaucrats to accept a significantly different kind of school lunch program. Nor was the educational bureaucracy any more disposed to favor the change. Finally, the workers on the line in the school food service business viewed with understandable alarm a proposal that could only result in a reduced number of patrons. Just a few years after the initial try at redirection, however, a legislative, journalistic, and public interest lobby developed in support of an expanded lunch program. Expansion does not pose comparable threats to school food service workers. It is a cause in their self-interest, and one which they embrace.

The National Education Association, the American School Food Service Association, and most of the state school-food directors follow a carefully drawn line when confronted with the redirection issue. For example, NEA's legislative consultant told an interviewer around the time of the Johnson proposal that the association supported the lunch and special milk programs, but would not want them extended to poor children "at the expense" of other children in the schools.[16] Lunch and milk programs were not originally designed as measures to aid the poor, the argument went, but as ways to help dispose of surpluses and, consequently, were intended for all children. Moreover, school feeding had other values: the program taught children manners and principles of nutrition, and introduced them to foods they might not eat at home. Happy with the Department of Agriculture and its state- and local-control orientation, uneasy about the U.S. Office of Education which had a different view of proper federal-state balance, NEA saw troubles ahead if existing arrangements were disturbed.

That attitude was neither less nor more enlightened than the position of the American School Food Service Association. A year after the redirection crisis, John Perryman explained that "whether all the powers-that-be have gotten the message yet or not, in the thinking of the vast majority of the people in our nation, school lunch is here to stay." Reporting with satisfaction that what he termed the threat of budgetary demise for school lunch had produced the greatest outpouring of mail to the Congress on any issue since termination of rent controls after World War II, Perryman explained that the popularity of school feeding was the inevitable consequence of working mothers; busing of children to "destinations culturally or geographically distant from their homes"; heavy traffic around urban schools; and the need to maximize class time during the school day.[17] Nor was convenience overlooked. Like the automobile, electricity, and cake mixes, school food service, Perryman claimed, was welded firmly to family convenience.

The School Food Service Association's goal is to be involved in distributing a product accorded treatment equal to that accorded other products of public education. In Perryman's view, for school food service workers not to be paid from regular school district funds constitutes a "unique indignity" in school fiscal practices. "Our nation's educational history," he claims, "abounds with evidence that public education in this country faltered and failed so long as it confined itself to the pauper's offspring."[18] Obviously, if food service were to be treated in a manner

16. Interview with Mary Condon Gereau, Nov. 29, 1967.
17. John Perryman, "The Shame of Being in the Black," *School Lunch Journal*, January 1968 (reprint).
18. John Perryman, "Log of the Executive Director," *School Foodservice Journal*, January 1972, p. 26.

indistinguishable from the generality of educational services, redirection would automatically fall away in favor of expansion to a universal lunch program comparable to universal education.

Expansion of school feeding is as clearly in the association's self-interest as redirection to the poor alone is not. The ASFSA is not a lobby intent on social altruism; it is an association of workers behind the counter intent on maintaining job opportunities and improving wages and working conditions. Association leaders are explicit on the self-interest question as they describe the work of ASFSA to their own members:

ASFSA works to upgrade the status and income of Association members.

ASFSA has helped create 350,000 jobs in school food service in the nation and has helped to bring these jobs under minimum wage.

ASFSA works to bring about legislation and federal funds that make the school lunch program and *your* job possible.

ASFSA has helped to bring about $1 billion a year in federal funding.[19]

The association serves its 58,000 members—one-sixth of all school food service workers—on a day-to-day basis by helping plan low-cost menus, finding new food ideas, recipes, and time-saving work techniques, and assisting in training kitchen employees and student help. Organized on the industrial union model, ASFSA reaches out to include school lunch directors and supervisors on the state and local levels, lunchroom managers, food service workers, and other educators in all fifty states. The great bulk of the members are production line workers or "assistants." These salad makers and pot scrubbers, together with managers (described by ASFSA staff as "the first echelon of administrators" with responsibility for personnel decisions) make up 93 percent of ASFSA membership. The remaining 7 percent are school lunch directors, those with responsibility for two or more schools in a district.

Spokesmen emphasize that the association is a professional organization, not a trade union. It does not bargain or work directly for higher salaries. The ASFSA clearly is in an ambiguous position in regard to salaries. Because most school food service personnel are paid from the school lunch account, higher salaries generally mean higher lunch prices. The interrelationship of the two may tend to discourage efforts to increase salaries because as school lunch prices go up, participation goes down— not something the ASFSA wants to encourage. Association spokesmen readily acknowledge the dilemma. In order to keep programs solvent, ASFSA's director of education explained to an interviewer, "we encourage the wage rate to go up gradually. We can't be too forceful" because

19. Ibid., March 1972, p. 25.

if it is increased too radically, the effect would be to run programs out of business.[20] Similarly, Josephine Martin, a long-time legislative spokeswoman and administrator of the Georgia school food service program, contends that before the advent of section 11's special federal funds for free and reduced-price lunches, school food service workers "felt guilty" about asking for salary increases—presumably because success would have meant either higher priced lunches, fewer programs, or both.[21] That attitude of self-restraint, still evident to a significant degree among association leaders, borders on the company union approach; workers accept company (school board) wage decisions because the association worries less about its members than it worries about management's sales figures.

Left to its own devices, the association's bureaucracy probably would continue to encourage moderation in salary demands in order to encourage growth of the lunch program. There is also a barely suppressed fear that better salaries will make school food service workers more attractive to organized labor unions, competition the association does not relish. One way to push off the union threat in the short run is to provide members with psychic benefits, an approach that takes particular form as a program for certification of school food service workers. Those pushing the certification scheme do not regard unions as a present threat to the ASFSA because, it is said, with pay scales so low, "there is no money in it yet" for the unions. School food service workers are simply not able to pay union dues from their salaries. If certification can be accomplished now, the argument goes, ASFSA will have an advantage later when salaries improve and competition from unions becomes more immediate a problem.

While certification clearly has much to offer the ASFSA national organization, it is sold to the rank and file as a way of improving their status— "a way of saying 'I'm a professional.' " School food service has always suffered from an inferiority complex within the educational community, and it is no doubt to this sense of inferiority that the certification program appeals. Still in the pilot stage in 1975 with activity in thirteen states, the program permits ASFSA members to be certified in one of three classifications: director-specialist, manager, and assistant, with in-grade steps within each classification. Only ASFSA members are eligible to participate in the various ASFSA-sponsored training activities and workshops leading to certification, a status that must be renewed every three years. If ASFSA membership expires, certification automatically expires also. The revenue-raising potential is significant. In addition to the basic ASFSA member-

20. Interview, Jay Caton, March 14, 1975.
21. Interview, Aug. 8, 1974.

ship fee, fees are associated with the workshops and training sessions leading to certification, and a small fee is levied for certification itself ($5.00 for assistants for the three-year period, $7.50 for managers, $10.00 for directors). Initial certification precedes the qualification activities or earning of points. One pays the fee, gets the certification card, and then must earn the requisite number of credits to be recertified at the end of the three-year period.

Certification seems to have had a prompt impact on ASFSA membership. In two of the three states where it was piloted, membership increased significantly. In North Carolina the number of members grew from thirteen hundred to twenty-three hundred in three months; in Colorado from six hundred to eleven hundred. An informed proponent projects a 30 percent increase in total membership once certification really gets started. No one is yet suggesting explicitly that an ultimate objective of certification is to limit school food service employment to "certified" workers. One reason to obscure that issue is that it could make current ASFSA members anxious about their tenure if they remain uncertified. National leaders already sense anxiety among many food service employees who fear certification may ultimately mean only college-educated persons will qualify for school food service jobs. By allowing certification to precede the requisite education and training activities, ASFSA is deliberately making it as easy as possible for members to become certified, and thus to acquire a status symbol that association executives believe is as important to school food service workers as is more money. ("Besides my driver's license," the association's journal quotes a worker as saying of her certification card, "that's the most important thing in my wallet."[22])

If it is true, as a member of the association's home office staff put it, that for many years ASFSA spokesmen bowed submissively at congressional hearings because "no one wanted to rock the boat," more recently the association's confidence and sophistication have increased. The ASFSA is not a stumbling group of bewildered little people lost in the lobbies of Congress or the administrative agency. Its monthly journal carries a volume of advertising that makes communicating with members no financial problem, and makes it possible to keep annual dues for rank-and-file workers at $5, a sum about half the actual cost of servicing each member. It has hired a New York public relations firm to do battle against proposed school lunch financing regulations that might limit participation.

22. *School Foodservice Journal*, July–August 1974, p. 90.

It shifts its efforts, in sophisticated fashion, from the Department of Agriculture to the Congress as necessary, depending on where receptivity to expansion is likely to be greatest. It rarely misses an opportunity to testify on legislative proposals, and runs legislative action workshops at which members of the Senate and House typically discuss the need for a national nutrition policy, a universal feeding program, and how to get involved in legislative activity.

The ASFSA, in short, must be reckoned with in any effort to change school feeding arrangements. It cannot be dissuaded from its drive for universality and for recognition of school feeding as an integral part of the public education system, deserving equality of treatment in the allocation of public resources. It could be and has been an effective force assisting political leaders interested in program expansion; it can marshal and has marshaled an army of "little old ladies in tennis shoes" to oppose redirection. The association's preferred objective is a universal program which would greatly expand its membership potential and would recognize the importance of the service. ("The war never will be won, the battlefield will continue to be joined, skirmishes, altercations, victories and losses will continue to be the order of the day until our nation once and for all sets aside its divided mind in the matter of feeding children and establishes a Universal School Foodservice Program."[23]) The status quo, on the other hand, which preserves the jobs of all members, is to be preferred to redirection to the poor. ("The affluent citizen is paying more into the tax structure in the first place—why should his child have to take extra money in his pocket to participate in any of the day's activities in school, including proper nutrition?"[24]) Redirection would probably mean fewer jobs. While job security is not necessarily the dominant ASFSA concern, it just happens to work out that in the association's view what is good for the country is good too for the association's members.

## Social Altruists and School Lunch Policy

President Johnson's proposal to redirect school lunch subsidies to the poor was rejected everywhere in 1966, but less than a decade later a redirection policy seemed less intolerable to some child feeding advocates. Redirection is clearly incompatible with the expansionist interests of the

23. "Log of Executive Director," School Foodservice Journal, January 1972, p. 26.
24. Ibid., p. 25.

ASFSA. Redirection is not similarly incompatible with the objectives of at least some of the social altruists who organized to give policy specificity to the new national social-consciousness of the mid-sixties. In that period, one such group of social altruists organized as an ad hoc Committee on School Lunch Participation, and another as the Children's Foundation. Both are important to a policy debate that is now effectively restricted to redirection versus expansion.

The stated purpose of the Committee on School Lunch Participation was to find out why "so few children participate in the National School Lunch Program or are denied the opportunity to participate, and why the School Lunch Program is failing to meet the needs of poor children." Five women's organizations, each with a religious orientation or connection, and all asserting a "special affinity for the needs of children" sponsored the resulting inquiry.[25] A small grant from the Field Foundation and a large number of volunteer interviewers made it possible to study the program in operation in forty communities.

The committee's widely publicized report, published in April 1968, concluded that the problem of the school lunch program was not in the individuals who ran it but in the system which limited or even prohibited their effective functioning. As a long-range plan, the committee suggested a universal free lunch program, a suggestion that could be warmly embraced by ASFSA. Pending a universally free lunch, the committee proposed a plan that included reduction of the maximum price of lunch to twenty cents, an amount then lower than the average price in virtually every state; an increase in the federal contribution; a new matching formula that would require the states to match federal contributions from state revenues, relieving full-price customers of the cost of the free and reduced-price lunches; and a uniform standard of eligibility for free or reduced-price lunches.[26] Whether the pieces in the short-run plan were separable was unclear, and it made a difference. For example, a uniform standard of eligibility alone might serve to increase the tax bite on paying children. A mandatory state contribution alone to cover the needs of poor children might simply drive some states out of the program entirely. The School Food Service Association could embrace the long-range plan for a universal, free school lunch proposed by the women's groups. But the

25. *Their Daily Bread*, a study of the National School Lunch Program by the Committee on School Lunch Participation under the direction of Florence Robin (Atlanta: McNelley-Rudd Printing Service [1968]), p. 3.
26. Ibid., p. 6.

short-run goals of the two groups differed in an important respect. For ASFSA, the short-run objective was to maximize the number of type A lunches consumed; for the Committee on School Lunch Participation, the short-run objective was to maximize the number of type A lunches consumed by poor children.

In its impact, the methodology of the Committee on School Lunch Participation is as important as are the committee's specific proposals. Simply by involving middle-class women residents of forty cities and counties in the conduct of fifteen hundred interviews with school lunch administrators, school principals, classroom teachers, and parents, the committee performed an educational service of consequence. Moreover, through their organizational connections the interviewers became instructors to an even larger ring of previously uninvolved, probably uninformed persons, thereby multiplying the size of the reform lobby. (It is a technique emulated several years later by Mary Keyserling in her inquiry under the auspices of and with volunteer help from the National Council of Jewish Women, into the quality of day-care services in local communities across the country. And a few years after that, Marian Wright Edelman's Children's Defense Fund organized Junior Leaguers to inquire into the circumstances under which children are jailed, confident that Junior League indignation would more likely result in reform than would indignant protests from social activists.)

By the time of the 1968 election, the school lunch reform movement was trifurcated. The federal budgeters sought redirection, the food service workers sought universality, and the hunger lobbyists sought universality as an ultimate objective while espousing expansion—not redirection—to more of the poor as an immediate objective. At the same time, other groups pinpointed deficiencies in both the structure and administration of the food stamp program initiated in the Kennedy-Johnson administration. Food and nutrition had become an important political question.

School lunch—like food stamps—benefited in two ways from the results of the 1968 election. First, Agriculture Department officials and poverty warriors who had served the Johnson administration, often defending the administration's food relief efforts whatever their private judgments, now became watchdogs and critics of programs they understood very well. (A case in point is Rodney E. Leonard who moved from a defensive posture as deputy assistant secretary of agriculture to an offensive posture as executive editor of the *Community Nutrition Institute Weekly Report*, an antihunger newsletter that focused particularly on deficiencies in U.S. Department of Agriculture programs and administration.) Second, in the fashion of a new administration, President Nixon's appointees searched for new policies and new ideas that might permit a distinctive Nixon stamp to appear or for which the new administration might claim appropriate credit. With food, nutrition, and hunger very much in the spotlight because of the combined impact of a television special on the subject, the publicity attendant on activities of a Senate subcommittee, the publication of a report on *Hunger, USA* by a so-called Citizens' Board of Inquiry (financed primarily, like the Committee on School Lunch Participation, by the Field Foundation), and the publication of the school lunch report, the fresh Republican administration could deny responsibility for the failure of earlier policy, and demonstrate its skill in putting things in order.

Just such a scenario unfolded in 1969—the first year of the new administration. Its supporters dominated House Education and Labor hearings on legislation to establish eligibility standards for free and reduced-cost lunches, to authorize advance financing for the program, and to require for the first time that states provide matching funds from state tax revenues, thus opening the way to a reduction of the "bite tax." These were major elements of the short-run program of the Committee on School Lunch Participation. By March 20 the bill had passed the House with little opposition. Early in May, President Nixon sent Congress a message on food assistance programs for the needy that included proposals for reform in the food stamp program and an expressed intention to call a White House Conference on Food and Nutrition. That message continued the emasculation of the Johnson approach to food programs with the disclosure of a plan to reorganize the administration of federal food programs, perhaps through the creation of a new Food and Nutrition Service with an exclusive concern in this area. Later in the year, Jean Mayer, professor of nutrition at Harvard, who was on record as a supporter of free food stamps and expanded day-care and school feeding programs, became the President's special consultant and chairman of the December 1969 conference.

Exactly the right combination of political forces had come together to effect the flowering of school lunch. The organized hunger lobby—including in the early 1970s both an efficient group of social altruists misleadingly named the Children's Foundation, self-described as the "only national anti-hunger organization in the country which is independent of government funds"—kept feeding programs under attention.[27] In addition, success in the battle against redirection spurred the Food Service Association to a more aggressive role as lobbyist for expansion. Congress had rejected redirection; some influential members were showing interest in expansion. Because the administration was new on the scene, it did not have to apologize for or deny past failures. The politic approach was to deplore its inheritance, and undertake to put things in order. It is no wonder, then, that school feeding was to grow as it did in the early 1970s.

### Is There a Case for Reform?

There can be no disagreement with the conclusion of federal budget officials that the enactment of five significant laws between 1970 and 1974 expanded school lunch and left it more costly and more complex a program than it had been at the beginning of that period.[28] Important legislation adopted in 1975 continued the trend. Not surprisingly, however, there is substantial disagreement over whether expansion, increased costs, and increased complexity point to the need for reform. The reformers fall into the old camps: expansion to achieve universal school feeding, on the one hand, and redirection to concentrate on the poor alone, on the other hand. But the most persuasive case is the one to be made for rejecting both reforms—the universal feeding and the redirection position—in favor of a school lunch policy based on the status quo.

Consider, first, the nature and consequences of five years of statutory change. Priority to needy children, including a minimum eligibility standard for free and reduced-price meals, and a maximum permissible price for the latter, was mandated in 1970. That act provided the opening wedge for the ensuing series of school lunch amendments raising minimum federal-reimbursement rates to the states for free and for reduced-price lunches, and for general cash-for-food assistance payments.

The average reimbursement for all lunches served moved upward from a statutory rate of 6 cents per meal in 1971 to 8 cents in 1972 to 10 cents in 1973, and finally to an indexed figure based on semiannual readings of

27. "The Children's Foundation Annual Report—Overview: 1974" (Oct. 31, 1974; processed), p. 43.

28. *The Budget of the United States Government, Fiscal Year 1976, Appendix,* p. 200.

the consumer price index of the cost of food away from home. By 1976 that rate had reached 12.5 cents. Similarly, the reimbursement rate in special cash assistance for free lunches—the section 11 program for which Senator Philip Hart had managed to secure a total of $2 million in 1965— was mandated at 40 cents per lunch in 1971, increased to 45 cents in 1973, and after indexing came to 56.75 cents by 1976, and reimbursement payments for reduced-price lunches were pegged just 10 cents below the free lunch rate. A 1974 statute provided that the national average value of the commodities donated to the program or the cash payments made in lieu of commodities should be not less than 10 cents per lunch; in 1976 it was 11 cents. Eligibility for free and reduced-price meals extended in 1976 to children whose family incomes exceeded poverty-level guidelines by 25 percent and 95 percent respectively.

What all of this meant was that on an average school day early in 1976, about 23 percent of children attending elementary and secondary schools were served a free or reduced-price lunch. Or, to put it differently, 39 percent of children participating in the school lunch program were served free or at a reduced price. The number of children provided such lunches increased by 3 million over the five-year period despite a declining school population. Moreover, school breakfasts—almost 85 percent of which were served free or at token charges to children—reached more than 1.5 million children in 1975 compared to under 800,000 in 1971. While gaps continue to exist—1,400 schools still had no food service facilities in 1975[29]—the special assistance program is a major element in the package of federal benefits available to poor families. A universal free-lunch program would also encounter problems in providing meals at schools without lunch facilities, and there is no reason to believe that it could more promptly overcome those difficulties than the present provision for nonfood assistance under which schools in low-income areas are supplied food service equipment.

The case for a universal free lunch must rest on some grounds other than its ability to provide lunch benefits to needy children not being served under existing programs. It is sometimes argued that it would eliminate real or imagined stigma associated with receiving a free or reduced-price lunch, sometimes that a balanced type A lunch is of superior nutritional value, sometimes that it offers economies of scale—the mar-

29. Agriculture—Environmental and Consumer Protection Appropriations for Fiscal Year 1975, Hearings before a Subcommittee of the Senate Committee on Appropriations, 93:2 (GPO, 1974), pt. 1, p. 1090.

ginal cost of a lunch declines significantly so that twice as many school children could be fed with a public investment much less than double the present public investment. None of these propositions is persuasive.

Stigma was one of the issues addressed by the comptroller general's 1973 report on progress and problems in achieving objectives of the school lunch program. To determine why about 1.5 million needy students attending participating schools did not eat free or reduced-price lunches, the General Accounting Office (GAO) identified 183 needy students at twenty schools and interviewed them or members of their families. "We were told," the GAO report says, "in 14 interviews that students did not want to take the school lunches free or at reduced prices because of their reluctance to be identified as needy."[30] Without drawing conclusions from these few observations, GAO also cited findings made in 1972 by Agriculture's own inspector general that confirmed administrative insensitivity to the problem of stigma in the implementation of the free and reduced-price program: "Some needy students had to work for their meals; some were required to use a medium of exchange, such as a voucher, which differed from that used by paying students; and some had to use identification cards which clearly indicated their status as free-lunch participants."[31] Although the data are fragmentary, they do serve to indicate that the issue is a real one.

But it is possible to neutralize the problem of stigmatizing poor children short of universalizing the benefit. The inspector general's report that the anonymity of students approved for special assistance lunches was protected in a substantial majority of the school districts audited suggests the remedy is to prohibit work-for-meals, distinctive identification cards, or the use of a separate medium of exchange. Such prohibitions are in effect and are effective in most jurisdictions. Further rigorous enforcement of the existing prohibition on discrimination against any child because of his inability to pay the full price is both possible and more rational than extending a free-lunch benefit to at least thirty million children without regard to need.

A different case is advanced by expansionists who see the universal free school lunch as the only way to provide that all children—without regard

30. Comptroller General of the United States, *Progress and Problems in Achieving Objectives of School Lunch Program* (June 29, 1973); reprinted in *National School Lunch Act*, Hearings before the General Subcommittee on Education of the House Committee on Education and Labor, 93:1 (GPO, 1973), p. 78.

31. Ibid., p. 79.

to income—have access to the food they need for good nutrition and good health. Senator Hubert Humphrey takes this position, noting that "health and nutrition experts from throughout this country have concluded, based upon scientific studies and surveys, that income alone is no guarantee of good child nutrition."[32] The argument is unassailable. Some of the middle income and the rich either do not like or do not know enough to buy what they need for good nutrition. But why should it be assumed that those same people either are willing to or are able to persuade their children dutifully to eat up the components of a type A nutritionally balanced lunch? Again, it is one thing to make federal reimbursement contingent on regulations that require school cafeterias to serve every purchaser every component of the lunch, and another thing to assume that what is served is consumed. One can lead a child to a type A lunch, but one cannot make him eat all of it. Public education is universal and free, yet everyone does not accept the free good over the private school option. Nor does every user accept all of the free education that is offered. Surely there is enough experience with the resistance shown by Americans to costless ways of improving their health to cast doubt on a strategy that insists on giving the middle class what it now can afford but chooses not to buy.

Finally, the universal-free-lunch case is sometimes couched in terms of economy of scale. The marginal cost of a type A lunch declines significantly as the number of lunches served increases. To provide such a lunch free for the half of the school-aged population not now using the program and to eliminate charges to present users would not result in a total bill twice the amount of present public and private expenditures. For only a billion dollars or so over current public costs, the argument runs, a universal-free-lunch program could be put in place. Before that argument can be persuasive, however, it must be shown why such a program should be put in place. Proponents have not yet coped with that more basic issue.

### Full Cost, No Cost, or Low Cost?

Veterans of the agency argue that the Office of Management and Budget (OMB) will sometimes propose fiscal restraint in a particular field far beyond OMB's real expectation of what can be accomplished. This strategy, it is said, anticipates a more satisfactory compromise than

32. *Congressional Record*, vol. 117, pt. 26 (1971), p. 33591.

might otherwise be possible with groups urging higher expenditures. That would be a logical—if speculative—explanation for the comprehensive block grant program the 1976 budget proposed to substitute for "the fragmented, overlapping, and administratively complex provisions of the Child Nutrition and School Lunch Acts." Under the administration's block grant proposal, nutrition subsidies were to be provided only to needy children. Politicians found it unappetizing. Months after the budget message, no sponsor had been found for what, in effect, was a bill to increase the daily price of type A lunches to middle-class children by twenty cents. Lyndon Johnson had discovered in 1966 that even then it was too late in the evolution of the lunch program to turn back to pricing lunches at actual cost, and to limiting the federal subsidy to the poor. Gerald Ford made the same discovery almost a decade later.

But the expansionists also overplayed their hand in 1975 as they moved to put a nationwide ceiling on the price of a type A lunch. As the strength of the present arrangement that couples a large benefit for the poor with a small benefit for all consistently has smothered efforts by budget-makers to redirect to the poor alone, so it also smothered efforts by the school food service community and some congressional liberals to edge toward the universal approach via a ceiling price. The first try at a ceiling in the House of Representatives put it at twenty-five cents. When that figure ran into serious trouble, proponents quickly fell back to thirty-five cents, reducing the cost of the proposal by half a billion dollars. But thirty-five cents could not be sustained either. "Congressmen do not need to have their children's lunches subsidized," one of them told the others. "Neither do corporation presidents, South American diplomats, and others who would be eligible under this bill."[33]

Supporters of the ceiling found themselves whipsawed. The objection on equity grounds came both from conservatives and from liberals like Thomas Ashley (Democrat of Ohio) who described himself as "wondering why it is that the taxpayers in Toledo who are earning $7,000 or $8,000 should be obliged to pay for the lunches of my children."[34] From the center, moderates like Albert Quie complained that "$521 million extra would have practically paid for the total authorization for aid for the handicapped this year."[35] Equally surprised by and unprepared for the outpouring of opposition from all sides, Education and Labor Committee leaders made all the wrong moves. Although Chairman Carl Perkins

33. *Congressional Record* (daily ed.), March 25, 1975, p. H 2296.
34. Ibid., p. H 2280.
35. Ibid., p. H 2285.

argued the desirability of steps to arrest an asserted decline in participation, his own statistics showed only that a 2.7 million drop in paying lunch participants was counterbalanced by an increase of 9 million free and reduced-price participants with some increase in total participation each year.[36] The reasonable response was that needy children had moved over from the paying side to the nonpaying side, that school populations had been declining, that à la carte service was increasingly available, and that taking these several factors together meant a fall-off in type A paying customers was to be expected. The response carried more than ordinary impact because it came from William Goodling (Republican of Pennsylvania), who was a former school superintendent. Nor was the cause helped by supporters like Lloyd Meeds (Democrat of Washington), who only embarrassed other liberals with the suggestion that it was time to do something nice for the middle class who are "footing the majority of the bills in this country, and they ought to be entitled to something which gives them and their children some benefit."[37] A succession of members recorded themselves as giving a higher priority to handicapped children, to older Americans, to nutrition programs for pregnant women, infants, and preschool children, and to sundry other causes than to an increase in the lunch subsidy.

Perkins's disposition to be secretive and to bypass open channels did not help the cause. The Ninety-fourth Congress had been in session only two months when the lunch ceiling was argued. The large group of new members, in particular, was taking pride in bringing a spirit of openness to House activities. Three committee chairmen suspected of autocratic behavior had been deposed by the Democratic caucus. While Perkins had an impeccable history as sponsor and supporter of liberal causes and as chairman of a committee that tended to be to the left of the House itself, he missed the signal in 1975 that called for open decisions, openly arrived at. The perfunctory attention given to the ceiling idea outraged committee members like Goodling and Quie:

We did not listen to children, we did not listen to principals of schools, we did not listen to teachers, we did not listen to guidance counselors. The only people we listened to were the food service people who were trying to promote their own product. I certainly do not fault them for that. I would wish we as Congressmen would do the same.[38]

36. Ibid., p. H 2280.
37. Ibid., p. H 2294.
38. Ibid., March 24, 1975, p. H 2235.

It was not a part of the bill that came out of the subcommittee. There was a quick hearing one morning in which some individuals came in and made a recommendation for a 25-cent limit on the lunch, and that was quickly adopted in the full committee. There was no deep consideration, no opportunity for witnesses who were in opposition to the 25-cent amendment to appear before the committee. That is all the consideration that the committee gave.[39]

Perkins proceeded to compound his error. With a twenty-five-cent cap clearly impossible to sustain, he decided to fall back to thirty-five cents hoping to capture those who objected to the original proposal as too costly. But he continued to misread the mood of the House where there was basic unease over the committee's quick acceptance of the ceiling without an opportunity for opposition witnesses to be heard. Changing the figure in a secret, late-night meeting from which Republican committee members were excluded neither calmed the unease over a procedure that John Anderson (Republican of Illinois) correctly called "cavalier and casual" nor blunted the opposition's substantive claim that the principle was wrong. The mix of procedural and substantive objections produced a lopsided vote (260–144) to strike the ceiling provision entirely. The effect of Perkins's bad judgment was to chill the expansionist movement for the indefinite future, to raise doubts about the strength of the American School Food Service Association, to boost the morale of Republicans in the House as they discovered that with a respectable case they could win, and to alert new Democratic members to be wary of the Education and Labor Committee. All in all, the precipitous decision to try for a school-lunch-price ceiling, to bring it to the floor without adequate preparation, and to change the proposed ceiling price in a private session combined bad politics with bad policy.

### Breakfast as a Reform Objective

There will be no wholesale expansion of school lunch via a universal free program or a nationwide ceiling price. Nor is it likely that the present subsidy for the middle class will be eliminated. Starting from those politically realistic premises, the Department of Agriculture, school food service workers, and members of Congress interested in child nutrition and school lunch might look to reduced-price meals and to the school breakfast program as mechanisms for shoring up their reputations.

39. Ibid., March 25, 1975, p. H 2298.

When created in the Child Nutrition Act of 1966, school breakfast was pinpointed to schools in poor areas and areas in which children must travel long distances to school. Although only 150,000 or so children were served by 1968, Secretary of Agriculture Orville Freeman termed school breakfast "a magnificent success."[40] In fact, for the first several years, it was little more than a token program. Participation did grow briskly after an amendment adopted in 1972 made the program available "in all schools which make application." By December 1974, over 1.75 million children participated, of whom 86 percent were served free or at a reduced price. In that respect, an early fear that the cost of the program would get out of hand because it would not be restricted to the poor turns out to be groundless. So does another expressed concern that breakfast would lead to supper, and then to a program to supply all meals to all people.[41]

Enlarging the breakfast program to reach more poor children is the reform now most likely to be accomplished and most to be desired. With about 5 million school-aged beneficiaries of aid to families with dependent children in any one month, and with a total of 1.5 million free or reduced-price breakfasts served early in 1975, it is clear that breakfast failed to reach 3.5 million children "certified" as poor. A reasonable test of eligibility should go beyond AFDC status. If reduced-price lunches are to be available to children in families with incomes 95 percent above the poverty level, logic suggests parallel eligibility for reduced-price breakfasts.

Heretofore, there has been a peculiar reticence to push the breakfast program stemming from a belief that breakfast should be a family affair. The American Parents Committee, for example, distinguishes between "the mother's primary responsibility to see to it that her school-child starts his day off well-clothed and well-fed" and the imperative need for schools to have lunch facilities available to all students.[42] A spokeswoman for the committee does acknowledge "actual need" as a reasonable criterion for school-breakfast participation, in the same breath, however, deploring fragmentation of the family unit. The legislator or bureaucrat reluctant to support a breakfast program can take satisfaction in saving the public money and shoring up the family unit all at once.

In recent years there has been a preoccupation with lunch rather than

40. "Secretary Freeman Details Domestic Food Aid Progress," U.S. Department of Agriculture press release USDA 326-68, Feb. 1, 1968 (processed).

41. Congressional Record, vol. 112, pt. 12 (1966), p. 15272.

42. Agriculture—Environmental and Consumer Protection Appropriations for Fiscal Year 1973, Hearings before a Subcommittee of the Senate Committee on Appropriations, 92:2 (GPO, 1972), pt. 2, p. 2345.

an explicit reluctance in the administration or in Congress to expand breakfast. Department of Agriculture officials have tended to argue that the breakfast program should remain secondary to lunch, "the basic meal to provide the major away-from-home supplementation of the diet for school-children."[43] Congressional interest in getting lunch participation increased has also obscured the breakfast program. Now, however, school lunch is reasonably stabilized. Brown-baggers—those who bring a sandwich—will not be bribed with a twenty-five-cent or thirty-five-cent ceiling on a type A lunch. Free lunches are reaching much of the population they should reach. The reformers should be seeking to achieve a comparable result for both reduced-price meals and for school breakfast. It is a timely and politically realistic goal.

43. *Nutrition and Human Needs—1972*, pt. 1: *School Breakfast Survey*, Hearings before the Senate Select Committee on Nutrition and Human Needs, 92:2 (GPO, 1972), p. 50.

# 9

# Child Health:
# Programs without Policy

Political accidents and back-door approaches rather than rational responses to rational proposals explain most federal actions on child health questions. One after another important child health measure has fallen into place without legislative consideration of child health as a discrete policy problem and without discussion of what the objectives of federal activity should be.

In the absence of a national strategy in child health, there are four separate streams of federal activity: a child health research institute within the National Institutes of Health; grants to the states for maternal and child health services; screening and treatment of welfare-eligible children; benefits to handicapped children. The separateness of the four streams and some incompatibility within each stream prevent them from achieving the momentum and impact that a more unified policy might engender. In the child health institute, a high-level determination to keep its research separate from the generality of policy questions concerning child health has meant that the institute has shunned a leadership role in the area. The maternal and child health program, traditionally aimed at rural areas and "all" children regardless of need, has come to focus on the health problems of children in urban ghettos as well—a not very comfortable union. In welfare medicine the federal-state partnership, casually mandated by an unknowing Congress, has displeased a substantial number of states and thus hindered the development of programs for medically indigent children. And the cause of handicapped children is weakened by the absence of a unified strategy among the disparate groups working—indeed even competing—in their behalf.

The basic program of federal formula grants to the states for maternal and child health—enacted first in 1921 and reenacted in 1935 in the Social Security Act—originated in part from the need of a newly created Children's Bureau to avoid the controversy that a focus on child labor would have engendered. The 1921 act drew its political strength from the ratification of the women's suffrage amendment a year before. In the early 1960s a National Institute of Child Health came as an add-on to balance proposals for medical care for the aged, and special project grants for services to poor children in urban areas came through the back door of a drive to combat mental retardation. The strength of that drive was another political accident—traceable to an assumption that a retarded sister would cause President Kennedy to have a special interest in the subject. Restructuring the Social Security Act in 1967, Congress wrote a Child Health Act that removed child health from Social Security's aid to dependent children title. The new act's principal purpose was to fuse grant programs for maternal and child health and for crippled children's services. Once more through the back door, what was called a conforming amendment mandated medical screening of all welfare-eligible children.

No administrative or legislative mechanism exists for bringing these several program elements within the purview of a single federal agency or of a single legislative committee in either the House or Senate. In 1975, responsibility for research and services in child health—not including the special case of child abuse—was distributed among four agencies in the Department of Health, Education, and Welfare: the National Institute of Child Health and Human Development, the Medical Services Administration, the Health Services Administration, and the Bureau of Education for the Handicapped. Congressional responsibility, no less diversified, involved subcommittees of the House Ways and Means and Senate Finance Committees, a House Commerce Committee Subcommittee on Public Health, three Senate Public Welfare Committee subcommittees on the Handicapped, on Health, and on Children and Youth, and a House Education and Labor Committee Subcommittee on Select Education. For all of the diffusion of responsibility that introduces the subject to an unusually large number of congressmen, neither a subcommittee nor any member takes a continuing and protective interest in child health.

When its focus is on those health issues that cut across class and race, child health usually gains a receptive ear from politicians—as in the mandating of the use of silver nitrate to protect infants against unnecessary blindness, or in the outreach program to locate and serve more crippled children. But modern preventive medicine has sharply limited the number of child health causes that derive strength from the democratic character of contagious ophthalmia or crippling disease. Lowering the

infant mortality rate—now at an all-time low of 16.5 per 1,000 live births—
and combating the incidence of mental retardation continue to be agreed
national goals over the long run, but immediate issues in child health
tend to be more divisive: for example, how and whether to provide routine
medical screening to all economically disadvantaged children no matter
what the costs relative to the benefits; how to resolve competition for help
among potential beneficiaries in a broad functional group like children
with a developmental disability; how to divide finite fiscal and professional
resources between services to well children and to children with irreversible
damage.

### Infant Mortality as "Safe" Cause

Long before the Social Security Act, child health provided the children's cause its beachhead at the national level. Although child labor also
agitated early reformers, infant mortality studies headed the statutory
list of nine charges given the Children's Bureau upon its creation in 1912.
When Julia Lathrop, the bureau's first chief, called together a little group
of advisers—Lillian Wald, Jane Addams, Florence Kelley, and Edward
Devine—to consider priorities, they confirmed that infant mortality should
be the bureau's starting point because the subject was of fundamental
importance and of popular interest, and it involved a real human need.[1]
Additional advice came to Lathrop to avoid controversy—in particular,
to steer clear of child labor for a time—and establish a reputation for scientific disinterest and factual accuracy.[2] Accordingly, the study of why
babies died became the bureau's first piece of work, "an entirely democratic inquiry, since the only basis for including any family within it was
the fact that a child had been born in the family during the selected year,
thus giving a picture not of a favorable or an unfavorable segment of the
community, but of the whole community."[3] The bureau's pursuit of factors leading to infant and maternal mortality "had repercussions far beyond the Bureau," Dorothy Bradbury has written. "They gave great
impetus to the drive for improved sanitary conditions in towns and cities

1. Dorothy E. Bradbury, *Five Decades of Action for Children: A History of the
Children's Bureau*, U.S. Department of Health, Education, and Welfare (1962), p. 6.
2. Walter Trattner, *Homer Folks: Pioneer in Social Welfare* (Columbia University
Press, 1968), p. 111.
3. Julia Lathrop, quoted in Bradbury, *Five Decades of Action*, pp. 6–7.

and for extending the pasteurizing of milk. They were used as an argument for minimum wage legislation and for widows' pensions."[4]

With the ratification in 1920 of the women's suffrage amendment, those early reports on infant and maternal mortality also had repercussions for the young agency itself. The reality of women voters combined with the interest taken by women's organizations in the bureau's work stimulated political responsiveness. Anxious to tie down the new voters, President Harding, in his first message to Congress, explicitly endorsed a maternal and child health bill and asked his party's congressional majority to pass it. Over vigorous medical association objections, Congress proceeded to enact one of the first federal grant-in-aid programs in the public health field. Proponents of the so-called Sheppard-Towner Act like Representative Alben Barkley (Democrat of Kentucky)—later senator, Senate majority leader, and vice president of the United States—related support to "startling facts" about infant mortality revealed by the investigations of the Children's Bureau.[5] Opponents characterized it as paternalistic, socialistic, and meddlesome. "It is now proposed," complained Senator James Reed, "to turn the control of the mothers of the land over to a few single ladies holding Government jobs at Washington."[6] The American Medical Association (AMA) found this plan of grants for the promotion of maternal and infant health and welfare to be "an imported socialistic scheme unsuited to our form of government."[7] At that, both the AMA and Senator Reed expressed judgments less harsh than one printed in the *Illinois Medical Journal* where the bill was called a "menace" and its sponsors termed "endocrine perverts" and "derailed menopausics."[8]

Despite the exaggerated fears of its critics, Sheppard-Towner managed to pass and to survive for eight years under Children's Bureau administration. States lacking maternal and infant hygiene divisions in their health departments established them as a condition for qualifying for federal funds. With Sheppard-Towner both the only federal children's program

4. Bradbury, *Five Decades of Action*, p. 9.

5. *Congressional Record*, vol. 61, pt. 5 (1921), p. 7933; reprinted in Robert H. Bremner, ed., *Children and Youth in America: A Documentary History* (Harvard University Press, 1971), vol. 2, pts. 7–8, p. 1012.

6. *Congressional Record*, vol. 61, pt. 9 (1921), p. 8765; reprinted in Bremner, *Children and Youth*, vol. 2, pts. 7–8, p. 1016.

7. *Journal of the American Medical Association*, vol. 78 (1922), p. 1709; reprinted in Bremner, *Children and Youth*, vol. 2, pts. 7–8, p. 1020.

8. *Illinois Medical Journal*, vol. 39 (1921), p. 143; reprinted in Bremner, *Children and Youth*, vol. 2, pts. 7–8, p. 1020.

and the only federal grant program in the children's field, Congress and the states as well as women's, religious, and medical groups came to associate child health with Children's Bureau administration. But that tie disturbed the doctor-dominated Public Health Service as well as many other doctors who considered Children's Bureau personnel to be laymen engaged in professional work.[9] Those forces, joined by Catholic church spokesmen, persuaded Congress to allow the act to expire in 1929.

No other federal agency took over the child health cause. Five years later, when Children's Bureau leaders were invited to propose the portion of the social security package assuring security for children, child health was still in their minds. Bureau recommendations eventuated in the four programs for children included in the Social Security Act: aid to dependent children (ADC), child welfare services, maternal and child health services, and crippled children's services. The bureau lost in the maneuvering for administrative control of the aid program but held the three services. The latter, unhappily for bureau prestige, were eclipsed before long in the competition with ADC for money and political attention.

Denied administrative responsibility for cash relief, the bureau could concentrate on maternal and child health services, in effect a revival of the Sheppard-Towner Act. "With consummate skill," Edwin Witte has written, the bureau's women worked out the program and overcame the opposition that had killed the Sheppard-Towner Act just a few years earlier. Catholic church objections anticipated by President Roosevelt never developed, a result Witte attributes to the "personal friendly relations" that Katharine Lenroot—named chief of the bureau in November 1934—had developed with Monsignor John O'Grady, longtime secretary of the National Conference of Catholic Charities and church spokesman in Washington.[10] The American Medical Association's earlier worries about maternal and child health services as an "imported socialistic scheme" gave way to more pressing new worries about health insurance. As for the Public Health Service, Lenroot struck a deal whereby the Children's Bureau pledged consultation with the doctors in administration of maternal and child health services. The program sailed through both committee sessions and floor consideration without a question being raised.

Between that political triumph of the mid-thirties and a series of politi-

9. Edwin E. Witte, The Development of the Social Security Act (University of Wisconsin Press, 1963), p. 165.
10. Ibid., pp. 166 ff.

cal disasters that overcame the bureau in the late sixties, it administered formula-based grants to state agencies for basic preventive maternal and child health services and for services to crippled children. Both programs, according to the 1935 statute, were to emphasize coverage in rural areas and in areas suffering from severe economic distress. Back in the business of combating infant mortality, the bureau doled out grants to all the states to pay for doctors, nurses, nutritionists, and medical social workers working in prenatal and child health clinics and in school health services. For fifteen years, maternal and child health apparently fulfilled its bureaucratic and programmatic missions: authorizations increased, appropriations nearly always equaled authorizations (although both were relatively paltry even by the standards of the time), statistics showed significant declines in infant mortality rates. While infant mortality in the United States had fallen at an annual rate of 2.5 percent during the first thirty years of the century, the annual rate of decline accelerated to 4.3 percent between 1935 and 1950.[11]

Yet there was less there than met the eye. Maternal and child health programs surely did no harm, but most of the accelerated decline in infant mortality must be credited to a combination of the discovery of sulfa drugs and an improvement in living standards. Bound by statute and by tradition to spread small amounts of federal money through all the states, the bureau's child health program attracted less and less interest. It fell into a category of routinely accepted activities of no particular consequence. After 1950, appropriations started to fall behind authorizations. Coincidentally—not even bureau people suggest cause and effect—the Children's Bureau was deprived of its most effective statistic in the child health field: the average annual decline in infant mortality slowed to only 1.1 percent in the fifteen years between 1950 and 1965.[12] During the latter part of that period, the civil rights revolution and the growth of the aid to dependent children welfare category focused public attention on child health problems of the urban poor. Child health, clothed as a poverty and race issue, was certified as too serious a social problem to be left to the Children's Bureau. But no new agency, whether the National Institute of Child Health, the Health Services Administration, the Social and Rehabilitation Service, or any other unit of HEW, has taken a leadership role in child health policy.

11. Victor Fuchs, *Who Shall Live* (Basic Books, 1974), p. 32.
12. Ibid., p. 33.

## The National Institute of Child Health

"As an important new step in a broader program for the improvement in family and child health and welfare services," President-elect John Kennedy was told by his Task Force on Health and Social Security, a national institute of child health should be established within the National Institutes of Health. "Such action would recognize the Administration's concern not only with the welfare of the aged, but with its children and youth," the seven-member group chaired by Wilbur Cohen reported.[13] The language is reminiscent of that urging the creation of the Children's Bureau fifty years earlier. For the old emphasis on infant mortality and child labor, Kennedy's advisers substituted the high incidence of mental disease, problems of juvenile delinquency, and "the burden on family and community resources for the care of the mentally retarded." All of these were said to attest to the need for a concentrated attack on problems of the development of the child. For Florence Kelley's interest at the turn of the century in an agency to make available and interpret the facts concerning "the physical, mental, and moral conditions and prospects of the children of the United States,"[14] Wilbur Cohen's task force substituted an assertion that "research into the physical, intellectual, and emotional growth of the child is at present severely handicapped by the absence of a central focus for research that exists in other fields."

The task force also urged an administrative reorganization that would have transferred the child health grant program from the Children's Bureau—an agency about which Wilbur Cohen had his doubts—to the Public Health Service, and transferred the child welfare services program from the bureau to the Social Security Administration. Deprogrammed, the bureau would then have been elevated in the hierarchy to the Office of the Secretary of Health, Education, and Welfare as a staff agency concerned with "all the problems of child life and the promotion of new programs to meet them."[15]

13. "Social Welfare Frontiers," in *New Frontiers of the Kennedy Administration: The Texts of the Task Force Reports Prepared for the President* (Washington: Public Affairs Press, 1961), p. 61. Other members of the task force were Dean A. Clark, James Dixon, Herman M. Somers, Robert E. Cooke, Joshua Lederberg, Elizabeth Wickenden.
14. Quoted in Bradbury, *Five Decades of Action*, p. 2.
15. *New Frontiers of the Kennedy Administration*, p. 63.

Wilbur Cohen became assistant secretary of HEW for legislation in the Kennedy subcabinet. Three weeks after the inauguration, President Kennedy's special message on health and hospital care went to the Congress. Particularly concerned with health care for the aged, the message adopted the Cohen task force's idea for balancing—however unevenly— the initiatives on behalf of the aged with a program for children, the National Institute of Child Health and Human Development (NICHD): "While meeting the health needs of the older groups in our population, we cannot neglect the needs of the young."[16] But the institute of the Kennedy message was not that envisaged by the task force. As Cohen and his colleagues—especially Dr. Robert Cooke, then professor of pediatrics at Johns Hopkins and principal sponsor of the idea for an institute of child health—had quickly discovered, the logic of the proposals for creating a child health institute and for restructuring and relocating the Children's Bureau was more attractive to the authors than to the leaders and friends of either the National Institutes of Health or of the Children's Bureau. In the fullness of time, Congress enacted legislation creating an institute with a human development focus instead of a targeted children's focus. And in the process, any underlying belief that the new institute would dislodge the Children's Bureau was also laid to rest.

National Institutes of Health Director James Shannon subsequently explained the basis for the NIH's unwillingness to accept Cohen's first formulation:

We felt there was very little in child health, as such, that could not be encompassed in the many programs of the other institutes, but we felt that if the Department was willing to take a broader look at the problems of child health, primarily in the context of development of the human being from birth through differentiation of species, then we felt it could cover an area in which new emphasis should be placed and where we could really put the best brains to work right away.[17]

Broadening the institute's focus beyond child health alone was easy. The White House offered only perfunctory resistance to adding human development to the institute's purpose.[18] The addition has made a difference

16. *Congressional Quarterly Almanac*, 1961, p. 871.

17. *Departments of Labor and Health, Education, and Welfare Appropriations for 1964*, Hearings before a Subcommitee of the House Committee on Appropriations, 88:1 (Government Printing Office, 1963), pt. 3, p. 306.

18. Interview with Elton Woolpert, formerly legislative assistant to surgeon general of the U.S. Public Health Service, April 2, 1974.

in at least two respects. First, it avoided putting an NIH imprimatur on pediatrics at a time of increasing professional skepticism over pediatrics as a specialized field of research—a contrary decision could have had a negative effect on the NIH's own professional standing. Second, the broader charge facilitated a shift away from child health per se in the distribution of research support over the years. From the beginning, and until the creation in 1974 of a separate Institute on Aging, about 11 percent of the NICHD's budget went to support research on aging. While child health support dropped from almost 80 percent to just half of the institute's research budget, population research grew from 10 percent to 38 percent.[19] Although the search for a safe and effective method of contraception might have been carried on without fanfare by researchers under the aegis of an institute of child health, such work could be considered an integral part of the job of an institute officially concerned with human development.

As the way was smoothed with the professional public health community, so was it also smoothed with the other group threatened by the tone of the Cohen task force report. Before the bill to create an institute got to the congressional hearings stage, an agreement had been reached with the Children's Bureau delineating the respective areas of interest of the bureau and the Public Health Service in child health research. Ultimately signed by the two parties, the agreement stipulated that Children's Bureau research would be directed toward program evaluation and improvement of maternal, child health, and crippled children's services, while Public Health research would be concerned with the development of new knowledge in the field of child health and human development. A representative of the Children's Bureau would serve as a member ex officio of the proposed institute's advisory council. Further to allay Children's Bureau fears and to forestall objections from friends of the bureau, the administration developed companion legislation "to strengthen and reinforce the present research activities and programs of the Children's Bureau."[20]

19. Labor-HEW Appropriations Subcommittee Chairman Daniel Flood (Democrat of Pennsylvania) recorded his distress about the distribution of research funds in *Departments of Labor and Health, Education, and Welfare Appropriations for 1975*, Hearings before a Subcommittee of the House Committee on Appropriations, 93:2 (GPO, 1974), pt. 4, p. 821.

20. *Child Health Institute, HEW—Additional Secretaries*, Hearings before a Subcommittee of the House Committee on Interstate and Foreign Commerce, 87:2 (GPO, 1962), p. 36.

## Tranquillity on the Campus

Not unlike a new academic department dedicated to the study of a fashionable, emerging field, the NICHD faced start-up and early-life problems. Because its subject is not one of the traditional fields of learning, its jurisdiction is not entirely clear. Because it has borrowed a little here and a little there from established departments, it is not entirely sure of its popularity among its peers. Because it knows that in order to survive it must act like a real department, it cannot agree to circumscribe or otherwise limit the research staff it selects. Nor can it allow any of the groups under study to control its priorities. For most of the first decade of its existence, the NICHD did very well on all counts. Its constituents were largely unorganized, or so splintered as to be unable to mount a challenge to the institute's decisions about research priorities, and those who paid the bills doubted their own ability to challenge the scholars. Aside from complaints about its failure to do more in aging—a problem resolved by the establishment of the Institute on Aging—life has been pacific for the NICHD since the sparring associated with its establishment.

Three major areas of child health research—mental retardation, growth and development, and perinatal biology and infant mortality—benefit from roughly equal support. Twelve Mental Retardation Research Centers established by the institute are concerned with retardation that is organic or physical in nature and also that which is the result of cultural deprivation, or other learning handicaps. The growth and development program focuses on the nutritional, social, and psychological needs of children and ways to insure optimal development despite social deprivation. The institute's perinatal biology and infant mortality research deal with problems of pregnancy (for mother and child), of prematurity, and of the newborn child.

Few congressmen will be recorded against research to combat birth defects, mental retardation, or premature births. To oppose child health research could suggest an indifference to sick children. Moreover, much of the NICHD's research is long term; results do not become available for years. Most of it is also hard to evaluate, certainly beyond the technical grasp of its legislative overseers. Taken together, all of this allows the institute to go on untroubled by any kind of legislative oversight or fiscal control other than an occasional comment at an appropriations hearing about the institute's leisurely pace, or a plea for greater emphasis on aging

("I was hoping . . . you fellows would come up with something so the next 20 years would be a little more beautiful,"[21] a sixty-eight-year-old New Jersey congressman once told NICHD leaders).

Recent congressional action seeming to indicate that the institute may be in for less tranquil years than those it has previously enjoyed actually poses no substantive threat. The decision in favor of an Institute on Aging is one case in point. Leading congressional supporters of the new institute like Senator Thomas Eagleton (Democrat of Missouri) simply saw it as a way of providing greater budgetary clout for research on aging without cutting the NICHD budget.[22] Carving a new unit out of the old portends no new congressional stance on the NICHD's freedom to fix its own research agenda.

A second case, potentially more troubling for the NICHD, involved the effort of a group concerned with the sudden infant death syndrome (SIDS) to persuade Congress to guide the institute's research priorities. Badly in need of issues, the Senate's Children and Youth Subcommittee took up the SIDS cause. The NICHD resisted. If parents whose children were victims of the syndrome could succeed, how many other groups concerned with one or another disease would be stimulated to comparable organization and action? The consequent battle and its resolution confirmed both the NICHD's desire and ability to be left alone and congressional unwillingness to get deeply involved in a child health issue.

### Caution at the Top

Coincident with but unrelated to the results of the battles over the Institute on Aging and over SIDS research priority, Gerald LaVeck, a mental retardation researcher, resigned as NICHD director after eight years. His successor, Dr. Norman Kretchmer, a Democrat surprised to be appointed in a Republican administration, chose not to disturb the existing style of the institute. Nor did Kretchmer—described by a close friend and professional colleague as "volatile, hyperactive"—reach for federal-level leadership of the children's cause despite an evident leadership vacuum. While recognizing that neither child development, child nutrition, nor other child health agencies with responsibility for any aspect of children's affairs gave promise of succeeding to the leadership role once

---

21. *Labor-HEW Appropriations for 1975*, Hearings, p. 868.
22. *Research in Aging and Nutrition Programs for the Elderly*, 1971, Hearings before the Subcommittee on Aging of the Senate Labor and Public Welfare Committee, 92:1 (GPO, 1971), p. 287.

exercised by the Children's Bureau, then briefly assumed by the Office of Child Development, Kretchmer quickly decided not to allow himself or his institute to be used as a leader. At the beginning of his tenure at the NICHD, Kretchmer spoke of his belief that the National Institute of Mental Health (NIMH) had overreached itself in moving beyond research into mental health services and in taking on a mental health policy leadership role.[23] The NIMH, according to the Kretchmer analysis, wound up cut off from power and with the loss of the separate identity essential to scholarly independence. Coordinated child development policy—an inevitable and reasonable goal for anyone taking on a leadership function to pursue—would assign a minor place to the NICHD, Kretchmer believes, because the NICHD function is less flashy than some other child development programs, certainly including child care. Accordingly, a fragmentation of child development activity throughout the federal structure is in the institute's best interests.

Kretchmer is clearly not indifferent to the children's cause. He is convinced of the importance of NICHD research and is fearful that the agency's work would be jeopardized by more aggressive leadership action. In the early days of the NICHD, its advisory council gave a good deal of time to discussing the scope and origin of children's problems in America, and possible approaches to their solution. Such grand issues no longer concern the institute. Its current self-image is of a modest, apolitical, professional agency. Asked about friends in Congress, an institute budget officer responded: "We don't really have anybody—unlike aging. Witness the fact that they now have their own institute."[24] And friends out of Congress, this respondent goes on, splintered into disparate groups concerned with mental retardation, perinatal biology, and sudden infant death syndrome, tend to compete against each other rather than coalesce on behalf of the NICHD. Left unsaid was that the establishment of the Institute on Aging did NICHD no harm whatever, and that the outcome of legislative action on SIDS makes it possible for the NICHD to command its own destiny, exactly what it has wished to accomplish.

### The Case of Crib Death Legislation

Sudden infant death syndrome—sometimes called crib death—kills up to ten thousand babies a year. The leading cause of death among children from one month to twelve months old in the United States, the

23. Interview, April 30, 1974.
24. Interview, Anne Osborne Summers, May 16, 1975.

syndrome appears without warning. An apparently healthy child dies in his sleep without giving any sign of trouble. No one knows the child had the syndrome until after he has died. Hiding behind recent legislation dealing with this tragic phenomenon are disagreements between the Senate Subcommittee on Children and Youth and the NICHD, between the Senate subcommittee and the House Subcommittee on Public Health and the Environment, and even between groups of SIDS parents.

A handful of letters of complaint first provoked interest in the sudden death syndrome around the time of the veto of the children's subcommittee's child development bill. Apparently sent to Senator Edward Kennedy's health subcommittee and then redirected to the less-busy children and youth group, these charges by parents of victims that the NICHD was unresponsive to inquiries about the syndrome led Kennedy and Walter Mondale to ask HEW Secretary Elliot Richardson for a report. An NICHD response that forty-two projects and $1.8 million of research "relevant to SIDS" were being supported that year brought a complainant's rebuttal challenging the institute's account as misleading, and charging that the institute had shirked its responsibilities on SIDS.[25]

Ensuing activity should cheer writers of letters to Congress. For all practical purposes Kennedy withdrew, but Mondale, at a hearing, challenged the NICHD's style: "I get the impression that basically the role of NICHD with respect to research applications is to wait for the applications to come in."[26] And again, "Can't the NICHD encourage interest in this field by its funding policies, by soliciting responsive research activities, by engaging the interest of the top medical schools?"[27] Using the hearing as a forum, two organizations founded by parents of SIDS victims underscored Mondale's complaints. One, the International Guild for Infant Survival, adopted a generally aggressive—even abrasive—stance against the NICHD, scorning the procedure for peer review of grant applications as likely to produce standard techniques where bizarre or nonconformist approaches might be preferred.[28] The guild's style weakened the strength of its case. But the rival National Foundation for Sudden Infant Death knew better how to make an impact, perhaps because Dr. Abraham

25. The correspondence is reproduced without comment in *Rights of Children*, 1972, Hearing before the Subcommittee on Children and Youth of the Senate Committee on Labor and Public Welfare, 92:2 (GPO, 1972), pt. 1, pp. 91–103.
26. Ibid., p. 11.
27. Ibid., p. 25.
28. Ibid., p. 74.

Bergman, its president, had served as a health policy adviser to Senator Warren Magnuson (Democrat of Washington), the influential chairman of the Senate's Labor-HEW Appropriations Subcommittee. Bergman, a Seattle pediatrician and political activist, took the line that the NICHD should assume an active role in soliciting crib death research proposals:

When it was known that there were not enough qualified investigators working in the infant death field, active efforts to solicit them should have been made. The Institute should have taken the initiative in contracting for scientific work that needed to be done instead of passively waiting for grant applications to come in.[29]

By June 1972, Mondale seemed to be scoring as the Senate passed his imprecise resolution directing the institute to make SIDS research one of its top priorities. That same resolution also directed HEW to distribute educational and counseling literature on SIDS and to work on improved statistical and autopsy procedures. The House took no action, but, a year later, proposals authorizing grants and contracts for SIDS research centers, information services, counseling, and training appeared in both chambers, giving the NICHD and the HEW administration a specific proposal to which to react. They did, claiming in classic bureaucratic fashion both that the bill was unnecessary and that the agency was "already engaged in an aggressive effort to understand and remedy the problem of SIDS."[30] Beware, HEW spokesmen said to the Congress, of intruding on the independence of researchers. Trust the experts:

What we are trying to avoid is tying the hands of the researchers into one specific thing while there are some attractive opportunities here that today don't look related but in history will be related. We are not avoiding an ability to solve the problem, but developing a mechanism that will let us best solve it. I think this is what we are testifying against in this bill, not against finding an answer to SIDS.[31]

The NICHD's claims about its support of research related to SIDS have produced disagreement between congressional committees and the NICHD. While the agency claimed to be spending $4.1 million on SIDS

29. Ibid., p. 37. A year later Bergman concluded that as a result of the 1972 Senate hearings, "there has been a decided improvement." Sudden Infant Death Syndrome, 1973, Joint Hearings before the Subcommittees on Health and on Children and Youth of the Senate Labor and Public Welfare Committee, 93:1 (GPO, 1973), p. 63.

30. Sudden Infant Death Syndrome, Hearing before the Subcommittee on Public Health and Environment of the House Committee on Interstate and Foreign Commerce, 93:1 (GPO, 1973), p. 12.

31. Ibid., p. 35.

research, it pinpointed only $600,000 in research grants and contracts for studies specifically concerned with SIDS. Using the $600,000 figure, the Senate committee then reported itself "disappointed and not satisfied with the magnitude and the scope of the SIDS program administered by DHEW."[32]

Comparable differences obtain over whether the NICHD is encouraging researchers to work on SIDS. The institute has pointed to the twenty-one grant applications it received for SIDS work in 1973, compared to thirteen in the previous nine years, an effect it attributes to its research workshops.[33] Yet some congressmen seized on the gap between twenty-one applications and eleven grants as evidence that rather than encouraging SIDS research, the institute turns down grant applications.

Superficially, Congress rejected the proposition that it should stay out of the NICHD's domain. Legislatively, it accepted the argument. So, Representative Paul Rogers spoke for his House committee: "I'm not sure we agree with those judgments" that NICHD makes on what diseases to study. "If you have people concentrating specifically on this disease, we think you will have a better chance of finding the answer."[34] The subcommittee, despite that judgment, proceeded to report and the House to pass in January 1974 a weak bill reflecting lack of interest in SIDS research. It provided for a public information program, for grants and contracts for the collection of information on the causes of SIDS, and for counseling of parents. The three-year authorization was $6 million. Research was not mentioned. A month earlier, the Senate had adopted a hard-line measure that designated the NICHD to carry out SIDS research and authorized $24 million over three years for research. An additional $12 million was authorized over the three years for grants for regional centers for SIDS counseling, information, educational, and statistical programs and for grants for developing and disseminating public information about SIDS. An annual report on the administration of the act was required.

Differences between the bills were reconciled by the staffs of the two committees, a procedure used when a bill is noncontroversial, or when there would likely be difficulty assembling a quorum of conferees from one chamber and sponsors in the second chamber are anxious for a bill. In this case, House members were understood to be not interested in

32. *Sudden Infant Death Syndrome Act of 1973*, S. Rept. 93-606, 93:1 (1973), p. 8.
33. *Sudden Infant Death Syndrome*, Hearing, p. 31.
34. Ibid., pp. 35 and 37.

proliferating funds for specific disease categories and so might not have attended a conference. The compromise designates the NICHD to carry out SIDS research, but earmarks no money authorization for research. Instead, to satisfy the Senate Subcommittee on Children and Youth that research would be done, the staff added a provision for detailed annual reports on grant and contract applications. The secretary of HEW is required to send to the appropriations committees a special estimate of the budget amount requested for SIDS research each year. The three-year authorization—close to the House figure at only $9 million—covers information collection and counseling activities as it did in the House bill. The Senate's reference to the establishment of centers was dropped to avoid any implication that construction of new facilities was intended.

For his efforts on SIDS, Mondale received a letter from the Guild for Infant Survival accusing him of "selling out." The NICHD goes on about its business.

### Early Screening

Both congressional approval in 1967 and subsequent delays in implementation of a program of early and periodic screening, diagnosis, and treatment (EPSDT) of all medicaid-eligible children epitomize back-door policymaking. President Johnson's 1967 message on welfare of children included a child health section that recommended "legislation to expand the timely examination and treatment" of additional children under the crippled children's program.[35] The President's separate request for added medicaid funds including increased money for medical care of needy children stemmed from his stated expectation that twenty-three additional states would be joining the medicaid program. The administration's draft bill amending the Social Security Act provided for EPSDT effective July 1, 1969, for individuals under the age of twenty-one who were eligible for medicaid. Whether by design or by chance, however, the accompanying analysis and explanation of provisions included no estimate of costs of EPSDT for children. It did tie a $15 million increase in the authorization for crippled children's services to a proposed periodic screening and diagnosis requirement in that program. No hook-up between screening and medicaid appears in the message. Taken all in all, there was little reason

35. February 8, 1967 Message on Children and Youth, *Congressional Quarterly Almanac*, 1967, p. 56-A.

for EPSDT to attract more than casual congressional attention, and it did not.

Earlier identification of crippled children and a more extensive use of the old program of services to crippled children did get explicit attention from Congress in 1967—to the limited extent that Congress dealt with any aspect of this issue explicitly. Senate Majority Leader Mike Mansfield characterized the requirement for early identification as mandating states "to work harder to find children with handicapping conditions."[36] A formal summary of the legislation made available to both House and Senate subsumed the provision under the heading of "additional requirements on the states under the federal grant program." Following specific reference to the new requirement for states to provide for early identification and treatment of crippled children, "Title XIX [Medicaid]," the summary goes on, "is amended to conform to this requirement."[37] Congressional discussions of the conference report included no mention of the conforming amendment. No mention was made, it is reasonable to conclude, because there could not have been half a dozen members of Congress aware of the importance of the early and periodic screening, diagnosis, and treatment provision—or even of its existence.

Anne-Marie Foltz, its most careful student, describes EPSDT as "ambiguous federal policy."[38] Its origins have been traced by Foltz to a program analysis memorandum prepared in the Office of the Secretary of HEW in 1966. Of three possible programs for screening and treating poor children considered in that analysis, the most extensive would have served five million children—newborns and children aged one, five, and nine years living in health-depressed areas—at an estimated cost of $150 million. Less expensive alternatives would have served only newborn children or only premature infants at costs of $30 million and $5.3 million, respectively. "This was the first and last time a federal document put a specific price tag on a specific nationwide screening or preventive care program for specified child populations," Foltz has written. Tracing the subsequent legislative history, she concludes that "during its eight-month legislative history, EPSDT's details were scarcely touched on. The scope of screen-

---

36. *Congressional Record*, vol. 113, pt. 27 (1967), p. 36925.
37. Ibid., p. 36313.
38. "The Development of Ambiguous Federal Policy: Early and Periodic Screening, Diagnosis and Treatment (EPSDT)," *Health and Society* (Milbank Memorial Fund Quarterly), Winter 1975, pp. 35–61. See also John K. Iglehart, "Health Report," *National Journal Reports*, June 29, 1974, pp. 969 ff.

ing and the eligible population were hardly mentioned."[39] The Department of Health, Education, and Welfare was left to write regulations and guidelines for a program barely considered in congressional hearings, and never negotiated out with either the interest groups involved or the states responsible for implementation and for a significant part of the costs.

The program involves child health appraisal on a wholesale basis. In this case, the "wholesale" aspect refers to the universe of medicaid-eligible children. Many of the issues that had to be resolved in order to put EPSDT in place might have been anticipated, however, had there been explicit attention to other kinds of efforts to accomplish wholesale child health appraisal. One example is the universe of school-aged children. To be sure, there are important differences between screening school-aged children and screening all medically indigent children of any age. School-children are captive subjects who, unlike at least the preschool component of the EPSDT clientele, can easily be found. On the other hand, all medicaid-eligible children, unlike all schoolchildren, would seem to be in special jeopardy and thus represent a more appealing collectivity. These differences do not diminish the pertinence of some troublesome questions long evident in school health appraisals that might have been aired: who shall perform the appraisal, how often shall it be performed, what tests shall be included, who shall provide follow-up services, are the benefits of wholesale child health appraisal greater than the costs?

Rather than highlighting the importance of these routine questions, and lacking either an agreed plan or alternate plans to deal with them, high-level HEW program leaders chose to take advantage of a perceived opportunity to legislate good intentions. They used—and Congress approved—a big bill concerned principally with important changes in social insurance and with cash assistance as a back-door entry way for an undeveloped idea.

The subsequent history of EPSDT must be read against this background: an innovation of unknown complexity and cost, without a congressional sponsor, buried in a massive bill not principally concerned either with children or with health, and scheduled by one administration to be implemented by its unknown successor. The sponsors of EPSDT in HEW clearly believed this strategy best suited to result in legislation benefiting the child health cause. Since the legislative achievement, actual screening and treatment of children has come hard. The program is char-

39. Foltz, "The Development of Ambiguous Federal Policy," pp. 49 ff.

acterized principally by the search for an accommodation among a few congressmen who know that EPSDT is law, a dying National Welfare Rights Organization—understandably outraged over an apparent decision by HEW to flout the law, yet happy to have a cause with wide appeal— and several groups of troubled bureaucrats within HEW. Among the latter, one group, disposed to respond to pressure from federal budget planners and from state governments, espoused a narrow approach that would minimize costs; another group, believing their mandate is to use the law to "do good things for kids," reached for ways to accomplish that goal.

No congressman's baby, EPSDT had no congressman to cherish it and nurture it during gestation. While the social security amendments approved by President Johnson in January 1968 anticipated implementation of EPSDT by July 1969, the act also tied implementation to HEW regulations. Thus, of two preconditions, one—the coming of July 1, 1969— could not be affected by bureaucratic behavior. Writing and issuing the regulations was another matter. Nothing could happen without first resolving understandable uncertainty over whether these regulations should be developed by the Maternal and Child Health Service (MCHS), which claimed specialized experience with the crippled children's program, or by the Medical Services Administration (MSA), the Social and Rehabilitation Service's unit responsible for medicaid, or perhaps even by the Children's Bureau, which was still interested in child health, its first love. In the summer of 1968, the job went to the MSA with the MCHS serving as consultant; the Children's Bureau was left without a role.

The MSA had never drafted regulations before, but its inexperience is less significant as an explanation of subsequent delay than is the American electoral cycle. If proposed regulations had been written by October 1— an extraordinary accomplishment, even for an experienced group dealing with a far simpler problem—publication in the *Federal Register* and the required thirty days for comment would have brought the calendar up to the 1968 election. It is fanciful to speculate over whether HEW Secretary Wilbur Cohen would have promulgated final regulations over state protests before leaving office in January 1969. In fact, the option was not available to him, either because the job was too complicated to be rushed or because MSA bureaucrats also knew that there was an election in November 1968, or both. Even as the MSA began its job, the medicaid program itself was under attack in the Congress with Senator Russell Long (Democrat of Louisiana), chairman of the Finance Committee, pushing efforts to cut back on federal matching and promising to renew those efforts the following year. After the November election, one of President-elect Nixon's task forces warned him that any medicaid change that would "exclude people already receiving benefits" or would "shift program costs to already overburdened state and local governments" would pose a major problem to the new administration.[40] The EPSDT activity, of course, would further overburden state and local governments, even under the existing federal-state cost-sharing formula, by adding significantly to the total number of services mandated for medicaid beneficiaries.

Had the EPSDT program been nursed through Congress by even a back-bench member who tied his name to it, an occasional inquiry to HEW could have been expected during the early period of the MSA's efforts, with much more frequent and intense questioning after July 1, 1969. No such pressures on the MSA and HEW were applied. The pressures that eventually led to completion of the guidelines were internally generated. The department now views the time between 1968 and 1971 as an "embarrassingly long period," but it is not clear just when embarrassment became a factor in moving things along.

Without congressional or judicial pressure to push it along, the Social and Rehabilitation Service still managed to send HEW Secretary Elliot Richardson a draft set of regulations on October 30, 1970. With his approval, they were published early in December.[41] Although the tentative regulations allowed for a delay in providing EPSDT services to children over six until July 1973, state protests over likely costs still rolled in. The secretary agonized. Neither the proposed regulations nor a revised version appeared in final form. And for seven months thereafter, apparently the only messages from the Hill urging the work along came from Senator Abraham Ribicoff, the former HEW secretary; but even Ribicoff, who tended to spread himself over many social policy issues, did not press hard. Some members may have restrained themselves, knowing that in the first half of 1971 the Nixon HEW and Management and Budget staffs were trying to relate EPSDT to the administration's plan for a limited health insurance program, and believing that a reasonable time should be allowed for that effort. Others, however, were hearing from their state capitols that HEW should be restrained lest the financial burden on the states be

40. "Report of the Pre-Inaugural Task Force on Public Welfare" ([1968]; processed), p. 9.

41. *Federal Register*, Dec. 11, 1970, pp. 18878–89.

intolerable. In the meantime, HEW was getting a similar message about federal costs from the Office of Management and Budget. Estimates of how much the proposed regulations would cost ranged wildly, from $25 million to an estimate of $900 million by MSA Administrator Howard Newman.[42]

A New York City congressman, William F. Ryan, finally wrote Richardson on August 18, 1971, that he found "this dilatory action extremely distressing" because "it appears to contravene the intent of Congress" and because delay "means the continued lack of adequate medical services to the more than 6 million children which your Department's own press release designates as the eligible group."[43] A month later, an article in the *Washington Star* mentioned the Ryan inquiry, reviewed the HEW December 1970 draft regulations and the department's accompanying press release, and characterized HEW's announced plans as "sham."[44] Five days after that unwanted newspaper publicity, Richardson responded to Ryan's letter, expressing "concern" for the program and telling Ryan that he had signed regulations which would be published "very shortly."[45]

But, in the meantime, a skeptical National Welfare Rights Organization readied a suit to compel the secretary to implement the law.[46] Nor was Richardson, already having trouble over the child development bill, and with EPSDT regulations still awaiting OMB clearance, helped by a *Washington Post* editorial on EPSDT that found the "alibis and stalls" to reveal "a bleak record of federal indifference to the poor and to the basic logic of preventive medicine."[47] For the second time within two months, action on the regulations followed an unfavorable account in the Washington press: Richardson dislodged the final EPSDT regulations—requiring only treatment services within a state's medicaid plan plus treatment for visual, hearing, and dental care—on November 9, 1971, to become effective three months later for children under six, and by July 1, 1973, for older children.[48]

42. Nick Kotz, "Poor Children Await Medical Care," *Washington Post*, Oct. 24, 1971.

43. *Congressional Record* (daily ed.), Sept. 16, 1971, p. H 8566.

44. Robert Walters, "What We Really Need Is Action," *Washington Star*, Sept. 16, 1971.

45. *Congressional Record* (daily ed.), Nov. 2, 1971, p. H 10247.

46. *New York Times*, Oct. 24, 1971.

47. November 2, 1971. The editorial followed Kotz's "Poor Children Await Medical Care."

48. *Federal Register*, Nov. 9, 1971, pp. 21409–10.

All the administrative indecision over regulations can at least be rationalized if not justified by a conjunction of circumstances: statutory ambiguity, an electoral calendar that brought a new administration, and state reluctance to accept the costs of congressional action. But the only rationalization for the absence of a challenge by Congress is the possibility that Congress had not understood what it had legislated in the first place. That explanation gained credence with the Senate Finance Committee's vote in March 1972, a month after the legal (but not actual) effective date of the regulations, to postpone the requirement for services to children over six by two years and to free states from the requirement in the regulations that visual, hearing, and dental treatment be provided for defects discovered in the screening process.[49] On the effective date of the regulations, only nine states were known to have operating programs; just fifteen states had submitted plan amendments indicating compliance. A little while later, Secretary Richardson acknowledged that the department lacked an inventory of states' efforts to assure that all eligible children were receiving the benefits of the program.[50] But the Finance Committee's approach changed before it actually reported a bill in September 1972. Rather than postponing and weakening requirements for EPSDT, the committee reiterated the 1973 target date for putting EPSDT in place for older children, and proposed a penalty on delinquent states. Only a perfunctory explanation of the penalty appeared in the committee report. Without discussion in either Senate or House, a provision of the Social Security Amendments of 1972 legislated the unthinkable in federal-state relations: effective July 1974, HEW "shall" reduce by 1 percent the federal share of AFDC to any state failing to implement EPSDT.

It quickly became an open secret that for some states the 1 percent penalty arrangement would constitute a cheap "buy-out" rather than a compulsion to act. Over a seven-month period, only five state agencies, eight organizations, and one congressional delegation responded to tentative penalty provision regulations. After Richardson's assurance to Senator Mondale early in 1972 that "we will do our best to see that it is effectively implemented by the States,"[51] and the passage of the penalty clause later that year, EPSDT again disappeared from congressional consciousness.

Richardson moved out of HEW in January 1973, and Caspar Wein-

49. *Congressional Record* (daily ed.), March 30, 1972, p. S 5240.
50. Letter from Elliot L. Richardson to Senator Walter F. Mondale, March 23, 1972.
51. Ibid.

berger—termed by Senator Lee Metcalf (Democrat of Montana) "chief architect of impoundment" as director of OMB[52]—moved in. Weinberger claims that he established EPSDT as "the major objective for the Medicaid program" after he became secretary.[53] It could not have been immediately after because a year and a half later, Senator Ribicoff again pressed the case. His June 1974 inquiry to Weinberger—written while the secretary was still sitting on penalty regulations proposed the previous December—was followed by an August letter to the chairman of the Senate's Labor-HEW Appropriations Subcommittee complaining that fewer than 10 percent of the thirteen million eligible children had received screening services. "Despite the rhetoric of HEW spokesmen," Ribicoff wrote, "there is little evidence that the Department has placed more than token staff resources behind that effort."[54] If the congressional wind stayed mild, harsher blasts came with increasing frequency from new directions: HEW's own regional directors pushed vigorously for compliance at a high-level management meeting on March 28; by that time, at least eleven law suits had been filed against individual states by public-interest law firms and state welfare rights organizations; in June, a comprehensive account of HEW's troubles with EPSDT—partly based on material obviously leaked by department personnel—appeared in National Journal Reports, then reappeared, predictably, several times in the Congressional Record;[55] a draft report of a General Accounting Office investigation of EPSDT came to Weinberger on July 11.[56]

The department's interest in discharging its responsibilities accelerated. (Later, Weinberger would acknowledge that "Considering that the law requiring it was enacted in 1967, it is certainly true that the present effort is long overdue."[57]) Weinberger issued final regulations on August 2, 1974, implementing the penalty provision for delinquent states, then promptly convened a series of conferences with state and HEW regional staff to emphasize the department's seriousness of purpose. As John

52. Congressional Record (daily ed.), Feb. 8, 1973, p. S 2486.
53. "A Communication from Caspar Weinberger," Washington Post, Feb. 24, 1975.
54. Letter from Ribicoff to Senator Warren Magnuson, Aug. 1, 1974.
55. Iglehart, "Health Report"; and Congressional Record (daily ed.), July 16, 1974, p. S 12575, and July 18, 1974, p. S 12872.
56. Comptroller General of the United States, Improvements Needed to Speed Implementation of Medicaid's Early and Periodic Screening, Diagnosis, and Treatment Program (Jan. 9, 1975); hereafter cited as GAO Report.
57. "A Communication from Caspar Weinberger," Washington Post, Feb. 24, 1975.

Young, HEW's comptroller, explained it in a memorandum suggesting stepped-up effort by the department, "push has come to shove, as far as the financial penalty is concerned."[58] And Weinberger himself said to the state managers that while not eager to penalize states, "we will apply the penalty where it is warranted."[59] The GAO report, based on data from eight states as of June 30, 1973, but issued in January 1975, led to another round of criticism of HEW's performance even as the high-level attempt to implement EPSDT progressed. Insisting that intensive efforts had been under way since August 1973 to screen and treat medical problems of poor children, Weinberger called the program "close to my heart" and "one of my highest priorities." It took the penalty provision, he explained, to generate real movement in states reluctant to pursue EPSDT.[60]

With the secretary privately and publicly committed, there could be no further backing away. For at least seven states, the EPSDT drama subsequently played itself out. In mid-1975, Weinberger, by then a lame-duck secretary, ordered the federal penalty invoked against Hawaii, Indiana, Minnesota, Montana, New Mexico, North Dakota, and Pennsylvania. Six other states were still under study. Not places with a history of repressing welfare, those penalized include several states that provide among the most generous AFDC payments in the nation. Pennsylvania's case is as interesting as any because it was already threatened by a judicially imposed penalty over EPSDT. The Pennsylvania Welfare Rights Organization (PWRO) had filed suit against the state in February 1973 after PWRO counsel became suspicious about whether the state's expressed good intentions would ever become actual policy.[61] When a judicial order issued in September 1973 setting up a schedule for action went unfulfilled and a contempt order seemed imminent, Pennsylvania's welfare commissioner and the PWRO agreed in March 1974 on a consent decree obligating the state, beginning two years later, to pay eligible but unserved recipients 133 percent of the cost of a screening. With that additional problem only eight months in the future, Pennsylvania had not come far enough along to avoid the HEW penalty in June 1975.

Indiana officials had been enjoined in March 1974 from continuing

58. Iglehart, "Health Report," p. 973.

59. *Washington Post*, Aug. 30, 1974; and *GAO Report*, p. 44.

60. "A Communication from Caspar Weinberger," *Washington Post*, Feb. 24, 1975.

61. Eric Peterson, "Legal Challenges to Bureaucratic Discretion: The Influence of Lawsuits on the Implementation of EPSDT," Yale Health Policy Project, working paper no. 27 (April 1975; processed), pp. 27 ff.

to administer their program in violation of the statute and regulations. That order coupled with a federal appellate decision in October made it especially hard to overlook the extent to which Indiana was out of compliance on EPSDT. The district court found that there was neither evidence of a comprehensive program, "nor even any semblance of any screening program however minimal."[62] Sustaining the lower court, the circuit court of appeals ruled that injunctive relief was appropriate, that the sole remedy was not merely the reduction of payments to the state; the court also passed unflattering judgment on the Indiana program: "Indiana's somewhat casual approach to EPSDT hardly conforms to the aggressive search for early detection of child health problems envisaged by Congress. . . . By the time an Indiana child is brought for treatment it may too often be on a stretcher."[63]

The obvious lesson is that providing health services to poor children is too complex, too expensive, and too consequential a matter to be legislated without a plan. Neither the federal carrot nor the federal stick accomplishes the federal objective. In view of the history of federal-state grant relationships and disputes over noncompliance, even the penalty already imposed is likely ultimately to be rescinded. And rescinded or not, neither the administrative nor the judicial penalty is desirable. The federal goal of screening and treatment will not be accomplished by $45 payments to whatever limited number of unscreened children can be located and for whom claims can be pursued, or by withholding money used to provide essential relief payments to families with dependent children, or by holding state officials in contempt of court.

Beyond the irrelevance of possible penalties to the purpose of the legislation, a more basic issue should be confronted. The EPSDT program has now become an enforcement challenge, a test of relative determination, not a cooperative effort to accomplish an agreed objective. Suppose the resisting states have a persuasive substantive case, that is, that this arrangement for wholesale screening of children is more costly than it is beneficial. "EPSDT did not become so politically salient as to attract substantial attention from elected political leaders, either in the formulation of

62. *Bond* v. *Stanton*, memorandum opinion (U.S. District Court for Northern Indiana, March 22, 1974); quoted in Peterson, "Legal Challenges to Bureaucratic Discretion," p. 53.

63. *Stanton* v. *Bond*, 504 F.2d 1246 (Oct. 30, 1974); for a detailed account of another state's implementation problems, see Anne-Marie Foltz and Donna Brown, "Child Health Policy: The Case of EPSDT in Connecticut," Yale Health Policy Project, working paper no. 23-1 (November 1974; processed).

policy or its implementation," Eric Peterson has written.[64] But Peterson understates the issue. As long as medical assistance for the poor remains part of the social security program, the fraction of the $1 billion per month medicaid program targeted to children will command relatively little attention. But there should be some way to learn whether reluctant states after seven or eight years of involvement are right, and the HEW leadership in 1967 was wrong.[65]

## Project Grants

The oldest and still most consequential of federal child health activities is the maternal and child health grant-in-aid. Enacted first in 1921 as a way to help reduce high rates of infant mortality, reenacted in the Social Security Act with allocations according to formula and with insufficient regard to geographic variations in the infant mortality rate, the program was modernized in the 1960s by the inclusion of modest categorical grants for projects in low-income areas. The projects get good marks from all evaluators. Yet, these are little programs that could get lost in big departments.

Child health, the title of the Social Security Act least relevant to its principal purpose, gets comparatively little legislative attention. Internally logical in providing social insurance as protection against income loss due to old age, disability, or death, and in providing public assistance protection where insurance is inadequate or inapplicable, the act can reasonably accommodate medical care for the aged (medicare) and medical assistance for the indigent (medicaid) as in-kind benefits intimately related to income security. No comparable case can be made for federal grants to help states extend and improve maternity clinics, classes for expectant parents, well-child clinics for health supervision of babies and children, school health examinations and screening tests, and similar services for mothers and children; for grants to assist in diagnosing and caring for children with handicaps requiring orthopedic or plastic treatment, and

64. "Legal Challenges to Bureaucratic Discretion," pp. 3 ff.

65. For the delineation of "a number of unanswered questions (including those about delivery, yields, costs and payoffs, among others)," and an agenda for research into several significant areas of uncertainty about screening services, see Kathryne Bernick, "Issues in Pediatric Screening," Harvard Child Health Project working paper (May 2, 1975; processed).

chronic conditions affecting muscles, bones, and joints; or for grants to sustain preventive health services to children in urban ghettos.

Statutory purism is not the issue. The Social Security Act is perhaps disfigured but it is not debased by an irrelevant title. The Child Health Act can fit as title V of the Social Security Act as well as in any other statute and is no less the law because of its statutory heritage. What is important is the inability of the child health cause to attract a fair share of attention in an environment dominated by complex issues of social security, unemployment insurance, and public assistance. An irrelevant title's program gets short shrift in committee and floor consideration.

The validity of this proposition has been demonstrated consistently since 1935 when the leaders of the Children's Bureau easily accomplished a renewal of the maternal and child health grant program as part of the Social Security Act's security-for-children package. In the ensuing twenty-five years, old age insurance flowered, the groundwork was laid for medicare, disability coverage was added to old age and blindness, and appropriations to support child dependency grew sharply. But child health services—the ignored stepchild of social security—just survived.

Ironically, mental retardation, a cause no less noble and no less irrelevant to the principal purposes of the Social Security Act than child health, ultimately provided the handle for modernizing the act's child health provisions. Mental retardation had a preferred political place early in the 1960s. Months before his February 1963 special message proposing legislation, President Kennedy, calling for a "full national commitment" to discover the causes and means to cure retardation, had created a Panel on Mental Retardation, sought out expert help for it, followed with a special message proposing federal aid, received his panel's report, and appointed a special assistant to develop and coordinate programs to combat retardation. In the February message, Kennedy proposed doubling the annual maternal and child health authorization, "a significant portion of which will be used for the mentally retarded," and asked for a new five-year program of project grants for prenatal care of low-income expectant mothers. (Subsequent statutory language to establish those project grants begins: "In order to help reduce the incidence of mental retardation caused by complications associated with child bearing. . . ."[66])

No more appealing cause could have been suggested to Congress.

66. Public Law 88-156 (1963). The Kennedy Special Message on Mental Illness and Mental Retardation may be found in *Congressional Quarterly Almanac*, 1963, p. 1003.

Neither House nor Senate bothered with hearings on the administration bill embodying the steps to combat retardation outlined by Kennedy. According to Chairman Wilbur Mills, of many comments to the Ways and Means Committee by individuals and organizations, a single negative letter argued that retardation should be left to private charity, while the bill's basic idea brought approval from "practically every national organization dealing in the field of health and medicine, by a great number of nonmedical national organizations, and by a great number of State agencies engaged in this field."[67] Apparently capturing the reaction of the House, Ohio's Thomas Ashley concluded that "no bill before the present session of Congress appeals more to our humanitarian sympathies or to our approval of intelligent social action than this measure."[68] With self-congratulatory speeches, both chambers passed the maternal and child health retardation planning amendments by voice vote. Their importance is inversely proportional to the ease of passage. Maternal and infant care (M&I) special projects authorized at an escalating rate—$5 million the first year, $15 million the second year, and $30 million each of the remaining three years—became the first federal project grants for child health designed predominantly for urban areas. In addition, these projects broke other new ground by expanding the range of potential sponsors to health agencies of political divisions below the state level.

If mental retardation was political magic for John Kennedy, so poverty was for Lyndon Johnson. The peak year of the Great Society, 1965, not only saw formula funds increased but a second program of urban special projects grafted onto the Social Security Act's title V—this one for the health of school and preschool children, generally referred to as children and youth (C&Y) projects. Designed to provide continuous, comprehensive medical and dental care to children and youth through preventive services, screening, diagnosis, treatment, and aftercare, these projects also carry an urban service emphasis. Eligible sponsors, moreover, extend beyond state and local health departments to include medical schools and teaching hospitals. Two years later, the Social Security Amendments of 1967 authorized an even wider list of eligible sponsors, and also wrapped the special projects together, expanded them to a total of five by adding dental health, and broadened M&I to allow grants for intensive infant care and for family planning projects. Further modernizing federal involvement in child health, the act fixed project grants authorization at a

67. *Congressional Record*, vol. 109, pt. 12 (1963), p. 16000.
68. Ibid., p. 16009.

level 80 percent that of the preexisting maternal and child health and crippled children's services authorization.

As it did for other social programs easily initiated in 1965–67, trouble for project grants came later. In this case, administrative paralysis and child health's low place in congressional concern combined to bring the new style maternal and child health program to the edge of disaster. Project grants, having been established as variants on the older formula grants, fell under the Children's Bureau's administrative umbrella. At the time the projects began, however, defunctionalizing the bureau continued to interest those policy planners who rejected age-grouping as an organizational principle and who also rejected the Children's Bureau's nonaggressive style. These "influential people within HEW," as Dr. Arthur Lesser, then director of Maternal and Child Health Services told an interviewer, argued for administrative organization on a functional basis.[69] Children's Bureau stalwarts held off reorganization until the first year of the Nixon administration, when HEW Secretary Robert Finch established the Office of Child Development and simultaneously cut bureau functions. One element involved shifting maternal and child health programs to the Health Services and Mental Health Administration (HSMHA) of the Public Health Service (PHS) "in order," an administration health spokesman explained, "to tie them more closely to other activities concerned with the delivery of health care."[70]

For several years, Lesser and his staff considered themselves well enough treated in PHS as Maternal and Child Health enjoyed a reasonable degree of support and an organizational status equivalent to that of a bureau. Things went so well, in fact, that MCHS simply failed to take appropriate steps to meet the 1967 congressional mandate for a July 1972 transfer to the states of basic responsibility for providing health services to mothers and children. Federal financing would continue, but a single special revenue-sharing program in child health was to substitute for the separate state-administered formula grants and federally administered project grants.

Maternal and Child Health personnel, viewing with alarm the prospect of this shift in decisionmaking authority and anticipating that it would result in fees being levied for M&I and for C&Y services theretofore pro-

69. Milton Senn interview with Arthur Lesser, Oct. 11, 1972, in oral history file, National Library of Medicine.

70. Assistant Secretary Roger Egebert, in *Departments of Labor and HEW Appropriations for 1971*, Hearings before a Subcommittee of the House Committee on Appropriations, 91:2 (GPO, 1970), p. 5.

vided free, nevertheless sat on their hands while two politically shrewd and energetic C&Y project directors mounted a campaign to continue the categorical grants. In an informal but effective division of labor, Dr. Fred Seligman, chairman of an Association of Children and Youth Project Directors, undertook to secure descriptions of individual M&I and C&Y programs and analyses of the consequences of termination; Dr. Frederick Tunick, director of a C&Y project in Brooklyn, New York's Bedford-Stuyvesant section, where fewer than 100 private practicing physicians serve a population of 450,000, interested a hard-working second-term Democratic congressman from New York, Edward I. Koch, in Tunick's comprehensive approach to child health (CATCH) project, an interest that escalated to congressional leadership of the effort to extend the project. Dr. Lesser and his MCHS, whether by design or by chance, did nothing, in their case a most effective contribution to scuttling child-health revenue sharing.

Koch, at the time a junior member of the House Banking and Currency Committee, not a strategic spot from which to lead a child health effort, compensated for that deficiency with single-mindedness and good sense. Beginning in April 1971, in the course of the subsequent fourteen months he persuaded eighty-five members of the House to cosponsor his proposal to extend projects for five years. When Edward Kennedy and sixteen cosponsors offered comparable legislation in the Senate, Kennedy referred to Koch and pinpointed only two C&Y projects: Tunick's CATCH preceded mention of the project in Boston's Dimock Health Center.[71] The project descriptions Seligman generated were ultimately packaged for distribution to congressional offices, but first dribbled into the *Record* by Koch over a period of two months. The MCHS contributed further to the project build-up with a glowing progress report on the fifty-nine C&Y projects, making no mention of the scheduled end of categorical grants.

After House Ways and Means Committee Chairman Wilbur Mills asked the General Accounting Office for a review of HEW and Senate plans for an orderly transition from combined project and formula grants to formula grants alone, some kind of extension became certain. The comptroller general subsequently reported that

officials responsible for planning at the Federal level anticipated that the authority to fund special project grants would be extended beyond June 30, 1972, and that plans had not been prepared to provide for an orderly transition.

71. *Congressional Record* (daily ed.), June 23, 1971, p. S 9750.

In addition, States were not notified officially of the possible changes in their title V allotments so that they could make plans. . . .

To determine the extent to which plans had been made by the States, we met with, or sent a questionnaire to, officials in each State. Responses from 50 States showed that few had adequate plans to provide for a smooth transition in funding methods. Many States were not aware of the degree to which their title V allotments would change.[72]

To achieve an orderly transition, GAO told Mills, the termination date for project grants would have to be extended beyond 1972. They were. The project staff had in mind, however, something better than the one-year extension subsequently voted. Pleased with Wilbur Mills's compliment, "There are mothers-to-be and children yet unborn who will owe him a debt of gratitude,"[73] Koch persisted, the job made easier by statements of support from the American Academy of Pediatrics. By March 1973, Mills was committed to another extension. But perpetuating a project grant approach in a program that had from its origins in the Great Society been scheduled to change to a formula approach did not fit well with the Nixon administration's predisposition toward revenue sharing. Mills, who took pride in explaining that during his tenure as chairman no Ways and Means Committee bill bearing his name had ever been vetoed, made no move to put that record in jeopardy. Meanwhile, on the Senate side, firm support for an extension of project grants came from the most respectable of sources. A letter to Senator Russell Long signed jointly by the executives of the American Academy of Pediatrics, the American College of Obstetricians and Gynecologists, and the American Medical Association said the shift to formula support would be "premature and is not in the best interest of achieving maximum program results."[74] Using as its vehicle the veto-proof bill increasing the debt limit, Senate Finance brought another one-year extension to the floor just before the end of the fiscal year and the expiration of project grant authority. One of the few nongermane amendments added by the Senate at which the House did not balk, maternal and child health project grants were saved for the second successive year at the last possible moment. Gambling on June 30 extensions is far too dangerous a game to play indefinitely, however, so

72. Comptroller General of the United States, *Maternal and Child Health Programs Authorized by Title V, Social Security Act* (June 23, 1972), p. 20.

73. *Congressional Record* (daily ed.), June 30, 1972, p. H 6465.

74. Letter to Long from Drs. Robert J. Frazier, Michael Newton, Ernest B. Howard, May 21, 1973; reprinted in *Congressional Record* (daily ed.), June 27, 1973, p. S 12146.

project grant proponents—foreseeing the end of the line in 1974—wrote language into this extension modifying the allocation formula to assure that no state and no individual project would be financially disadvantaged during 1975 because of the termination of direct federal financing of projects.

After a while it will become clear whether the project proponents and their congressional supporters can continue to be winners in the skirmishing against formula grants. The MCHS's Arthur Lesser, however, did not survive the 1973 round. With the fate of the rider to the debt limit bill still uncertain but an administrative reorganization already announced that would cut up the HSMHA and simultaneously cut away at the size and scope of the MCHS, Lesser spoke out against the reorganization. Claiming that his staff would be reduced from a hundred and sixty to seven, Lesser said: "Reorganization is the first step in the elimination of categorical programs. It is another disregard for the intent of Congress.... It's as though they [administration officials] had actually gotten [child-health] revenue sharing through Congress."[75]

Lesser's superiors were content to stand mute, the most sensible strategy during last-minute maneuvering over the extension issue. A reasonable comment might have been that child-health revenue sharing had indeed gotten through Congress, under the terms of the authorizing legislation passed six years earlier. Whatever the differences between Lesser and his political superiors over the merits of formula versus project grants, the Child Health Act specified that the latter were to be folded into the former. Congress voted several reprieves, but a reprieve is a delay, not a pardon. As an agency to disperse about $250 million annually according to formula, the MCHS hardly merited the bureau-equivalent status Lesser had been happy with when the agency ran a total of a hundred and fifteen M&I and C&Y projects. Under the reorganization, Maternal and Child Health—over the protests of its staff—did become one of six responsibilities of the Bureau of Community Health Services within a new Health Services Administration, a step down from its designation as one of eleven major operating components of the HSMHA.

Project grants, twice rescued on successive June 30s, deserved a better fate than ultimately to be handed over to the mercies and the fiscal capabilities of the several states. The grant projects were capable of securing support on their merits from a broad spectrum of health providers and

75. *New York Times*, June 29, 1973.

government officials at federal and state levels, yet this grant program, which seemed to show important success in preventive health care, was never considered for a multiyear extension. Lesser, the highest ranking proponent in HEW, was not up to a leadership role that involved doing battle with the new federalism. Koch did very well in Congress, but this was Ways and Means business and he was an outsider lucky to be allowed on the inside briefly.[76] If the C&Y directors had not been organized—as the M&I directors were not—Koch would have been without a mechanism for getting the case together with which to appeal to individual members of Congress.

By 1975 the Ford administration was proposing sharp cuts in federal financing of community health services, including the now-unified maternal and child health grants. The case for a reduced appropriation hinged on a belief that increased amounts of money could be recovered from recipients of care and from third-party (insurance) payers. Congress will not accept that proposition. One active congressional nonbeliever, Edward Roybal (Democrat of California), argued that HEW has no field evidence to substantiate that belief. Citing a health survey of his Los Angeles district and of the state of California as well as a more extensive study by the American Academy of Pediatrics covering eleven states and four cities, Roybal says there is no laxity in recovering fees either by direct reimbursement to the program or by direct payment to providers.[77] Other members are distressed to hear the international rankings in infant mortality: fourteen countries report lesser rates than the United States. Still, support is shallow enough that inconsequential shifts in the comparative infant mortality rankings and a few horror stories involving failure to collect from third-party payers could result in a cut-back in the program.

### From Programs to Policy

The disarray characteristic of federal activity in child health is inevitable in the absence of a comprehensive child health policy. There is now no mechanism for formulating such a policy. In its absence, neither a review of the way Congress usually reaches important decisions on child

76. "It is the clear consensus of his colleagues," Martin Tolchin has written in the *New York Times*, "that Mr. Koch has become not only the best liked member of the New York delegation, but also, all things considered, the most effective." April 18, 1975.
77. *Congressional Record* (daily ed.), June 27, 1975, p. E 3577.

health legislation nor a review of the way HEW responds to congressional decisions inspires confidence. Congress acts in episodic fashion and HEW seems unwilling or unable to participate in aggressive new forms of child health work. Programs result more from the momentary strength of a particular group than from systematic consideration of the trade-offs that may be necessary between services and research; federal and state financing; preventive care and treatment.

Those concerned with child health should look to ways of broadening and increasing the political attention paid to the subject. To accomplish this, high priority should be assigned to locating and educating political leaders who would be willing to keep a watchful eye on how HEW implements child health programs; who will maintain contact with the interest groups that propose and develop program ideas; and who will actively try to attract more political interest in child health, including interest in a rational restructuring of congressional committee responsibility. Getting policymakers interested in the subject is the only way to meld otherwise disparate programs into a child health policy.

# 10

# Is a Children's Policy Feasible?

The flurry of activity on behalf of comprehensive child development legislation aside, health and welfare of children—a subject of continuing significance to most Americans—generates relatively little political attention. The absence of a theory legitimizing a place for family relationships on the public rather than the private agenda discourages grand designs. A paucity of tested ideas about how government actually can act to advance the children's cause limits the volume of proposals for serious consideration. The failure of social altruists and program providers to make common cause diminishes the political strength of each. Division of responsibility for children's programs among congressional committees and among administrative agencies impedes evolution of a focal point of concern about policy. Unlike the universal programs for older Americans, children's programs are selective responses to selective needs.

The children's cause can boast of few absolute successes, but it is inaccurate to conclude that the cause is not compelling, and it is overly emotional to conclude that Americans are not a child-loving people. What is certain is that aside from aid and services to children who are orphaned, abandoned, neglected, physically handicapped, mentally retarded, emotionally disturbed, or abused, disagreement continues over where governmental intervention should be offered, where mandated, where prohibited. Those who are constantly exposed to needy children, to children provided substandard day care, to children suffering disabilities of function, and to children without permanent family attachments insist that the level of intervention is inadequate. Those who are troubled by the idea of making judgments about other people's family relationships are more likely to be reluctant to promulgate day-care standards or to give legal sanction to permanent removal of a child from his natural parents or to faciliate tonsillectomies that are too often unnecessary. One group is not composed

240

of decent people and the other of insensitive people, nor is either group necessarily more "child-oriented" than the other. Both groups can find the children's cause compelling, and both are probably composed of child-loving people. A democratic society that emphasizes the privacy of family life and worries about the dangers of state control over child development should welcome honest disagreements over the appropriate limits of public intrusion in parent-child relations, an area in which privacy has always had a favored place.

## The Agenda Problem

What the best and wisest parent wants for his own child, John Dewey once wrote, we should want for all children. The sentiment is as resistant to translation into legislative policy as it is unexceptionable. So are more recent observations by officials and program advisers in the Office of Child Development (OCD) favoring "everything good for kids." Children's issues are too often the province of social reformers and child-welfare workers whose support for an increased public role in children's lives invariably shows enthusiasm, compassion, and a sense of mission but is less frequently accompanied by specific and tested plans for implementing their goals.

The reformers and the professionals keep trying to avoid the hard choice between limiting their goals and limiting their political strength. Construction of an orderly agenda with defensible priorities still eludes spokesmen for increased public activity. Discussing the activities of the coalition that came together to draft a comprehensive child development bill in 1971, Marian Edelman reports that welfare mothers and middle-class women "almost came to blows." The former saw the program as a way of insuring the highest quality care for their children while the mothers were working out of economic necessity. The latter thought they should have equal opportunity to be relieved of child-care responsibility if they wanted time to go to an art gallery.[1] It is an instructive story because it underlines an old and still unresolved dilemma: efforts to set priorities inevitably weaken a coalition; failure to set priorities reduces the responsiveness of policymakers. Since government can rarely afford to accommodate both groups, it will probably satisfy neither. Important

1. "An Interview with Marian Wright Edelman," *Harvard Educational Review*, vol. 44, no. 1 (February 1974), p. 69.

federally financed groups invariably seem to believe they can have it both ways: the Joint Commission on Mental Health produced a compendium urging everything and emphasizing nothing; the 1970 White House Conference on Children joined its 1950 and 1960 predecessors in dealing with too much; an advisory committee to the OCD on child development could barely get a report together because it would not deal with priorities. As for the product of Edelman's coalition, the most strident veto message of the Nixon administration both nullified congressional passage of a comprehensive child development bill and for years discouraged some supporters from making a serious second try. It has become commonplace since then for proponents to worry aloud about political indifference to the children's cause.

Yet, the record of responsiveness to specific proposals on behalf of children will not sustain so depressing a conclusion. In recent years, policy responses in the areas of child abuse, sudden infant death, school lunches, and programs for handicapped children have come promptly. Project grants in maternal and child health have been initiated and retained. Foster care and adoption policy is under scrutiny with a view to quickly finding permanent families for a maximum number of waiting children. And, for all of the expressions of outrage about cheats, chiselers, and high costs, aid to families with dependent children has come to support a constantly increasing number of children. Some responses in specific fields— early and periodic screening, diagnosis, and treatment of medically indigent children is an example—came so promptly that the administrative and professional apparatus involved could barely manage the task. None of the problems addressed by these responses will simply disappear, but none of them has been turned aside by a political system often characterized as indifferent to children because they are nonvoters, noncampaigners, and nonlobbyists.

At the same time, some highly touted demonstrations and experiments turned sour. Any failure to expand Parent and Child Centers or Home Start or Health Start cannot be characterized as political indifference. Neither child advocacy nor community coordinated child care could survive the transformation from concept to reality. Financing of programs to train so-called child development associates continues although both the falling birthrate and the substance of the programs dictate that it should not. The truth is that inventing workable programs for children is hard. If by some great miracle, children's lobbyists became federal policymakers, they would not be ready with a large stock of fresh ideas. They would be well advised to nourish and perfect existing programs.

Whether what is now on the books will just survive, flourish, or die over the next decade depends on how much attention is paid to the lessons of the past decade. No lesson seems more important than that of involving groups with a self-interest in the children's cause. School food service personnel have been important to school feeding; project directors have been important to maternal and child health projects. And any prospects for child development legislation depend on the comparable anxiety of public school teachers to protect their job opportunities by reaching for younger clients to keep the pool full.

## Combining Self-Interest and Social Altruism

In the early seventies, as enthusiasm for the antipoverty effort began to fade and so-called welfare reform turned out to be a goal widely sought but difficult to accomplish, some social reformers concluded that progress was more likely if programs for children became the vehicle.[2] It appeared that public child-care programs could become a major social innovation of the decade comparable to medicare and medicaid of the sixties. The argument was logical enough. The traditional system of mothers staying at home with small children involved social, psychological, and economic costs contrary to the interests of many of the groups involved: the absence of a child-care system was a most formidable impediment to the "workfare" goals of the national administration, a frustrating problem for low-income mothers themselves, a manifestation of indefensible sex discrimination from the viewpoint of the women's liberation adherents, a wasted opportunity according to child development experts. The convergence of the crisis in welfare, the pressures for equality of opportunity, and the legal and logical appeal of this aspect of the women's liberation movement stimulated legislators and budget planners to search for a federal policy in child care, theretofore considered one of the fields in which public activity was inappropriate or politically unlikely.

A theory on which to base greater federal involvement in child rearing grew out of the Head Start program. Because, for a short period at least, Head Start was thought to have an important effect on children's cognitive development, some parents and some politicians concluded that virtually all preschool children should be considered public rather than private responsibilities. All those who were not provided early education

2. Elizabeth B. Drew, "Reports and Comment: Washington," *The Atlantic*, January 1973, p. 10.

experiences, the argument ran, were being deprived of benefits they could not subsequently acquire because of the supposed special character of the first five years of life. Head Start served as the linchpin holding together various conceptions of intervention at the preschool level: out-of-home child care, early cognitive development, parent and community involvement. But Head Start could not carry that heavy a social burden. Its evaluators spoke of fading cognitive gains; observers found parent and community involvement did not often come up to the level of the Mississippi Child Development Group. Compensating for what Edward Zigler terms "naive environmentalism,"[3] federal officials turned to "continued improvement and innovative thrust in Head Start, coupled with intensive efforts to prevent and correct program deficiencies."[4] The benefits of replicating the Head Start model on a grand scale could not be predicted with confidence; the certainty of high costs could.

These conclusions led to outright hostility to child development legislation in some political circles, to indifference in some others, and to the general decline of child development as a public issue. Although the inventors of child development legislation never dissolved their organizational apparatus, the political strength of the child development coalition peaked in 1971. Unable to mount another major drive since then, the coalition has met, talked, worried, and looked to the future. It has paid insufficient attention to problems of political strategy, to finding the child development equivalent of school lunch's School Food Service Association. If there is to be a renewal of the child development issue and a national program, it will occur because self-interest specifically joins social altruism as a driving force.

## Keeping the Coalition Together

The child development coalition that spearheaded congressional action in 1971 accepted Marian Edelman's insistence on local community control because Edelman was the most knowledgeable leader among them. While organized labor provided the lobbying strength, it was Edelman who organized the drafting of legislation and who had the clearest con-

3. "Is Our Evolving Social Policy for Children Based on Fact or Fiction?" (speech delivered at the meeting of the Education Commission of the States, Denver, Colo., Dec. 7, 1972; processed), p. 2.
4. *The Budget of the United States Government, Fiscal Year 1974, Appendix*, p. 465.

ception of what might be accomplished, particularly for poor black children. For most of the coalition, however, poor black children were a social cause, not a personal experience, and community control was not an ineradicable principle. More recently, an important segment of the labor movement has found child development to be in its own self-interest—but not on Edelman's original terms.

Social altruists who supported earlier efforts are badly divided over how to react to a determined effort by a new leader of the AFL-CIO's American Federation of Teachers (AFT) to co-opt child development for the public schools and, by so doing, to meet the job needs of teachers being "excessed" in the face of a declining total of school-aged children. Albert Shanker had barely displaced David Selden as AFT president in the summer of 1974 when Shanker announced that as its major education priority the United States should develop a universal system of early childhood education. If the schools can only get children at age five or six, it is often too late to correct undesirable patterns, according to Shanker. "We now have the teachers and the classroom space for early child education because of the declining student population. It has to become part of the American public education system."[5] After this and a subsequent *New York Times* article by Shanker also calling for early education under public school control,[6] the old coalition had to reexamine its stand.

Of the three components of the original child development coalition, one concerned especially with cognitive development has little trouble embracing a primary role for the public schools. While some early education specialists will argue that the training of personnel for this purpose involves appreciably more than a casual short course, there is no disposition to argue that public schools and cognitive development are incompatible. Thus, the educationalists in the coalition can line up with the AFT.

Those who see child development as primarily a problem in the physical care and supervision of children fall both ways on the public school question. There is no inherent inconsistency between the recommendations of the day-care needs and services study, *Windows on Day Care*, directed by Mary Keyserling, and an approach that accepts a public school as prime sponsor. Mrs. Keyserling calls for full- and part-day develop-

5. *Washington Post*, Aug. 23, 1974.
6. "Early Childhood Education Is a Job for the Public Schools," *New York Times*, Sept. 8, 1974; reprinted in *Congressional Record* (daily ed.), Sept. 24, 1974, p. E 6063, and again Oct. 3, 1974, p. H 9921.

mental services available in the neighborhood and not "welfare" oriented. She concludes, too, that "both day care and elementary schooling will benefit to the extent that there can be a closer interrelationship of and continuity between these educational services."[7] Other day-care leaders see only trouble resulting from public school sponsorship. For example, Joyce Black and Marjorie Grosett, president and executive director of the Day Care Council of New York, pronounce it "a moral outrage that the education establishment seeks to solve its problem of empty classrooms and teacher unemployment by enrolling preschoolers in a system unable to meet their needs while refusing to acknowledge its obligation to older children."[8] Black and Grosett deny that public schools can effectively meet day-care needs and term a contrary view "blind self-interest." Clearly, those who have labored to shape the character of the free-standing day-care center or the facility located at the parent's work place will find it hard to share influence with the educational bureaucracy—itself not known for a cheerful willingness to share.

The original advocates of community control are ambivalent about a role for the schools under current circumstances. On the one hand, the need to use child development as an instrument of change—a way to provide depressed people a greater measure of control over their own destinies —is less great than it was in the sixties when the movement began. In addition, realists in the community-control group appreciate that there is little prospect that child development legislation can be accomplished without recruiting a major new interest group to the cause. So positions are reexamined as old community-control proponents consider whether social change has come far enough to permit support for a program of improved care and earlier education under public auspices, but without community control.

Tired of being proponents of a failing cause and reluctant to be divisive forces within the labor movement, a substantial number of the coalition's important participants have moved quickly toward the Shanker position as a practical course. Emphasizing the importance of a united front, the Amalgamated Clothing Workers' legislative representative has explained to her coalition colleagues that the public schools are not such a bad place and that a compromise with Shanker seems to represent the most likely path to legislative success. Her International Ladies' Garment Workers' Union counterpart speaks of efficiency as the appeal of the

7. *Windows on Day Care* (National Council of Jewish Women, 1972), p. 229.
8. "To the Editor," *New York Times*, Aug. 14, 1975.

schools, and points out that Shanker's position as advocate for the schools puts a burden on day-care spokesmen to be precise about the inadequacies of the school system as day-care provider. The representative of the AFL-CIO's social security department finds the possible use of the schools as prime sponsors "intriguing" because they may represent the best way to get universal day care and the best way to get quality control of that care all at once. Completing the union sweep, the assistant director of the AFL-CIO's department of legislation has told the coalition that he can see a role for the public schools, that Shanker is not a devil, and that instead of focusing on the community-control issue, discussion should move to questions of standards, comprehensiveness, and parent participation. The coalition, he says, must be kept together if legislation is ever to be achieved, but the feeling in Congress is that the coalition is "hopelessly divided" on all sorts of issues.

Whatever political success the child development cause has had is a result of the intellectual and organizational leadership provided by Marian Edelman and the lobbying activity contributed by organized labor. Because other members of the coalition are simply incapable of performing either of these critical functions, their disposition to hang back on the public school issue falls into the "interesting but not crucial" category. Even among these rank-and-file elements, however, the possibility of the public school as prime sponsor is not summarily dismissed as an intolerable deviation from child development orthodoxy. Spokesmen for the Child Welfare League, the Children's Foundation (concerned primarily with nutrition), the Black Child Development Institute, and Americans for Democratic Action do express reservations about schools as prime sponsors. The Black Child Development Institute's Evelyn Moore, for example, points out that the institute's constituents are grass-roots people and that the track record of public schools with black children in the grass roots is a poor one. Again, Barbara Bode of the Children's Foundation expresses reservations because of the historic unwillingness of the public schools to sponsor summer feeding programs and because they lack experience in child development.

But as Shanker and the AFT, supported by other parts of the labor movement, move on child development legislation, it is unlikely that overt opposition will come from any part of the coalition as long as some leeway, at least, is left for alternative sponsorship under special conditions. While not all members of the coalition understand the choice as limited to a public school bill or no bill, that really is the choice. By the summer of

1975, Shanker had managed to push a resolution through the AFL-CIO executive council praising the child-care programs developed by unions, church groups, local community organizations, and cooperatives, but terming them "scattered efforts . . . clearly far from enough." The only real answer, the resolution went on, is a massive federal commitment to the provision of early childhood development programs under prime sponsors who "must be responsible elected officials. The AFL-CIO believes that there is great merit in giving the public school systems this prime sponsorship role . . . with the responsibility for planning programs, distributing funds and monitoring programs."[9]

If this language was not as strong as Shanker and the AFT would have liked, it was not bad. In December 1974, AFT's own executive council had adopted a position paper positing an exclusive role for the schools: "Proliferation of private enterprise day care in nonschool social service programs is haphazard and even dangerous."[10] In view of its previous disposition to adhere to the community-control position—with a minimum population of five thousand for prime sponsors—that Marian Edelman had taken in 1971, the AFL-CIO executive council's May 1975 move toward the AFT position of December 1974 strengthened Shanker's case significantly. Hastening to consolidate his strength, Shanker made early child development a prominent item at AFT's 1975 convention where the delegates voted unanimously to favor a resolution calling for a national early childhood education program. Any reluctance must have been dispelled by a report on the job market for school teachers issued just a few days earlier by the National Education Association (NEA): in the 1974–75 school year, more than 175,000 elementary and secondary school teachers could not find employment.[11]

"Unions are at their finest," Shanker has said, "when they find issues representing a good combination of self-interest and public interest."[12] Whether a national system of early childhood education under public school or any other sponsorship is in the public interest has yet to be determined. That it is in the AFT's self-interest is irrefutable. So is the proposition that the entry of this group—espousing a cause in its self-interest—does more for the cause than could be done by social altruists alone.

9. American Federationist, June 1975, p. 5.
10. American Federation of Teachers, Early Childhood Education: A National Program (Dec. 17, 1974), p. 3.
11. New York Times, July 14, 1975.
12. Ibid.

## Mobilizing Social Altruists

The children's cause will not always lend itself to fusion with a politically consequential group pursuing its own self-interest. Providing educational benefits to handicapped children is a case in point. So is care of emotionally disturbed children. In these and comparable areas providers are politically weak and parents or caretakers are too few in number or too dispersed or too emotionally exhausted to be organized. Concerned leaders facing comparable circumstances should look to the way in which the National Council of Jewish Women's (NCJW) day-care project and the Children's Defense Fund's (CDF) children out of school project enlisted help from social altruists in a fashion that gave them a self-interest in accomplishing reform.

In both projects, professional leaders multiplied the size of the cadre of activists by reaching out for and thereby co-opting groups of volunteers. The volunteer-as-participant invariably becomes the volunteer-as-partisan. Thus, members of the seventy-seven NCJW sections—originally enlisted to contribute detailed reports to Mary Keyserling's day-care study—acquired a stake in the study, its reception, and programs to overcome deficiencies in day care to which they were exposed in the course of observing homes and centers and interviewing working mothers. The NCJW lacks an apparatus to follow through on its work and its project director had only a temporary attachment to the council. Nonetheless, if there is to be a drive for improved monitoring of the conditions under which day care is provided, the drive will involve NCJW members who have come to believe that they have a personal stake in reform.

Similarly, but even more skillfully because it has a continuing mechanism for exploiting its findings, the Children's Defense Fund utilized local community groups and individuals as well as the American Friends Service Committee (AFSC) in its survey of thirty areas where it found— to the dismay of both the CDF and of the AFSC and other volunteers —that 5.4 percent of all children aged six to seventeen were out of school.[13] Capturing AFSC members may be less of a coup for a reformist cause than is capturing NCJW members, but the model is no less sound. Those aspects of the children's cause that cannot in logic or in good conscience be tied to the needs of a preexisting interest group are likely to be overrun in

13. *Children Out of School in America*, a report by the Children's Defense Fund of the Washington Research Project, Inc. (October 1974), p. 43.

the policy process. Their proponents would do well to emulate the NCJW and CDF techniques for giving volunteers and altruists a stake in policy change.

## A Focal Point for Policy

Neither innovation nor marginal improvement in children's policy is likely without further development of a legislative or administrative focal point for policy growth. Paradoxically, however, that development has been hindered rather than enhanced by the creation of the Office of Child Development in the Department of Health, Education, and Welfare and by the establishment of a Subcommittee on Children and Youth of the Senate Committee on Labor and Public Welfare. Both the office and the subcommittee were created prematurely, and both suffer from the weakness that is a consequence of inadequate activity. With their joint drive for comprehensive legislation aborted by the firm Nixon veto, neither unit subsequently seemed credible, neither could hold key personnel, and neither has overcome the image of a loser. As the OCD continues downhill, other possibilities for policy leadership are not exploited in HEW. And as the subcommittee flounders, congressional institutions make it unlikely that alternate leadership of the children's cause will appear in the Capitol.

### The Jurisdictional Quandary in Congress

The congressional problem is easier to understand than is the vacuum in administrative leadership. Most—not all, but the major dimensions—of a congressman's agenda is fixed by the jurisdiction of the committee or committees to which he is assigned. It is considered unseemly and impolitic to invade someone else's jurisdiction unless a compelling constituency interest provides justification for doing so. Constituency interest is not a general license, however, so that the committee "outsider" who interests himself in child mental health, say, because there is a school for disturbed children in his district will be abided, but the outsider who pursues that kind of issue without comparable justification is more likely to be resented. The problem does not often present itself since most members have all they can do to deal with issues within their own committee's responsibilities and their own constituency's needs—the demands of the job limit the number of congressional busybodies.

Children are part of every member's constituency, and fit into no single committee's jurisdiction. The result is a distribution of responsibility for child health, nutrition, welfare, and development across standing committee lines. While a member might start from any of these perspectives and develop a general specialization in children's policy, that path is unlikely because the original toehold is both uninviting and small. Consider, for example, the work of the Social Security Subcommittee in House Ways and Means. Of the full range of issues covered by the Social Security Act, maternal and child health involves the fewest dollars and the smallest number of beneficiaries. What politician will take that problem as his own when his options include the payroll tax, old-age insurance benefits, medicare, and medicaid? If one be found, he quickly must come to realize that maternal and child health is only a fraction of the children's cause, and the bigger fraction remains distributed among at least three other committees.

Recognizing this circumstance as both reality and opportunity, Walter Mondale sought to effect new arrangements with the cross-cutting Subcommittee on Children and Youth. But neither is it immune to the jurisdictional problem, nor can it claim important legislative successes. Locating a focal point of congressional leadership of the children's cause is no less difficult now than it was before the subcommittee came into existence. The reality—satisfactory to noninterventionists, depressing to interventionists—is that barring a wholesale reorganization of Congress not likely soon to occur, there is no easy way either to improve congressional attention to the children's cause or to attract more members to a continuing concern about it.

## The Vacuum in Administrative Leadership

Before the limits of preschool programs were closely scrutinized, and before decisions were made about services and programs for children to add to or substitute for those already in place under Children's Bureau auspices, the Office of Child Development came into being—the consequence of congressional insistence that the Head Start program be shifted out of the Office of Economic Opportunity (OEO), and of doubts entertained by both the outgoing Johnson and the incoming Nixon administration about the vitality of the Children's Bureau. Political antipathy to the OEO and bureaucratic intrigue within the Children's Bureau resulted in the creation of a new agency without a program. While the architects of the OCD assumed that new purposes could be served, they were not explicit about those purposes. As it turned out, Head Start survived, albeit without growth, but other inheritances of the office—Parent and Child Centers and community coordinated child care—could hang on only temporarily and only for want of program alternatives. Symbolically, however, degradation of the Children's Bureau was complete with the establishment of the OCD.

The first five years of the OCD's life do not promise much for its future growth and development. The office made neither substantive nor political progress. The agency's style, to use the jargon of its own trade, is more custodial than developmental. One reason is that it had only an acting director rather than a director for its first year and again for another three full years beginning in mid-1972. In bureaucratic circles, that state of affairs is not considered an invitation to innovate. A second reason is that during the relatively brief period that the OCD had a real director rather than an acting director, the director was preoccupied with negotiating an agreement on child care under proposed welfare reform legislation. A third reason is that even by the time HEW Secretary Robert Finch formally created the OCD in June 1969, White House advisers were persuaded by the Westinghouse report that child development should not be rushed into. But Finch never got the word and proceeded to set up the OCD on the basis of an outmoded scheme. A fourth reason is that the experimental and demonstration efforts initiated by the OCD— including the child development associate credentials it sponsored for children's caretakers, and Health Start, Home Start, and a Child and Family Resource Program—have not worked out well enough to justify their expansion.

Of these several troubles visited upon the OCD, surely the hardest to understand is the failure to designate a leader between 1972 and 1975. Since the reorganization that downgraded the statutory Children's Bureau to a component of the OCD, the historically significant position of chief of the Children's Bureau has lost its importance. The absence of policy leadership in the Office of Child Development consequently deprives the children's cause of an in-house spokesman. Progress toward any kind of children's policy has been impeded by the shabby treatment the Nixon administration accorded its own creation, the Office of Child Development, by the silence of surrogate lobbyists for children who did not speak out on the issue, and by the consequent three-year leadership vacuum at the national governmental level. Throughout much of this period, the word-of-mouth network would report that one or another scholar or practitioner in the field had declined appointment as OCD director. Yet, as often as not, no offer was ever really made. The agency's acting director had neither substantive competence in the children's field nor any indication from his political superiors that he was expected to behave like a director rather than an interim administrator. Consequently unable to initiate or respond to proposals, the OCD's Saul Rosoff made no important speeches, avoided calling on appropriate congressional leaders, and simply concentrated on holding together an agency that grew progressively weaker—so weak that the prolonged failure to appoint a director did not even require a high-level explanation.

A cursory review of the dynamics of administrative organization in other children's programs makes it appear unlikely that leadership of the children's cause will soon be found in any of the agencies concerned with child health, nutrition, or welfare. In the case of child health, the most recent of the incessant reorganizations of the federal health apparatus turned what for a long period had been a Maternal and Child Health Service into an Office for Maternal and Child Health within a Bureau of Community Health Services (BCHS). While the new office will ultimately be responsible for approving a total of three hundred and seventy individual projects, executive reorganizations have done much, as Representative Edward Koch has put it, to reorganize the Maternal and Child Health Service out of existence. Premature withdrawal of federal technical assistance staff left the states largely on their own to put together programs or projects. No matter how good the case may be for this kind of special revenue sharing in child health, there is no chance that the director of a BCHS "office" with narrowly circumscribed authority and little staff can expect to speak for children's issues at high levels—nor is he likely to try. Comparable disabilities do not restrict the director of the National Institute of Child Health and Human Development. He has a protected post and comes from a powerful professional group. But the temptation to view the job as part of the National Institutes of Health's "campus" rather than as part of the HEW "jungle" is apparently irresistible. Recent directors have taken the attitude of medical research administrators rather than shapers of children's policy.

Agency heads concerned with other children's welfare programs have

other disabilities. Protective services are under the OCD umbrella. The Social and Rehabilitation Service (aid to families with dependent children) recruits its leadership from business administration, not social policy, and the time is long past when public assistance administrators could serve as advocates for their clients. In child nutrition, Agriculture's Food and Nutrition Service runs school lunch and school breakfast by the statute, largely oblivious to whether the ultimate beneficiaries are children or any other population group.

Experience between 1969 and 1975 shows that there is no sure way to guarantee children's policy leadership at a high level of the federal government. Without such leadership, the children's cause suffers at the HEW departmental level, and in turn in presidential program formulation. The OCD remains the logical home for a children's policy leader. At a minimum, the children's lobby should put together an interorganizational committee that can serve as watchdog over the OCD directorship —offering a panel of suitable appointees, publicizing failure to keep the job filled, issuing an annual evaluation of OCD performance. The goal should be exactly that stated when the OCD was established in 1969: to unify federal-level responsibility for children's programs and to strengthen those programs. "There are few programs so bad that they can't be improved," Elliot Richardson once said while secretary of HEW.[14] But it does take leadership.

### Is a Children's Policy Feasible?

Grace Abbott's observation with which this book began—that all children are dependent but only a relatively small number are dependent on the state—bears repeating at its end. In the distribution of public goods and services, some children should be favored over others because some parents are less well able than others to cope with their children's needs. Public policy should focus on two objectives: to define minimum standards of needs and to perfect mechanisms for meeting them according to an established set of priorities.

Reasonable progress toward meeting these objectives has been made through improvements in old programs of cash relief for poor families and feeding of poor schoolchildren. For divers reasons, the public agenda is expanding to include the needs of children in foster care for a perma-

14. *Washington Post*, March 30, 1973.

nent family setting and to include the educational needs of children who are physically, mentally, or emotionally handicapped. But places on the public agenda are assigned in haphazard fashion. In the extreme case, it will be a consequence of a chance visit to an institution by an influential senator to repay a political obligation, or of the birth of a child with an obscure handicap to the legislative assistant of a member of the House. On the other hand, when agenda-building is specifically addressed by conferences or commissions, they collect items without limit, leaving public officials bewildered.

The children's policy most feasible—and most desirable—is one targeted on poor children, handicapped children, and children without permanent homes: unlucky children whose parents cannot provide them a start equal to that provided most children. The commission that makes the most useful contribution is one instructed to inventory that population. The lobbyists most needed are those urging programs targeted to those specific categories. The social altruists performing the most useful service are those who monitor the actual provision of compensatory benefits and services to unlucky children. Ultimately, a far more complex, universal program may be warranted. It may develop that private families really are not equipped to meet most children's needs. "There is serious thinking among some of the future-oriented child development research people that maybe we can't trust the family alone to prepare young children for this new kind of world which is emerging," Reginald Lourie told a congressional committee a few years ago.[15] Unless and until that case is made more persuasively than it has been, however, a children's policy will be successful enough if it concentrates on ways to compensate demonstrably unlucky children whose bodies or minds are sick or whose families are unstable or in poverty.

15. *Comprehensive Child Development Act of 1971*, Joint Hearings before the Subcommittee on Employment, Manpower, and Poverty and the Subcommittee on Children and Youth of the Senate Committee on Labor and Public Welfare, 92:1 (GPO, 1971), p. 184.